Facts On File Encyclopedia of

Black Women

IN AMERICA

Theater Arts and Entertainment

Darlene Clark Hine, Editor

Kathleen Thompson, Associate Editor

D1267190

☑® Facts On File, Inc.

Facts On File, Inc.
11 Penn Plaza
New York NY 10001

Library of Congress Cataloging-in-Publication Data

Facts on File Encyclopedia of Black Women in America / Darlene Clark
Hine, editor : Kathleen Thompson, associate editor.
p. cm.
Includes bibliographical references and index.
Contents: v. 1. The early yers, 1619–1899 — v. 2. Literature —
v. 3. Dance, sports, and visual arts — v. 4. Business and professions —
v. 5. Music — v. 6. Education — v. 7. Religion and community —
v. 8. Law and government — v. 9. Theater arts and entertainment —
v. 10. Social activism — v. 11. Science, health, and medicine.
ISBN 0-8160-3424-9 (set : alk. paper)
ISBN 0-8160-3436-2 (Theater Arts and Entertainment)

1. Afro-American women—Biography—Encyclopedias. I. Hine.
Darlene Clark. II Thompson, Kathleen.
E185.96.F2   1996
920.72'08996073—dc20   96-33268

Text design by Cathy Rincon
Cover design by Smart Graphics
Printed in the United States of America

RRD FOF 10 9 8 7 6 5 4 3 2 1

This book is printed on acid-free paper.

Contents

How to Use the Volume

SCOPE OF THE VOLUME

The *Theater Arts and Entertainment* volume includes entries on individuals and organizations in the following subject areas: comedy, film, musical theater, radio entertainment, television entertainment, theater, and vaudeville.

RELATED OCCUPATIONS

Related occupations addressed in other volumes of this encyclopedia include the following: broadcast journalists (*Business and Professions*), dancers and choreographers (*Dance, Sports, and Visual Arts*), musicians *(Music)*, producers of film, theater, television, and radio (*Business and Professions*), and teachers of theater arts (*Education*).

HOW TO USE THIS VOLUME

The introduction to this volume presents an overview of the history of black women in theater and entertainment. Musical performers are frequently included in this overview, but more extensive coverage of these entertainers can be found in the volumes of this encyclopedia that are devoted exclusively to music and dance. A chronology following the entries lists important events in the history of black women in theater and entertainment in the United States.

Individuals and organizations are covered in alphabetically arranged entries. If you are looking for an individual or organization that does not have an entry in this volume, please check the alphabetically arranged list of the entries for all eleven volumes of this encyclopedia that appears at the end of this book, in addition to tables of contents of each of the other volumes in this series.

Names of individuals and organizations for which there are entries in this or other volumes of the encyclopedia are printed in **boldface**. Check the contents list at the back of this book to find the volume where a particular entry can be found.

Facts On File Encyclopedia of

Black Women

IN AMERICA

Theater Arts and Entertainment

Introduction

Imagine the moment. It's 1964. You, a young black American, are sitting in a seat in a Broadway theater, front row center. It's opening night and everyone is dressed to the nines. All important critics are there as well as many famous actors, people whose faces you recognize from movies. They're conversing freely in the lobby, the aisles, and their seats. But then the audience becomes quiet.

The house lights dim, the curtain rises, and the play begins. On stage is a young Alan Alda. His fame as Hawkeye in television's *M*A*S*H* is years in the future. To you, he's just a tall, funny white guy. Playing the woman he falls in love with is Diana Sands, a beautiful, intelligent, funny, talented black woman.

You've never seen anything like it before.

In fact, it has never happened before. Diana Sands is on Broadway playing a role that was not written specifically for a black actress, and there is no reference whatsoever to her race or that of her white costar at any time during the play. Sands is just an actor playing a role, not a black actor playing a black role.

The play, *The Owl and the Pussycat*, was a big success. Diana Sands was nominated for a Tony, and the production moved to London. Sands had proved that a black actor could be accepted and successful in a leading role—a *romantic* leading role—in a play that wasn't about being black.

The first black American to create on Broadway a role written for an actress of unspecified race, Diana Sands was propelled by her success in The Owl and the Pussycat *into a brilliant career. Her 1968 performance in the title role of Shaw's* Saint Joan *was considered by some critics to be her best.* (SCHOMBURG CENTER)

Everything should have changed then. The lines of talented black actors waiting to walk on stage—any stage—should have moved forward, but they didn't. That is all part of the long, difficult, fascinating journey that black performers—especially black women performers—have taken in American entertainment.

1

SINGERS, MINSTREL SHOWS, AND ONE LONE WASHERWOMAN

On warm summer nights on plantations across the South, slave masters would call their workers up to the Big House to entertain them. Weary from their day's work in the fields, aching in their bodies and sore in their minds from the abiding sense of freedom lost, black women and men pulled from their memories the rhythms of Africa. They beat on single-headed drums. They danced. They sang.

Those long-forgotten artists must have experienced the paradox of black entertainment in America—finding the deep satisfaction of artistry and self-expression while performing for your oppressors, tailoring your performance to please the people who have enslaved you, persecuted you, and rejected your humanity. In the case of black women, that paradox was compounded in a country where entertaining has been a double-edged sword for any woman, whatever her color.

Throughout United States history, everyone has had trouble getting on stage. In 1750, the same year that British actor Thomas Kean appeared in New York in Shakespeare's *Richard III*, the General Court of Massachusetts passed a law prohibiting theatrical entertainment of any kind. A few years later, when a troupe of players, the Hallam London Company, came to the colonies to entertain, Pennsylvania passed a law calling for anyone presenting or acting in a play to be fined. Because the fine was more than most people in the colonies could earn in a year, and because actors aren't the wealthiest of peo-

ple, this law was very discouraging. But it wasn't the last. By the time independence was declared, there were only two colonies that had *not* passed some kind of law against theaters, and in 1778, a new federal law prohibited theater in any form.

Despite this, plays, concerts, and other forms of entertainment were presented. In many of them, female roles were acted by men; essentially women who appeared on stage were considered to be prostitutes. Black roles were acted by whites.

Gradually, the restrictions against women in serious drama lifted, but the ban on black performers, of either gender, did not, with one notable exception: One of the noblest theatrical efforts made by African Americans was the African Grove Theater. This group formed in Manhattan in about 1820 to present Shakespearean plays and the other classics, had a small theater at Bleecker and Mercer Streets in Lower Manhattan. Their audiences were primarily black, although they courteously provided an area for white audience members.

The company consisted of both men and women. A playbill for *Tom and Jerry, Or, Life in London* includes the names of Miss Peterson, Miss Johnson, and Miss Davis. The accompanying pantomime includes Miss Hicks.

It was the company's policy of allowing white audience members that eventually closed it. White hoodlums came to harass the players and made performance conditions impossible. Still, black women had appeared on stage in the United States for the first time, in serious drama.

In the commercial theater, however, they might as well not have existed. In the 1820s, when Edwin Forest wanted someone to play the role of a black domestic servant in a play he was producing, he could find no white woman who was willing to wear blackface and act a maid. He did not advertise for a black actress to fill the role; instead, he persuaded his own black washerwoman to play the part.

Still, though they were not accepted on theater stages, black women were performing and singing in churches. In 1776, the year of United States independence, the first black gospel singing by an organized choral group was heard at a black Baptist church in Petersburg, Virginia.

Women were singing on the plantations with their men, planting the roots of the only truly original American music, what Langston Hughes called "the hand-clapping, feet-stomping, drum-beating rhythms (related, of course, to the rhythms of the human heart) that Africa exported to our shores in the fifteenth century."

They were dancing in the slave quarters —the juba dance and the bambouche. Their white owners and neighbors came to spy, watching in complete fascination and some fear.

Many male slaves made money for their masters as entertainers. There were banjoists, singers, fiddlers. Their masters hired them out, keeping the fees for themselves. The most famous of these performers was probably Blind Tom, a child prodigy whose career as a pianist and composer continued after Emancipation.

It was the dancing and singing of black street performers in New Orleans that inspired the major continuous attraction in nineteenth-century American entertainment —the minstrel show. Its popularity began in the 1830s and continued for the next 80 years.

The minstrel show has to be one of the strangest theatrical phenomenons in history. It was, very simply, a bunch of white men, wearing burnt cork on their faces to make them look black, performing black dances and black music and acting out stereotypes of black personalities. This form of entertainment dominated the American theater for decades.

At the time, the legitimate theater in America featured mostly European plays, acted in the exaggerated European style. As the century went on, more American plays were produced, but they were primarily the hero-villain-maiden-tied-to-the-railroad-tracks melodramas we now associate with nineteenth-century theater. There were the saloons shows, but they hardly counted. While the performers struggled onstage, the waitresses were soliciting customers, and you might get shot for a bad joke. For music, comedy, and quality entertainment, people went to the minstrel shows. They presented all the best songs written by the best songwriters, the best dances, the best jokes. So, for most of the nineteenth century, if you wanted to go on stage to sing and be funny, you had to pretend to be black.

If you *were* black, you could forget it.

After the Civil War, there began to be black minstrel companies. They performed the same dances and songs and acted out the same stereotypes. Many of them even wore burnt cork over their own black faces. And, like the white minstrel shows, they did not include women. There was usually a female character, called "the wench," but she was played by a black man in bustle and wig.

In the meantime, however, a black woman was gaining great attention and success on the stage as a singer; a concert musician named **Elizabeth Taylor Green-**

field. From private concerts for wealthy white patrons, Greenfield went on to perform around the country, often appearing in theaters where the audiences were thoroughly white. In England, she gave a command performance for Queen Victoria.

Still, Greenfield's career belongs more in the history of American concert music than that of theater and entertainment. It was the Hyers sisters who were the first black women to gain success on the American stage, and, in essence, they were the founders of black dramatic theater in America.

Anna and Emma Hyers, like Greenfield, were opera singers, who began their stage career performing together in concerts of serious music. This strictly musical phase lasted for several years and was successful enough that the sisters decided to broaden their scope. In 1875, they formed a troupe called the Coloured Operatic and Dramatic Company and began to produce musical plays depicting the black experience, the first of which was *Out of Bondage.*

Out of Bondage followed black people in America from slavery to what the Hyers sisters called "attainment of education and refinement." It had a story line, making it completely different from the minstrel shows that flourished at the time. It also had characters who were consistent from the beginning to the end of the play and featured serious music. Costarring in the play with the Hyers sisters was Sam Lucas, a well-known black actor who spent most of his career in minstrel shows. However, when Anna and Emma Hyers presented *The Underground Railroad* and *Princess Orelia of Madagascar,* Lucas left his high-paying minstrel show and joined them again. Later, he want back to the blackface stage to make a living.

Not until **Anita Bush** founded her all-black dramatic company in 1915 would there a be significant breakthrough in black dramatic theater in this country.

Meanwhile, the American audiences' strange love for watching blackface performers continued. The minstrel shows faced their first serious competition from the "Tom Shows"—plays based on Harriet Beecher Stowe's novel *Uncle Tom's Cabin* —that began to appear in 1853. Again, white America flocked to watch black characters on stage, and again, those characters were played by white actors. It was not until 1877, almost a quarter of a century later, that a black actor, Sam Lucas, was finally cast as Uncle Tom. But in 1933, when the show was produced in New York, Topsy was still being played by a white woman.

However, as the nineteenth century drew to a close, black women were being seen on stage with the beginning of the black musical. It was the next stage in the development of black theater in America, and again, it was a woman who laid the groundwork.

Sissieretta Jones' beautiful voice was repeatedly compared to that of Adelina Patti, an eminent opera singer of the time. Jones' talent won her roles at the Metropolitan Opera in the 1892 season. But though her contract was signed, the plans fell through. Instead, Jones went on the road with a company called the Black Patti Troubadours. It was billed as a musical comedy, not a minstrel show, and in the second act, where the minstrel show had a cakewalk, the Black Patti Troubadours show had operatic arias.

The producer of Sissieretta Jones' show was Bob Cole, who next produced the first all-black musical show created, directed,

Sissieretta Jones, whose beautiful voice was compared to that of opera singer Adelina Patti, toured with her Black Patti Trouba-dours, a sensation around the country. (SCHOMBURG CENTER)

and managed by black theater professionals. Suddenly, black women were on stage!

VAUDEVILLE AND THE BLACK MUSICAL

The chorus line, a string of attractive women with long legs whose faces nobody ever notices, is a moving background for the stars. It's the place where everyone is inter-changeable and dispensable—the line everyone wants to get out of to move on and up.

Ironically, in the history of black women in entertainment, the chorus was the wedge driven into a solid wall of opposition that had lasted for more than a century.

As the nineteenth century drew to an end, white audiences finally began to tire of watching minstrel-show depictions of pre–Civil War black people. Toward the end of its far-too-long life, minstrel-show carica-tures began to change to show urban rather than rural stereotypes. The happy-go-lucky, good-for-nothing, lazy black from the old plantation was replaced by the finger-snap-ping, partying, cakewalking city dude. The guy on the banjo was replaced by the guy at the piano. The music got a ragtime beat.

Then, in 1890, *The Creole Show* ap-peared. It had the basic structure of a min-strel show and headlined a great star of the minstrel shows—Sam Lucas again—but it had that one new feature: a chorus line of 16 black women.

Over the next few years, the new black musicals, or "coon shows" as they were offensively called, drew large audiences. Their formula was always the same: Take the urbanized minstrel show, add acts from the saloon shows—now cleaned up and be-ing called vaudeville—set it all to a ragtime beat . . . and make sure you have a chorus line. What defined the musical comedy, as opposed to the minstrel show, was the cho-rus.

Bob Cole took a major step forward in 1898 when he wrote, directed, and pro-duced *A Trip to Coontown*. An all-black production that had a plot and characters, it was also one of the first American musical comedies, black or white.

Two strains of American musical theater came together in the 1890s, the burlesque shows and the minstrel shows. The burlesques were not, as they later were to become, strip shows. They were parodies of serious theater, enacted by women. The women played all roles, including the male characters. Of course, in order to play men, they had to wear pants—or tights. As a result, the burlesques were immensely popular with male audiences, who were accustomed to female costumes that showed nothing so daring as an ankle. Out of the burlesques came the first white musicals; out of the minstrel shows came the first black musicals: They appeared on the scene at about the same time.

The new black musicals accustomed people to seeing black women on stage. The chorus offered the opportunity to be seen, to learn, to develop talents, and while the male stars such as Lucas and later Williams and Walker still got most of the attention, here and there a talented woman moved from the chorus to center stage.

One of the first of these women was **Aida Overton Walker,** a talented dancer who had toured with the Black Patti Troubadours and had married George Walker just as he and Bert Williams were about to take off on

Aida Overton Walker became one of the first black international superstars. She perfected her performances while young, as shown here by her exuberant dancing with two unidentified male partners. (DONALD BOGLE)

Vaudeville and the Theater Owners Booking Association provided thousands of black entertainers with their only opportunity to perform. This group is Edwards and Delotch's "Bingham and Brevities." (SCURLOCK STUDIO)

the New York stage. The team recognized what an asset this lovely woman was: She could sing, dance, and act like an angel. She even choreographed their shows for them.

Aida Overton Walker appeared in all of the Williams and Walker musicals during the next decade. When Walker became ill and the team broke up, she helped Williams fulfill their bookings by dressing in men's clothes and performing her husband's biggest dance hits in every show. She went on to perform in vaudeville and later became a producer.

It would be another ten years before the next black woman moved from the chorus to the Broadway spotlight, one of the most disgraceful decades in this nation's history. From about 1910 to 1920, antiblack hysteria peaked. The Ku Klux Klan terrorized the South with lynchings and night riders; laws were passed to segregate every aspect of life; a large migration of black workers from southern to northern states threatened white workers and increased racial feeling. In *On With the Show*, Robert C. Toll reports that, in this atmosphere, the success of

Stump and Stello were among the black acts that toured the vaudeville circuits. (SCUR-LOCK STUDIO)

the black musicals triggered racist anger, and when Williams and Walker's *In Dahomey* opened, there were fears of a race war. But, he goes on, "Violence did not drive Negroes off Broadway. . . . Bias, insidious invisible bias and middle-class financiers and producers did. Although the exclusion was not a single, sudden event, 1910 can be pinpointed as the critical date."

The women of the chorus who had talents and aspirations to stardom would have to wait a while longer.

This was a critical moment in the history of black entertainment for another reason: In 1909, Anselmo Barrasso organized the Theater Owners Booking Association (TOBA). Black vaudeville was born.

Until TOBA was created, there was only one vaudeville. It had grown out of the

saloon shows that had been, since the early part of the nineteenth century, the dregs of show business. In 1875, Tony Pastor cleaned up this type of show and took it uptown. In 1885, Benjamin Franklin Keith and Edward Franklin Albee made it into big business.

A vaudeville show was a variety show. A three-hour program might feature acrobats, dog trainers, singers, dancers, comedians, magicians, and ventriloquists. Vaudeville producers paid non-entertainment celebrities just to appear onstage. Carrie Nation, the temperance leader who was famous for taking an axe to bars and saloons, ended up for a time in vaudeville.

Vaudeville also featured the cream of entertainers from Broadway musicals, the legitimate stage, and the concert halls: black performers Williams and Walker came to Broadway from vaudeville; Sam Lucas and his wife, Carrie Melvin Lucas, performed extensively in vaudeville, as did Bill "Bojangles" Robinson, Sissle and Blake, the Nicholas Brothers, Mantan Moreland, and Pigmeat Markham.

Black women who performed on the white vaudeville circuits before 1910 included Dora Dean, a famous cakewalk dancer; the De Wolfe sisters; **Hattie McIntosh**, a dramatic actress who toured with her husband Tom; and Aida Overton Walker.

When black performers began to disappear from white stages in the teens, TOBA was there to book them into theaters with black audiences.

It was on the TOBA circuit that the great blues queens reigned. **Ma Rainey** traveled with her Rabbit Foot Minstrels from Chicago to Florida, from Oklahoma City to Pittsburgh. She made her reputation on the TOBA circuit, and there she continued to perform all during her successful recording career. **Bessie Smith** was a TOBA headliner, as was **Ethel Waters**, under the name Sweet Mama Stringbean. Susie Edwards toured as part of the husband-and-wife team Butterbeans and Susie. Sippie Wallace toured in black vaudeville as part of a trio with her two brothers.

The "class acts" included the Whitman Sisters and operatic soprano Fanny Wise. The novelty acts included Wee Georgia Woods, a talented ventriloquist, and Allie Brown, who performed on the slack-wire (as opposed to the tightrope). Toy Brown was a pretty snake charmer, but she was not alone in this odd specialty: Madam Cow Cow Davenport charmed snakes as well. There was even a lion tamer named Bessie Coleman (not to be confused with the famed aviator).

The black vaudeville circuit offered opportunities for black women performers to hone their skills and, sometimes, to build a following. But conditions were rough and, throughout vaudeville, black women still had to work within the stereotypes established by the minstrel shows and enforced by theater owners and talent bookers. They could be lusty wenches, sexless mammies, or comic nags, and that was about it. The greatest performers stretched the limits of those characters as far as they could but seldom broke through them. The bitter paradox of the black entertainer continued.

As America came out of World War I, black musicals, chorus lines intact, moved back toward Broadway. In 1920, two teams of vaudeville heavyweights—the singing and piano-playing Noble Sissle and Eubie Blake and the comedy-dancing act of Flour-noy E. Miller and Aubrey Lyles—got together to write *Shuffle Along.*

After a considerable struggle, it reached Broadway. New York was dazzled: To that point, there had been only a handful of successful musical comedies on Broadway —*Adonis, A Trip to Chinatown, Florodora, Irene*—and there had never been anything like this new all-black musical hit. *Shuffle Along* had a silly plot and stereotyped black characters, but it had fabulous music written by Eubie Blake and spectacular dancing.

Ethel Waters was Sweet Mama Stringbean on the Southern vaudeville circuit, was the star of the Cotton Club *singing "Stormy Weather," and was the toast of Broadway in Irving Berlin's* As Thousands Cheer. (DONALD BOGLE)

Though the four male writers of the show were undeniably its stars, it followed the lead set by Williams and Walker, and featured an ingenue, first played by Gertrude Saunders. Later, she was replaced by **Florence Mills,** who was about to become the first real black female superstar.

Mills was only twenty-five, but she had been around. As a child, she had been part of a "pickaninny chorus," one of the many groups of black children who were used by white vaudeville stars to jazz up their acts. The "picks" would open the act with energy, provide it with excitement, and close it with energy, all for very little money.

Florence Mills was one of the best-known black singers in vaudeville and musical comedy. She achieved a first for blacks when she headlined at New York's famous Palace Theater. (MOORLAND-SPINGARN)

In *Shuffle Along,* Mills was a sensation. She quickly become as big a star as any black man on Broadway, as big as most performers of any color. However, after only seven years as a star of Broadway, London, and Paris, Florence Mills died, at the age of thirty-two. Her death was a great blow to the progress of black women in the theater. It was also a great blow to her admirers: At her funeral in Harlem, 150,000 people lined the streets.

The second black woman of the time to become a great star stepped directly out of the chorus of *Shuffle Along* into theatrical history. When she first auditioned, she was turned down as too young, too thin, and too dark. But she went back armored in light-tone face powder, and managed to snag a job as a dresser. Then she proceeded to learn all the songs and all the dances in the show. Sometime, the ambitious teenager figured, one of the chorus girls would drop out. She was right: Someone became pregnant, and the young dresser was ready to take her place.

When **Josephine Baker** went on stage that first night, however, she did not simply sing the songs and dance the dances; she mugged, she shimmied, she crossed her eyes—in short, she made everyone in the theater notice the sixth girl from the right in the chorus. The audience loved her; they continued to do so for decades. Baker's greatest success, however, came when she went to Europe in *La Revue Nègre*. She startled and enthralled Paris with her near-nude dancing, and as a European superstar, she saw no reason to come back to race-conscious America.

The second Sissle and Blake production, *Chocolate Dandies,* showed the progress women were making in black musicals. Among the featured performers, besides

When Josephine Baker first went on stage (in the chorus of Shuffle Along) *the audience loved her. She soon became a superstar in Europe and saw no reason to return to race-conscious America.* (DONALD BOGLE)

Josephine Baker, were **Amanda Randolph**, Pauline Godfrey, **Inez Clough**, Lottie Gee, Elisabeth Welch, and **Valaida Snow**. Women had moved out of the chorus for good.

The third black woman among the great musical stars of the twenties and thirties, along with Mills and Baker, had a much greater impact on American theater, musical and otherwise. She also came to stardom by another route.

Ethel Waters is one of many black women who came to acting through music. She established her reputation in vaudeville, black and white, as Sweet Mama String-bean, and then came to New York and sang in clubs. She started recording, first on a "race record" label, Black Swan Records, and then with Columbia Records. When Waters went on stage in *Africana* in 1927, she was already well known. As she went from success to success on Broadway, she became a star. She did *Blackbirds of 1930* and *Rhapsody in Black* and then went on to make her first film, *On with the Show*, in 1929.

Then in 1933 Irving Berlin cast her in the musical revue, *As Thousands Cheer*. She was the only black cast member and one of the shows biggest hits, singing such Berlin songs as "Heat Wave" and "Harlem on My Mind." She had taken a step that few black performers had ever taken; she had become a star in the world of white entertainment. She was now the highest paid woman on Broadway.

Waters, a black woman from a Philadelphia ghetto who had once supported herself as a domestic worker, was one of the great stars the musical theater in America had ever produced. And the best was yet to come, for her and for the theater.

A THEATER OF ONE'S OWN

Put yourself in Anita Bush's place: She was a black teenager in New York right before the turn of the century; her father was a tailor, and his reputation had got around in the theater crowd—he was always making a suit for a famous white actor starring at the Majestic or a dress for a glamorous black singer in *The Creole Show;* Anita saw some of the shows and even got to go backstage—her father knew everybody.

Perhaps she saw Maude Adams, the first Peter Pan—a small, beautiful woman who was one of the first to bring truthful, naturalistic acting to the American stage. Maybe she watched from backstage as Minnie Maddern Fiske interpreted the startling new women's lead roles in Ibsen's *A Doll's House* and *Hedda Gabler.* She could have met the new, young Barrymore girl, Ethel.

At any rate, Anita Bush fell in love with the theater. She decided that, more than anything in the world, she wanted to act. So, at sixteen years old, she talked her reluctant parents into letting her join the Walker and Williams company. Of course, it was a musical company, and Anita didn't know how to sing or dance, but Bert Williams told her father that she would "make a pretty picture on stage."

She stayed with the Walker and Williams company until it disbanded, working hard and learning everything she could. Then she sought work as a dramatic actor. There wasn't any. There were no parts for even the best, most experienced black actors. No Broadway producers presented plays about black life, and they certainly weren't casting black actors in any other kind of play, except for an occasional part as a maid or a handyman.

Bush survived by performing here and there in musicals. However, she didn't give up easily on her dream of being a "real" actor. Seven years after she left the Walker and Williams company, she formed the Anita Bush Players. By that time, she knew a great many black actors who were out there desperately looking for work and a chance to do what they had always wanted

to do. Bush brought them together at the old Lincoln Theater and began to present theater in Harlem. Within the year, they had moved to the Lafayette Theater and become the **Lafayette Players**.

The Lafayette Players was the most important milestone for serious black drama since the Hyers sisters' Coloured Operatic and Dramatic Company back in 1875.

The Lafayette Players, with Anita Bush as artistic director produced serious drama with all-black casts for the next seventeen years. A great many of the plays they did were the same plays that were being done on Broadway with all-white casts: *The Count of Monte Cristo, Dr. Jekyll and Mr. Hyde,* and *Madame X.* They presented the Jewish comedy *Potash and Perlmutter.* They played anything and everything that white actors did; they simply played them in Harlem.

An article in *Billboard* magazine in August 1921 said:

> It is beginning to dawn on the American public that the Negro, in a none too distant future, is destined to command respectful attention and win favorable consideration in the realm of drama. In the past the theatregoer had visualized the Negro on the stage only in comedy, dance and song, and colored comedians have made enviable reputations as exponents of buffoonery; but today there is every indication that the Negro is soon to invade the legitimate field. . . . For six years, colored actors have been appearing with great success in stock at the Lafayette Theater, Seventh avenue[sic], between 131st and 132nd streets, New York.

The article went on to report the favorable reactions of a white producer who was "profuse in encomiums" and of a white actor who was so thrilled with the company's work that she went backstage to compliment the players. But the really important reaction to the Lafayette Players came from the black community. When it became clear that black audiences wanted, needed, and were willing to pay for serious theater, a group of black capitalists formed the Quality Amusement Corporation, which sponsored the Lafayette Players, sent them on tour, and formed black theaters in other cities.

Over its seventeen-year existence, the Lafayette completely changed the situation of black women as actors. With a place to develop their skills and talents, they thrived, and the larger theater world soon heard from such Lafayette Players as **Abbie Mitchell, Evelyn Ellis, Evelyn Preer, Edna Thomas, Laura Bowman,** and Inez Clough. It would not be too much to say that **Anita Bush** changed American theater forever.

In 1917, several of the Lafayette Players appeared at the Garden Theater in a trio of short plays by white poet Ridgely Torrence: *The Rider of Dreams*, *Granny Maumee*, and *Simon the Cyrenian*. Theater critic and historian Emory Lewis calls Torrence "the first white playwright who presented blacks with artistry and truth."

As for the actors, they were uniformly praised by critics of the time: Robert Benchley of the *Tribune* raved. George Jean Nathan of the *American Mercury* put *two* of the actors—Opal Cooper and Inez Clough—on his list of the ten best performers on Broadway that year—not the ten best *black performers*; not the ten best women performers; but the ten best *performers* of the year.

The play might have had a greater impact, but the United States declared war the day after it opened, and nations at war don't particularly like plays that criticize their treatment of their own people. *Three Plays for a Negro Theatre* ran for only a few weeks.

Still, the success of the Lafayette Players and its members became an important part of theatrical history and of that period's movement, the Harlem Renaissance. For one decade—the 1920s—black literature, music, theater, and art thrived. It was as though seeds that had lain dormant for years had suddenly found just the right soil, sun, and rain and had burst up and into flower. It was the time of Langston Hughes, **Zora Neale Hurston,** Countee Cullen, Walter White, **Gwendolyn Bennett,** and hundreds of other black artists. In this atmosphere, black actors began to appear on the Broadway stage in dramatic roles.

Several plays by Eugene O'Neill featured black roles, including *The Emperor Jones*, and *All God's Chillun Got Wings*. **Rose McClendon** made her mark on Broadway in Lawrence Stalling's *Deep River* in 1926. Paul Green's *In Abraham's Bosom* that same year and *House of Connelly* in 1931 gave roles to McClendon and Abbie Mitchell. The cast of DuBose and Dorothy Heyward's *Porgy* in 1927 included McClendon, Evelyn Ellis, and **Georgette Harvey.** Marc Connelly's *The Green Pastures*, which opened in 1930, provided work for hundreds of black actors.

Indeed, during this one "golden" decade, there were several plays concerning black life on Broadway; however, only a few of them were written by black men.

For black women, getting a play produced was virtually impossible. For example, in 1879, a playwright named **Pauline Elizabeth Hopkins** wrote a music drama called *Slaves' Escape: or the Underground Railroad.* It was performed by the playwright's family and friends, calling themselves the Hopkins' Colored Troubadours, at the Oakland Garden in Boston. The play received a good review in the *Boston Herald*, but this was a far cry from the New York stage.

Fortunately, black women playwrights, actors, and other theater professionals did not put their faith entirely in the Broadway stage. Their search for a place to practice their art was aided by the spirit of the Harlem Renaissance when black leader W. E. B. DuBois called for black writers to use the drama as a tool for social change and enrichment. He called for "native drama," which meant, in essence, plays about black people written by black people.

DuBois backed up his call for native drama with the power of the NAACP's *Crisis* magazine, which he edited. With Charles S. Johnson, editor of the National Urban League's *Opportunity* magazine, he held a contest in 1925 for one-act plays. The prize would be publication in one of the two magazines and a cash award.

The first year the contest was held, two of the three winning plays that appeared in *Crisis* were by women—**Ruth Gaines-Shelton**'s *The Church Fight* and **Myrtle Smith Livingston**'s *For Unborn Children.* Four of the seven *Opportunity* winners were by women—Zora Neale Hurston's *Colorstruck* and *Spears*, **May Miller**'s *The Bog Guide*, and Eloise Bibb Thompson's *Cooped Up.* In the two years that followed, before the contest was discontinued, awards were won by **Eulalie Spence, Marita Bonner,** and **Georgia Douglas Johnson.**

DuBois also founded the Krigwa Players, a black theater company based in Harlem.

Georgia Douglas Johnson wrote one of the first two plays produced by the Krigwa Players. W. E. B. DuBois, who had called for black writers to write plays about black people, founded the Krigwa Players in Harlem to produce these plays. (SCHOMBURG CENTER)

Their philosophy of theater was stated by DuBois:

The plays of a real Negro theatre must be: *One: About us.* That is, they must have plots which reveal Negro life as it is. *Two: By us.* That is, they must be written by Negro authors who understand from birth and continual association just what it means to be a Negro today. *Three: For us.* That is, the theatre must cater primarily to Negro audiences and be supported and sustained by their entertainment and approval. *Fourth: Near us.* The theatre must be in a Negro neighborhood near the mass of ordinary Negro people.

This was a new idea that black theater artists should not focus their energies on getting white people to hire them as actors or produce them as playwrights, but that they should do their own theater in their own place. Even the Lafayette Players performed plays by and about white people, though the actors were all black.

Companies of Krigwa Players were formed in other cities as well, and many of the plays performed in the short history of this endeavor were written by black women. **Mary P. Burrill**'s *Aftermath* was produced by the New York Krigwa Players and appeared in the David Belasco Little Theater Tournament in 1928. Three of Eulalie Spence's plays were produced by the Krigwa theater—*Foreign Mail*, *Fool's Errand*, and *Her;* The first two were published by Samuel French. In Baltimore, the Krigwa Players produced the plays of May Miller and Georgia Douglas Johnson. Many other black women saw their plays produced on the stages of the Krigwa Players during the twenties. By the thirties, the Krigwa Players no longer existed.

But the tradition of black theater, of black people producing theater for the black community, has never died. Black theater ensembles began to spring up all over the country. Again and again, their founders or cofounders were women. In New York, the most successful black theater ensemble was yet to come.

TUNE IN TOMORROW

With radio's enormously growing popularity in the 1920's, the world changed: Here was communication on a scale never before imagined. Black women faced the same sort discrimination in this new medium that they had in others, and yet, they were there in one way or another almost from the beginning.

Bessie Smith was the first black woman to sing live in concert on the radio. She was broadcast on radio stations in Atlanta and Memphis in 1924. That same year, the Hampton Singers, a black group from the Hampton Institute in Virginia, was broadcast from New York. During the next few

Stage, screen, and recording star Ethel Waters was among the black entertainers who also performed on radio. (DONALD BOGLE)

decades, many black singers stepped up to the mike, including Eva Taylor, who had her own radio series on NBC in the 1930s, Ethel Waters, and **Adelaide Hall**.

Few black actors, however, made their way into radio dramas. There were some, including Rose McClendon, who performed with Dorothy Caul in a presentation of *John Henry, Black River Giant*. **Georgia Burke** performed in soap operas, including *When a Girl Marries*, and *Betty and Bob*.

Comedies provided more opportunities, but the roles were highly stereotypical. Both Amanda and **Lillian Randolph** appeared on the popular *Amos 'n' Andy Show*. Amanda played the mother of Sapphire and mother-in-law of the Kingfish. Lillian played Madame Queen. Sapphire was played by Ernestine Wade. When the show moved to television, the white male stars were replaced by black actors Tim Moore, Alvin Childress, and Spencer Williams. The Randolph sisters and Wade moved with the show.

Ruby Dandridge staked out her territory on *The Judy Canova Show*, playing the role of Geranium. She was Raindrop on *The Gene Autry Show* and Oriole on *Beulah*. When *Beulah* went to television, Dandridge went with it.

As the power and popularity of television rose in the late 1940s and early 1950s, radio drama gradually disappeared. In the new world of radio, where music was the primary programming tool, black women were more in evidence. In 1947, there were only seventeen black disk jockeys broadcasting in the United States. Four years later, there were at least nine black *women* who were pulling in listeners in markets that ranged from Homestead, Pennsylvania, to New York, Atlantic City, and Birmingham. **Una**

Mae Carlisle had a national show on the American Broadcasting Company.

When black women performed as themselves—when they were singers, instrumentalists, or disk jockeys—they were often able to frustrate the expectations of the white entertainment world. But for actors in the mainstream of theater, film, and—soon—television, the limitations remained stifling.

MAMMY AND THE MAID

By the 1930s in America, the minstrel show was dead, but all its stereotypes were alive and kicking. As the twenties and the Harlem Renaissance passed, the black roles available in the theater, and now in films were almost always extensions of those caricatures from the bad old days. That enormously popular aspect of entertainment had been successful because it pandered to the hates and fears of white America, and, in the process, had helped to form white America's view of black life. The theater occasionally broke away from the minstrel vision; films and television, for decades, did not. As Langston Hughes and Milton Meltzer put it in *Black Magic*, "The silver screen was for many years black America's daily betrayal before millions of people."

But what art those black actors made inside the constricting shells formed by prejudice and ignorance! What dignity and sweetness and humor they projected through the husks of bigotry that encased them. Nothing makes this point clearer than the careers of the black women who had to work within the skins of the mammies, maids, and sirens . . . or the newer stereotype, the tragic mulatto.

In Gone With the Wind *(1939), Hattie McDaniel played Mammy to the headstrong Scarlett O'Hara (Vivien Leigh). For her performance, McDaniel won the first Academy Award ever presented to a black actor, male or female. She was not allowed to attend the Atlanta premiere of the film, however.* (DONALD BOGLE)

The three great Mammy figures were probably **Hattie McDaniel, Louise Beavers** and, in the second half of her remarkable career, Ethel Waters.

As Catherine Clinton outlines it in *Black Women in America*, "The myth of the Mammy revolves around two basic principles. First, that a slave woman within the white household devoted her maternal instincts and skills to the white family who owned her and that she took pleasure and pride in this service. Second, that she gained status from this role and was revered within the black community." Physically, the Mammy was fat, dark, and of mature years.

There is little or no truth to this myth, but it has had a persistent life in American theater and film. Mammy was there in *Birth of a Nation* in 1915 when D. W. Griffith revolutionized the film industry technically with a film that plumbed the depths of racism, and she stayed there through the decades to follow.

Hattie McDaniel played the role in *Gone With the Wind* in 1939. For doing it, she won the first Academy Award ever presented to a black actor.

McDaniel started her career as a blues singer on the TOBA circuit. Later, she moved to Los Angeles, where she played a few bit parts in movies and a bossy maid, Hi-Hat Hattie, on a weekly radio show on a black station. Her pay for these show-business jobs was so low that she had to take other work to support herself—as a maid.

Before long, McDaniel was dusting and sweeping for Marlene Dietrich, Mae West, Will Rogers, and Shirley Temple, all on film. She played in *Alice Adams* with Katharine Hepburn and in *The Mad Miss Manton* with Barbara Stanwyck. Virtually all of her roles fit the Mammy/maid stereotype. When she played Mammy in the biggest box-office hit Hollywood had ever known and won an Oscar for it, she became the most visible depicter of that mythic figure in American entertainment history. In all of these roles, as Donald Bogle points out in *Brown Sugar*,

In the 1934 film Imitation of Life, *Louise Beavers is the servant whose family recipe is turned into "Aunt Delilah's famous Pancake Mix" by her employer (played by Claudette Colbert).*   (PRIVATE COLLECTION)

The servant Dilsey is a central character in William Faulkner's great novel The Sound and the Fury. *She is played superbly in the film version by Ethel Waters.* (DONALD BOGLE)

"Boldly, she looked her white costars directly in the eye, never backing off from anyone. . . . Sometimes, McDaniel seemed angry. Although the movies never explained it, her undercover hostility, even when coated with humor, was never lost on the audience."

There has been a great deal of controversy about McDaniel and the other black actors who played stereotypical roles. During her lifetime, she was the target of scorn from Walter White of the NAACP and others.

But we have seen the paradox that has existed from the beginning for the American black entertainer—"finding the deep satisfaction of artistry and self-expression while performing for your oppressors, tailoring your performance to please the people who have enslaved you, persecuted you and rejected your humanity." That was what it meant to be a black performer on the plantation in 1800. That was still what it meant in 1939 in Hollywood. If you wanted to perform in the American mainstream, you worked within the stereotype and used your talents to give it all the humanity you could.

Louise Beavers did just that in the Mammy/maid roles she played in hundreds of vehicles, from a 1927 silent version of *Uncle Tom's Cabin* to the fifties television show *Beulah*. She gave her characters wit and dignity, kindness and good humor. In *Imitation of Life* in 1934, she and **Fredi Washington** took a trite, melodramatic script and, in their scenes together, created genuine cinematic art.

It was Ethel Waters, though, whose artistry cracked open the shell of the stereotype and ultimately left it shattered. Her first dramatic role was in the play *Mamba's Daughters* by Dorothy and DuBose Heyward, the authors of *Porgy*, in 1939. Hagar, a mother who sacrifices herself to assure her daughter a chance in life, is not a Mammy role. She is seen in relation not to her white employers but to her own black family.

Waters played Hagar with such honesty and power that the critics were overwhelmed—except for the influential Brooks Atkinson, critic for the *New York Times*. This sole holdout liked neither the play nor Waters' performance in it. But Waters had had such a tremendous affect on others that a group of theater professionals took an ad in the *New York Times*. It read, in part, "We the undersigned feel that Ethel Waters' superb performance in *Mamba's Daughters* . . . is a profound emotional experience which any playgoer would be the poorer for missing. It seems to be such a magnificent example of great acting, simple, deeply felt, moving on a plane of complete reality, that we are glad to pay for the privilege of saying so."

The ad was an extraordinary tribute to Waters's achievement. It was signed by, among others, Judith Anderson, Tallulah Bankhead, Dorothy Gish, Carl Van Vechten, and Burgess Meredith. After reading it, Atkinson went back to see *Mamba's Daughters* and changed his opinion.

This role should have been followed by others that gave Waters scope for her remarkable natural gift. Instead, she spent the rest of her dramatic career playing Mammies—magnificently: Her role in the film *Pinky* in 1949 transformed soap opera into truth and won her an Academy Award nomination as Best Supporting Actress. She played Berenice in Carson McCullers' *The Member of the Wedding* on Broadway in 1952, a triumph that Waters re-created with equal success in the film version of the play two years later. She provided the strong moral presence of Dulcy in the film version of *The Sound and the Fury* in 1959.

"She gave an additional human dimension," said Langston Hughes, "to the con-

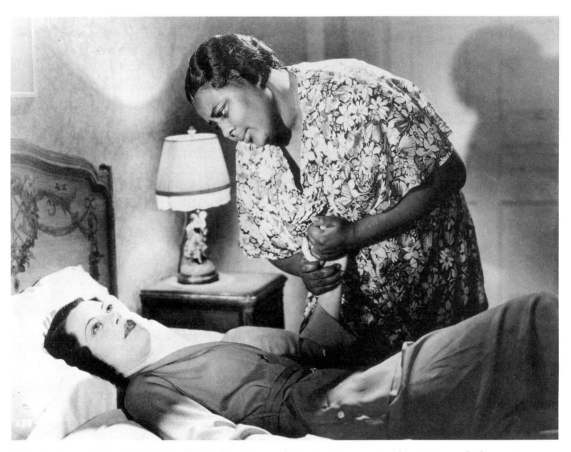

In Imitation of Life *(1934), Fredi Washington and Louise Beavers took a trite, melodramatic script and, in their scenes together, created genuine cinematic art.* (DONALD BOGLE)

Ethel Waters played Berenice in Carson McCullers' The Member of the Wedding *on Broadway in 1952. It was a triumph. Waters recreated the role with equal success in the film version of the play two years later.* (DONALD BOGLE)

ventional 'Mammy' of old—one of dignity and gentleness." But what was even more striking than her gentleness and what served more than anything else to leave the Mammy stereotype in shards on the stages where Waters played was her rage—the potential even for violence—that came through when she was pushed too far. Her performances foreshadowed those of the powerful black women in films to come—**Cicely Tyson, Ruby Dee, Rosalind Cash, Gloria Foster,** and **Oprah Winfrey** among others.

Another of the stereotypes left over from the minstrel shows was the wench, the black temptress, the siren. With her dark—though usually light-skinned—beauty she entices men, black and white, away from the path of righteousness, away from the good—though usually dull—wives and fiancées who truly love them. Unlike the Mammy role, the siren has a distinct white counterpart in the vamp. This is where the white fears and fascination with black people converge with the male fears and fascination with women. The combination is deadly.

The first of the black screen sirens was **Nina Mae McKinney.** When she was cast in the King Vidor film *Hallelujah* in 1929, she was a beautiful seventeen year old from the chorus of *Blackbirds.* Understandably, critics called her character "half woman, half child."

McKinney and her career set a pattern that would be repeated again and again in Hollywood: She was a beautiful, light-skinned woman who could not believably be cast as a maid. She was obviously a leading lady, and Hollywood was fascinated by what it thought of as her hypersexuality, but it would not use her as a romantic lead. She played small roles in two more films, *Safe in Hell* and *Reckless,* and then left Hollywood for a singing career, mostly in Europe.

Lena Horne started in films in the same kind of role, playing "the other woman" in the film version of *Cabin in the Sky* in 1943. Again, she was light skinned and beautiful and all set to be stereotyped as the mulatto siren Hollywood wouldn't know how to use.

What happened instead was that Horne, with the support of her father and of that of NAACP executive secretary Walter White, fashioned an image of sophistication, glam-

After giving Lena Horne (left) a seven-year contract, Metro-Goldwyn-Mayer cast her in only one speaking role, in the all-black film Cabin in the Sky (1943), *which also featured Eddie "Rochester" Anderson and Ethel Waters. Horne's other appearances in the studio's films were in musical numbers that could easily be edited out of prints of the film for showing in Southern theaters.* (DONALD BOGLE)

our, and cool unapproachability. At her father's insistence, her contract with MGM stated that she didn't have to play stereotyped roles. So, she didn't actually *have* roles in most of the films she made. Instead, she would come onto the screen in isolation from the plot and her fellow cast members, sing one song, and then disappear. The studio could then cut her appearance when the film was to be shown in the South. It wasn't until 1956 that she had her first speaking role in a mixed-cast film, *Meet Me in Las Vegas.*

In other words, she wasn't forced into the stereotype, but she also wasn't allowed to act. Lena Horne used her appearances in films to spark a long career singing and, in 1957, she went back to Broadway for the musical *Jamaica.*

A slight variation on the black-siren stereotype was the tragic mulatto, played by Fredi Washington in *Imitation of Life* in 1934. Washington had come to Hollywood after a career that began in the chorus of *Shuffle Along*, continued in a tour of Europe as a dancer, and then went back to the New York stage for a series of dramatic roles. She had also appeared in a number of films before *Imitation of Life*, but her role as Peola, a young woman who decides to pass for white, enclosed her in a stereotype from which she would never escape.

The idea of a black woman who looked so "white" had fascinated audiences in New York when she appeared in *Black Boy* with Paul Robeson, making her instantly famous. The same thing happened after she appeared in films as Peola: She was a sensation, not for her powerful performance, but because she was a curiosity, a novelty, almost a freak. The mulatto who just missed the great "glory" of being white was an utterly fascinating figure.

In addition, Washington's performance was so convincing that many people, black and white, identified her with the role. Donald Bogle, in *Brown Sugar*, tells what she faced after the film premiered: "On one occasion, as Fredi Washington sat in a beauty parlor, she overheard another woman telling a beautician that she knew Fredi Washington and that that high-yellar so-and-so was, in real life, just the way she had been on screen. Of course, the woman did not know Washington at all, and when Fredi introduced herself the lady promptly shut up."

But Washington was not there in every beauty parlor and drug store and dress shop to defend herself. In spite of the obvious fact that she was clearly capable of passing for white and had rejected that course out of identification with and loyalty to her black heritage, Fredi Washington developed a reputation for being antiblack.

The studio heads were not concerned with that aspect of the situation, but they were concerned with what to do with their glamorous new actor. Like McKinney and Horne before her, she was just not believable as a black maid. Of course, no one had the wit or courage to cast her regardless of race. So Washington went back to Broadway and her great success as Ethel Waters' daughter in *Mamba's Daughters*. Eventu-

Lena Horne chose to perform in nightclubs and radio, where she had more control over her art, than in films. [MOORLAND-SPINGARN]

ally, her interest turned towards political activism, and she retired from acting.

Black women in films fought for freedom from the limits of stereotyping in many ways. Louise Beavers, for example, appeared in independently made black films where she could get rid of her apron and also appeared in New York in a one-woman show. Lena Horne chose to perform in nightclubs and radio where she had more control over her art. Many black actors, such as Edna Mae Harris, Bee Freeman, and Ethel Moses, appeared almost exclusively in independently produced all-black movies.

The time when black women would begin to come into their own as actors, writers, designers, and directors in Hollywood was still many years away. But across the country in New York, many of the key players were beginning to appear on the scene.

THE FIRST LADY AND HER CHILDREN

The question: What does Spike Lee owe to the wife of a New York chiropractor? The answer: Ruby Dee, Ossie Davis, and a whole lot more.

Rose McClendon, wife of chiropractor Henry Pruden McClendon, was thirty-six years old before she ever appeared on a professional stage. She didn't even go to drama school until she was thirty-two. But from the time she walked down the stairs in a small part in Lawrence Stallings' *Deep River* in 1926, her dignity and distinction made her the black First Lady of Theater.

McClendon appeared in virtually every important play about black life that appeared on Broadway during the seventeen

years between her debut and her early death. She made a lasting mark in Langston Hughes' *Mulatto*, which had the longest run on Broadway of any black play before *A Raisin in the Sun*, but that wasn't her most important contribution to the theater. McClendon was deeply committed to changing the position of black actors and playwrights. It is for that commitment that Spike Lee is in her debt.

McClendon served on the board of the Theater Union, which ran the Civic Repertory Theater on West Fourteenth Street in New York City. She also directed plays for

Ruby Dee and Ossie Davis were two of the actors in the Rose McClendon Players, founded in 1937, the first important black theater in New York since the Lafayette Players, fifteen years earlier. (MOORLAND-SPINGARN)

the Harlem Experimental Theater and organized the Negro People's Theater, whose first production was a black version of Clifford Odets' social protest play, *Waiting for Lefty*. When Franklin Delano Roosevelt's Works Progress Administration (WPA) initiated the Federal Theatre Project (FTP) to help theater professionals survive the Great Depression of the 1930s, Rose McClendon was appointed codirector of the Negro Unit with white director John Houseman. She served in that capacity until her death from cancer.

In her honor, the first important black theater company in New York since the Lafayette Players was called the Rose McClendon Players. It was founded in 1937, and with her spirit of commitment to excellence in theater and equality for black performers, the modern black theater movement was born.

Ossie Davis and Ruby Dee were in the group. So were **Jane White**, **Helen Martin**, and others who would have long, distinguished careers in the black theater. The Rose McClendon Players produced for five years. When it folded, several of its members were involved in the founding of the American Negro Theater, training ground for **Rosetta LeNoire**, **Alice Childress**, **Isabel Sanford**, and **Clarice Taylor**, as well as for such male stars as Sidney Poitier and Harry Belafonte. The theater produced eighteen plays during the decade of its existence, including Katherine Garrison's *Sojourner Truth*.

The theater's biggest hit was *Anna Lucasta*, a play with an interesting history. It was originally written to be performed by a white cast, dealing as it did with a Polish family. But its author, Philip Yordan, was unable to find a producer to commit to it.

Abram Hill, artistic director of the American Negro Theater, suggested to Yordan that the play could be adapted for an all-black cast. It was, and the production, with **Hilda Simms** as Anna, was a smash hit in Harlem. Also in the cast was Alice Childress, soon to make her name as one of the first successful black woman playwrights.

The success of *Anna Lucasta* raised a question that was only to become more intense in the years following World War II: Did the future of black theater in America lie in the adaptation of proven white plays, or did it lie in the exploration of the black experience by black artists?

Looking at the issue now, half a century later, it's difficult to imagine how anyone could ever have thought that a black version of a white play was the answer to the position of blacks in American theater. It seems so clear that African Americans needed to find their own voice and speak from their own experience, just as DuBois had said. However, in the 1930s and 1940s, there were reasons to think that black actors could best avoid stereotyping by playing roles that were for white actors.

Besides the success of *Anna Lucasta*, there was also what was happening to the black musical. That was a truly remarkable situation.

SWING IT

Once upon a time, there was an Ethiopian princess who lived a very sad life in the Deep South of the United States during the Civil War . . . Doesn't sound too likely, does it? But it happened on Broadway.

It all started with a production from the Negro Unit of the FTP in Chicago in 1938.

That group presented *Swing Mikado*, a version of Gilbert and Sullivan's operetta *The Mikado* set in the South Sea Islands. It had an all-black cast and a few black touches in the choreography and arrangements of the music, and it broke box office records. Soon, the show was on Broadway. Three weeks after it opened, white producer Mike Todd opened a rival all-black show, *Hot Mikado*.

Todd's show had more swing than *Swing Mikado*. It had another advantage as well: Because the FTP was part of the WPA, Roosevelt's program to keep people in work during the Depression, it had to hire "unemployed" actors. So with its bigger budget and bigger stars, *Hot Mikado* was strong competition.

Both of the shows were successful enough to start a new trend in black musicals. In 1939, there was *Swingin' the Dream*, an adaptation of Shakespeare's *A Midsummer Night's Dream*, in which singer **Maxine Sullivan** starred as Titania and **Butterfly McQueen** was Puck. In 1943, Oscar Hammerstein II weighed in with *Carmen Jones*, based on Bizet's opera *Carmen* and starring, at alternating performances, Muriel Smith and **Muriel Rahn**. *Memphis Bound* (1945) was *H.M.S. Pinafore* in disguise. Edith Wilson was featured.

It wasn't until 1952 that the trend began to falter with *My Darlin' Aida*. This is where we come to the Ethiopian princess because that's what Verdi's *Aida* is about. Just hearing the title makes you wonder why anyone ever thought this was a good idea, and to make things even more absurd, most of the major roles in the "black" version of *Aida* were played by whites in blackface makeup! The producers auditioned and turned down New York City Opera singers Camilla Williams and Margaret Tynes as well as Muriel

Rahn, who had made such a great success of *Carmen Jones*, and then, declaring these divas inadequate, cast an inexperienced twenty-one-year-old white singer. The show was an abysmal failure at the box office.

Why did black actors become so involved in these productions, far as they were from an authentic black voice in the theater? Well, when the choice is between *Swing Mikado* on the one hand and yet one more successor to *The Green Pastures* and *Porgy and Bess* on the other, it's not surprising that there was a certain fondness for the Lord High Executioner.

Blacks in the theater were trying desperately to break out of past stereotyping. They were looking for a way to shatter the constricting images of black people and black life that had existed for so long. Gilbert and Sullivan's "three little maids from school" may have been light years away from the reality of black experience, but they were also light years away from the wench of the minstrel show and the Mammy of the early theater. At the time, it seemed a way to show that black performers could do anything; and as only one part of a rich, abundant black theater it would serve exactly that purpose. As the major representative of black people on stage, it was seriously lacking.

Cabin in the Sky, produced in 1940, was one of those white-owned-and-operated black musicals that tried to "interpret" black religion, folklore, music, and mythology. It was extremely successful commercially and critically, in large part because of the talents of its black cast.

At the center of the show was Ethel Waters. She did not begin at the center, but moved there as the play developed. Waters had just made her dramatic—in both senses of the word—debut as Hagar in *Mamba's*

Daughters, and was developing a new image of black womanhood in the theater and film. That image had at its core strength and spirituality.

As originally envisioned by the authors, Waters's character, Petunia, was the mildly funny, patient wife of likeable womanizer Little Joe Jackson. Her rival was Georgia Brown, played by dancer **Katherine Dunham**. Waters persuaded the producers that, since Petunia collaborates with God to save Little Joe's soul, she should have a serious, genuine faith. This change in the conception of one of the main characters gave the show a stronger impact, and the play went on to become a film. Waters remained in the cast as Petunia, but Dunham was replaced by up-and-coming film star Lena Horne, who scored a personal success in the role.

The Broadway show's major contribution to the American theater was Katherine Dunham. The great dancer, because of her role in *Cabin in the Sky*, was in a position to develop the dance company she had formed a few years before.

Dunham was not like any black woman the entertainment world had ever seen. She didn't come out of the chorus; she came out of the University of Chicago, where she had studied anthropology. As an anthropologist, she spent time in the Caribbean, studying dance forms of the West Indies. When she came back, she formed a company to perform dances inspired by the West Indies and Africa.

In the years that followed *Cabin in the Sky*, Dunham and her company presented the most entertaining—and genuine—Caribbean dancing on a Broadway that seemed to have gone West Indies wild. Her troupe appeared in *Tropical Revue, Bal Nègre, Blue Holiday*, and *Caribbean Carnival*.

Dunham choreographed and performed in *Carib Song*.

In the 1940s and 1950s on Broadway, it was safer to set musicals on a tropical island than deal with the issue of race in the United States. Still, there was one black musical of the period that was considerably different. Its composer, Harold Arlen, had been writing for black performers for at least a decade. He composed music for several Cotton Club revues, including "Stormy Weather," the song that became Ethel Waters's trademark. Arlen also wrote black performers into white shows such as *Bloomer Girl*, with Celeste Holm.

For *St. Louis Woman*, he turned to black writers Countee Cullen and Arna Bontemps. They adapted Bontemps' novel *God Sends Sundays* for the stage and retitled it. Ruby Hill starred as Della Green, the St. Louis Woman of the title, but it was **Pearl Bailey** as Della's rival who walked away with the show.

Important as Bailey's Broadway debut was, it may not have been the most important event connected with the production. That happened when the cast stopped the rehearsals, protesting offensive stereotypes in the show! They actually refused to go on until the characterization of the women in the play was changed.

Of course, black actors had complained before about stereotyping; still, most of them had little power and knew it. It was a sign of significant change when a whole cast refused to go on until their complaints were listened to. But one show and one cast were not enough; the essential problem remained. Shows about black life presented unacceptable stereotypes, while black versions of white plays failed to speak to the experience of either black performers or black audiences. This was a problem that the black theater movement would have to solve before it could grow.

AFTER THE WAR WAS OVER

During and after World War II, there was a new feeling in America. Many black men and women had fought for their country and had come back to share in the freedom. Many white men and women knew it. There were opportunities enough for everyone in the prosperous wartime and postwar economies and, for a while anyway, it looked as though there were even enough opportunities to go beyond the limits of race.

In the 1940s, quite a number of black actors found work on Broadway. There seemed to be a move toward integrating the New York stage. As John Lovell, Jr., discovered when he tabulated the figures, the number of black performers on Broadway grew steadily from a total of fifty-two in 1940 to 279 in 1946. His figures didn't show how many of those performers were women, but we know they included Muriel Smith and Muriel Rahn in *Carmen Jones* (1943), Pearl Bailey in *St. Louis Woman* (1945), Katherine Dunham in half a dozen musicals, Evelyn Ellis in *Deep Are the Roots* (1945), Jane White in *Strange Fruit* (1945), and Ruby Dee, Laura Bowman, and **Reri Grist** in *Jeb* (1946).

In the late forties, however, things began to look bleak again. By the 1951–52 season, only thirteen black actors had parts on Broadway, and almost all of them were bit parts.

America in the 1950s was eating up *Guys and Dolls*, *The King and I*, and *Can-Can*. It found *Pal Joey* just a little too dangerous. It certainly did not want the "problem plays" of the 1940s, such as *Mamba's Daughters*

Ruby Dee was one of a number of black actors who found work on Broadway in the 1940s. (LIBRARY OF CONGRESS)

and *Black Boy*, which dealt with serious racial issues. Broadway was also beginning to turn away from black musicals, which raised the thorny issue of stereotyping. And black actors were not yet accepted as the ordinary characters in life's drama—lawyers and druggists and shopkeepers, friends and colleagues and neighbors.

So, for a while, it was back to servants. Langston Hughes and Milton Meltzer sum it up nicely in *Black Magic*:

> In the Joshua Logan adaptation of Chekhov's *The Cherry Orchard* to a Louisiana

milieu under the title of *The Wisteria Trees*, Ossie Davis, Georgia Burke, and Alonzo Bosan played servants to the Dixie gentry. In Max Gordon's production of *The Small Hours*, John Marriott was also a manservant. In Lillian Hellman's *The Autumn Garden*, Maxwell Glanville portrayed the colored butler of a summer boarding house. P. Jay Sidney was a Pullman porter in the Hecht-Arthur farce *Twentieth Century*, and Ossie Davis played a handyman in the Kaufman-Ferber comedy *The Royal Family*. Eulabelle Moore was the comic maid in *The Male Animal*, Evelyn Davis supplied kitchen help in *Southern Exposure*. In *Four Twelves are Forty-Eight* Rosetta LeNoire was a black servant with a Ph.D. degree! . . . In Truman Capote's *The Grass Harp*, Georgia Burke played a cook who sat in a tree.

Playing a cook is not the ultimate ambition of any good actor, even if you get to sit in a tree, so the black theater movement in Harlem began to revitalize. Alice Childress, Ruth Jett, and others formed the Council on the Harlem Theater. Through this council, the small theaters of Harlem agreed to cooperate with each other in any way possible, sharing resources and arranging compatible schedules.

Soon, Alice Childress' play *Just a Little Simple* opened at the Club Baron. An adaptation of Langston Hughes' series of newspaper columns entitled "Simple Speaks His Mind," the show was a big success. In 1951, the Club Baron presented *A Meal for Willie* with Clarice Taylor and Helen Martin in a cast that also included Julian Mayfield and Eli Wallach.

Ruby Dee came back from Hollywood, where she had appeared as Jackie Robinson's wife in *The Jackie Robinson Story*, to act in Ossie Davis' *Alice in Wonder*. The show, which included two other one-act plays in addition to Davis', showed a remarkable spirit of cooperation and support. Famous black actor William Marshall donated money to help get it on stage. Sidney Poitier, who hadn't made it yet himself, sold tickets to the show in his restaurant, "Ribs and Ruff."

The Greenwich Mews Theater in Greenwich Village had a policy of casting regardless of race that provided black actors with a great many acting opportunities. Helen Haynes, for example, played a Jewish mother in *Monday's Heroes*. She also appeared in the theater's production of Alice Childress's brilliant, funny *Trouble in Mind* in 1955.

In 1953, the play *Take a Giant Step*, which featured Maxine Sullivan, Pauline Myers, and Estelle Hemsley along with star Louis Gossett, Jr., had a modest success on Broadway. But when it was revived in Harlem in 1956, with **Frances Foster**, Juanita Bethea, and Godfrey Cambridge, it was a hit. The black theater movement was coming into its own.

In the 1960s, it would explode. But, in the meantime, Broadway was about to welcome a classic, a play that would bring the Harlem actors downtown and then on to Hollywood.

A RAISIN IN THE SUN

The year was 1959. After the period of promise that followed World War II and despite such momentous events as the Supreme Court's *Brown* vs. *Board of Education of Topeka Kansas* decision, the United

States was once more mired in its ugly racist attitudes. Unable to wait any longer, to bear any more, black citizens had begun the fight for civil rights, but it was still a young movement. In Alabama Rosa Parks had sat down on the bus in Montgomery four years before, but Martin Luther King had not yet gone to jail in Birmingham. The days of rage had not begun, and the days of invisibility were still around.

So far, the only black characters on the brand new medium of television were Beulah, Amos and Andy, and Jack Benny's chauffeur, Rochester, although Pearl Bailey occasionally showed up to josh with Ed Sullivan. In the movies, it seemed that all the black people lived on islands in the South Seas called Tamango, and the women were always busting out of their clothes. You could look through most newspapers for months at a time without seeing a single black face outside the sports pages, and there weren't too many there.

Then suddenly, on Broadway, there was *A Raisin in the Sun.*

It wasn't a musical. It wasn't a comedy. It wasn't a social problem play. It was a simple story about a working-class family whose members want a nice place to live and a little hope for the future and who are becoming very frustrated.

A Raisin in the Sun by **Lorraine Hansberry** was more than an exceptionally fine play; it was a social phenomenon. It showed an ordinary family with ordinary feelings and relationships. They are black, and their blackness affects their lives, but their struggle is universal, and their appeal is universal. It was just the kind of portrayal of ordinary African Americans that segregation-minded America had been working overtime to keep off the stage, the screen, and the airwaves. It broke through the wall of hatred and fear and said, very simply and very clearly, "black people are *people.*"

From the reaction of audiences and critics, it was clear that the breakthrough was long overdue. The play was a hit, Hansberry

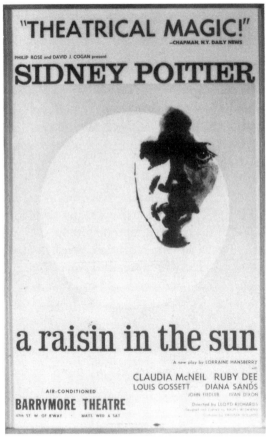

The Broadway production of A Raisin in the Sun *made Lorraine Hansberry a celebrity overnight. Drama critic Walter Kerr, in his opening-night review, stated, "The mood is forty-nine parts anger and forty-nine parts control, with a very narrow escape hatch for the steam these abrasive contraries build up."* (SCHOMBURG CENTER)

became famous, and virtually the entire cast was on its way to stardom.

Sidney Poitier, who played Walter Younger, would become the biggest black male star in movie history and keep that distinction for many years. Ruby Dee, who played Ruth Younger, would have a distinguished career on stage, in films, and on television, right up through Spike Lee's *Do the Right Thing* and beyond. **Claudia McNeil,** who played Lena Younger, would be recognized immediately as one of the great stage actors of her generation. Diana Sands, who played Beneatha Younger, would become a Broadway star, the first black woman to be given the opportunity to play such roles as Saint Joan. Even the actors who played smaller roles had fine futures ahead of them, actors such as Louis Gossett, Jr., Ivan Dixon, and Lonnie Elder III.

A Raisin in the Sun soon became a film. Poitier, McNeil, Sands, and Dee re-created their stage roles.

Success breeds success. In the years immediately following the play's conquest of Broadway, other black plays began to appear. In the three years before, there had been a total of five "black" plays on Broadway and off-Broadway, not all of them by black authors or with all-black casts, but all providing at least one principal role for a black actor. In the three years following the success of Hansberry's play, there were nine, and the 1963–64 season alone had ten black plays in Broadway or off-Broadway theaters.

Hansberry had benefited enormously from the groundwork laid by the black theater movement in the years before she began her career. When her play came along, she found a talented black director, actors, and backstage workers, as well as an audience that had been building for decades. Now that same movement was benefiting from her success.

Though there have been setbacks, the black theater movement has continued to thrive. As the civil rights movement pushed against the limitations of white society, the black theater reflected and inspired that movement.

A major new voice made itself heard when **Adrienne Kennedy**'s *Funnyhouse of a Negro* was produced by a group calling itself Theater 1964. The play takes place in the mind of a young black woman, played by **Billie Allen,** and traces her journey as her own conflicts about her race drive her to madness. The play and the production were very well received. Adrienne Kennedy won an Obie and became one of the first of a wave of new black women playwrights.

The **Negro Ensemble Company** was founded in 1968 and soon gained the reputation of a national black theater. Among the women who have worked with the NEC are Alice Childress, Rosalind Cash, Frances Foster, **Esther Rolle,** Ellen Holly, Ethel Ayler, Barbara Montgomery, Clarice Taylor, Allie Woods, **Mary Alice,** Roxie Roker, and **Hattie Winston**.

In 1969, Rosetta LeNoire formed her Amas Repertory Theater (from the Latin word *amas*, meaning "you love"). Its stated function, to encourage cultural pluralism and love, has remained LeNoire's guiding principle for more than twenty-five years.

The Free Southern Theater, organized in New Orleans, was one of many regional companies involved in the black theater movement. It began by touring to Southern black communities doing classic drama with black casts. Later, under the urging of members such as **Denise Nicholas,** it turned more to black folk life.

In Chicago, **Valene Grey Ward** organized the Kuumba Theater, which began producing ground-breaking musical and dramatic theater. **Jackie Taylor** formed the Black Ensemble Theater, which has produced steadily for twenty years, giving Chicago some of its most innovative and powerful theater, and Abena Joan Brown cofounded ETA, which also continues to illuminate the Chicago theater scene.

The National Black Theater Company, founded by **Barbara Ann Teer,** put its emphasis on spirituality and ritual. **Vinette Carroll**'s Urban Art Corps trained black and Hispanic young people. Through her work there, she developed a number of works that ended up on Broadway, such as **Micki Grant**'s *Don't Bother Me I Can't Cope* in 1972 and her own *Your Arms Too Short to Box with God* in 1976.

The New Federal Theater at the Henry Street Settlement produced the work of minority playwrights and had a special relationship with Joe Papp, who ran New York's Public Theater. In a number of cases, a play would start out at the New Federal and then move to the Public. One of the more important plays of the contemporary theater, **Ntozake Shange**'s *for colored girls who have considered suicide/when the rainbow is enuf,* followed this course in 1976. It then went on to the Booth Theater on Broadway. Its total run was 867 performances in New York. Shange won an Obie for the play, and Trazana Beverley won a Tony for her performance. The play was later produced on Public Television's *American Playhouse* series.

In 1971, the New Federal Theater presented *Black Girl,* by **J. E. Franklin.** It was so successful that it moved to the Theater de Lys, also in New York City, for 234 performances. Directed by **Shauneille Perry,** the play was a remarkable theatrical experience; according to Jeanne-Marie A. Miller in the *Dictionary of the Black Theater,* "Audiences waited after each performance to congratulate members of the cast. For black theatergoers, *Black Girl* was the play to see." It went on to become a film starring **Leslie Uggams.**

Franklin's next major work was a musical collaboration with Micki Grant. *The Prodigal Sister* opened at the Theater de Lys and was also very successful. Since then, Franklin has consistently given black women a strong voice in the theater with such plays as *Mau Mau Room* and *Cut Out the Lights and Call the Law.*

Shauneille Perry, director of *Black Girl,* formed the National Black Touring Circuit with Woodie King, Jr., which gave successful plays a place to go after their initial run in New York and helped to keep the black theater movement alive around the country.

Interestingly, black women who are theater professionals move in and out of the various entertainment media with a flexibility you seldom see among other groups. Ruby Dee, for example, has won among dozens of awards a couple of Emmies, an Obie, the Drama Desk Award. But what sometimes seems even more astonishing than the quality of her work is its infinite variety. She has done film, television, radio, and readings. She has been on soap operas and situation comedies. But again and again, she confirms her commitment to the theater in all its forms, old and new.

Dee is not alone. Black women such as Esther Rolle, Rosalind Cash, and Isabel Sanford remain connected to their roots in the theater as they explore film and television. There are probably a number of reasons for this, other than love of the theater; one reason becomes abundantly clear when we go back to Hollywood to see how far it's come since the days of the Mammy and the siren.

BLACK WOMEN IN FILM

For women, making it in Hollywood is a balancing act. For black women in the 1950s, few managed to walk the tightrope.

Pearl Bailey did. She came to Hollywood from Broadway after her success in *St. Louis Woman*, and her style was perfect for the situation. She was relaxed and funny and full of good humor. She *joshed*. Now, joshing is a very special talent. You're giving somebody a hard time, but the way you do it, they have to like it, because it's so clear that you like them. They also hear what you're saying.

Bailey was a master of joshing. After being featured in supporting roles in a few movies—*Isn't It Romantic?*, *Carmen Jones*, *That Certain Feeling*, *Porgy and Bess*, among others—she became an extremely popular and active performer on television. She didn't have her own show until the 1970s, but in the fifties and sixties she was on everybody else's: Ed Sullivan featured her repeatedly; she was able to transmit being relaxed enough for many appearances with Perry Como, and in the meantime, she had her successful nightclub act. She walked the tightrope without a false step. It was much later that Bailey made her indelible impression on Broadway and tour in the all-black production of *Hello, Dolly!*

Then there was **Eartha Kitt**. She danced along the tightrope with a daring that made people gasp. She had captivated Broadway audiences in *New Faces of 1952*, *Mrs. Patterson*, *Shinbone Alley*, and *Jolly's Progress*. Then she came to Hollywood to star in a film version of *Anna Lucasta*. She was sexy, sophisticated, playful. She seemed to do exactly what she wanted, the way she wanted to do it, and all the time, she was balancing carefully, never going too far, but coming close enough to seem dangerous.

Then, in 1968, she faltered. The wife of President Lyndon Johnson, Lady Bird, invited Kitt to a gathering at the White House, along with a number of other prominent women. While they were discussing the problem of juvenile delinquency, Kitt brought up racism, poverty, and an unjust war in Vietnam. Conservatives were scandalized, liberals were delighted, and, with the spotlight of controversy glaring, Kitt fell off the tightrope. Her subsequent disruption of a Senate session did not fortify her position.

Dorothy Dandridge was born on the tightrope. She grew up in Los Angeles where her mother Ruby had a small career in movies and a more significant one on radio. Dorothy Dandridge performed in churches when she was a child, at the Cotton Club when she was a teenager, and with Duke Ellington and Cab Calloway as a young woman. She had bit parts in a series of forgettable movies. Then, supporting herself by her singing, she set out to become an actor, to become a star.

She took classes, went to auditions, did whatever she had to do. She worked with the singing coach who had helped shape the styles of Lena Horne and **Diahann Carroll** and perfected a nightclub act. She was constantly compared to Horne. Her nightclub performances sold out, and her picture appeared in *Life* magazine, but this was all preparation. She was going to be an actor. She was going to be a star.

When Hollywood called, Dorothy Dandridge found herself cast in larger parts, though in still forgettable pictures. Then, in 1953, she was cast opposite Harry Belafonte in the film *Bright Road*. The role was that of a Southern schoolteacher. Dandridge played it with dignity and truthfulness, and the critics were impressed. Dorothy Dan-

Dorothy Dandridge was a prodigiously talented and charismatic actress who was forced into a destructive stereotype as a siren that wasted her talent and, eventually, her life. Her first important film role was as a Southern schoolteacher in Bright Road *(1953), in which she costarred with Harry Belafonte.* (NATIONAL ARCHIVES)

dridge had achieved her first goal: She had become an actor of the first rank.

However, when the film role of the decade for a black woman came up, it almost passed her by. Otto Preminger was casting the film version of *Carmen Jones*, he dismissed Dandridge as too "regal." He wanted a black temptress, a siren out of the old mold, the stereotype come to life. Dandridge put on a low-cut blouse, messed up her hair, dropped her regal, Horne-like bearing, and walked into Preminger's office. She got the role.

Dandridge was a huge success in *Carmen Jones*. She was the first black woman to receive an Oscar nomination in the Best Actress category. *Newsweek* called her "one of the outstanding dramatic actresses of the screen." She was a star.

As for the answer to the question "How far had black women in Hollywood come?" Dandridge did not have another role for three years. When she did appear onscreen again, it was as a black temptress in movies such as *The Decks Ran Red*, *Tamango*, and *Malaga*. In 1959, she played Bess in the film version of *Porgy and Bess*. Because she so successfully captured the various aspects of Bess's complicated character, she won the Golden Globe award for Best Actress in a Musical.

But that, for all intents and purposes, was the end of Dandridge's career. She successfully walked the tightrope only to discover that there was nothing at the other end of it. In 1965, she was found dead of an overdose of antidepressants. She had been a splendid actress, but there had been no place for her.

Indeed, the place for black women in Hollywood was becoming more and more limited. The 1960s were a time to get rid of the old stereotypes. Gone was the Mammy, gone was the maid, and gone was the black temptress. With the civil rights movement raging, the producers knew there would have to be a new image for black women on the screen.

Of course, Hollywood played it safe again, and so they got it wrong again. Their new black woman of the sixties was not an intensely human woman of intelligence and fire, of wisdom and dignity and foolishness and weakness and courage, the kind of woman Ruby Dee, Diana Sands, **Beah Richards**, and Clarice Taylor were playing in the theater. The new black woman in Hollywood was middle class, educated, refined, and completely unethnic.

Among the actors who became trapped by this new stereotype was Diahann Carroll, a gifted singer who won a Metropolitan Opera scholarship at the age of ten. She was studying psychology at New York University in 1954 when she was cast in a costarring role in the Broadway musical *House of Flowers*, written by Truman Capote and Harold Arlen. The show was not a success, but Carroll was. Her solo performance of the lullaby "A Sleepin' Bee" was met with raves. That same year, Carroll won a small role in the stage version of *Carmen Jones*. She studied acting with Lee Strasberg and sang in nightclubs. Her first film role was a small one in *Porgy and Bess* in 1959.

Then, in 1962, Carroll was cast in the lead of a Broadway musical that might have been written for her, Rodgers and Hammerstein's *No Strings*. She played a model in Paris who fell in love with a writer, played by Richard Kiley, a white actor. She and her clothes were fabulously glamorous, she sang beautifully, and the interracial romance seemed daring on Broadway. The show made Carroll famous. When she discovered that a film version was to be made with a Eurasian woman in her role, she accused Hollywood of racism, making something of a scandal in the press. (The film was never made.)

In 1968, after six years of nightclub engagements and television talk-show appearances, Carroll was cast in the title role of the television series *Julia*. The show was television history.

FROM *JULIA* TO *ROOTS*

Television is the great popular medium of the twentieth century. Almost from the beginning, it has tried to appeal to the widest possible audience. That has meant, for the most part, that it has ignored the preferences and sensitivities of minorities, including, of course, black women. When they appeared on the small screen at all, they found themselves in the same negative stereotypes they had been playing for years in films.

Of course, there were the mammies and the maids, the most famous being *Beulah,* which was originally a popular radio show featuring Hattie McDaniel. It focused on the comic trials and tribulations of a Mammyesque maid. Although Ethel Waters portrayed the television Beulah for the show's first season, McDaniel was slated to take over in the second season. When she became too ill, Louise Beavers—the third of the great Mammies—became the final incarnation of Beulah. Butterfly McQueen and then Ruby Dandridge played Beulah's brainless friend Oriole.

The emphasis on black women in service roles in white households continued with **Lillian Randolph**'s Louise in the long-running Danny Thomas vehicle *Make Room for*

Nichelle Nichols played Lieutenant Uhuru in the first Star Trek *series. Though she did little more than punch buttons at the command of Captain Kirk, she was very much a presence on the crew. Asronaut Mae Jemison says it was Nichols who first convinced her that she could travel in space.* (PRIVATE COLLECTION)

Daddy from 1953 to 1957. Even after the civil rights movement of the 1960s, black women continued to find themselves in subordinate roles in all-white environments. **Nichelle Nichols** as Lieutenant Uhuru in the NBC 1966–71 cult favorite *Star Trek* did little more than punch buttons at the command of Captain James T. Kirk.

One critically acclaimed series was more radical. In 1963, *East Side/West Side,* which featured Cicely Tyson, explored a variety of inner-city problems. In a guest appearance, Diana Sands won an Emmy for her role as the wife in a black couple trying to make ends meet in the ghetto. But *East Side/West Side* proved too sobering for the American television audience and was broadcast for only one season.

The role of Julia, on the other hand, eliminated everything anyone had ever complained about in the portrayal of black women on stage, film, or television. Julia was not a servant. She was not a temptress. She was not ignorant, lazy, foolish, or fearful. She had never been poor, never lived in a ghetto, never seen a child go hungry. By the time the writers and producers decided everything Julia was not, she was not much.

The show was successful and ran for three seasons. African Americans were proud of Carroll and happy to see a black woman with dignity on television. At the same time, a large part of the black community did not respond favorably to the implication that for a black woman to be respected and admired she had to be—well—not black.

Looking back, it seems clear that Diahann Carroll's Julia was a transitional figure. She cleared the stage for a new exploration of black women in film and television. Carroll herself went on to be part of that exploration.

The moderate success of *Julia* did not give rise to a rash of successors. There were two variety shows starring black women at the end of the sixties and beginning of the seventies, but they didn't last long. *The Leslie Uggams Show*, starring the now-grown-up child star, aired in 1969 and was canceled after thirteen weeks. *The Pearl Bailey Show* lasted only half of the 1970–71 season.

One move in the direction of a new image for black women starred a veteran of the black theater movement, Denise Nicholas. The series *Room 222,* which ran from 1969 to 1974, depicted a wide range of realistic issues concerning the multiracial student body of Walt Whitman High. Nicholas was the school's guidance counselor. The show sympathetically portrayed her character and that of her romantic interest, a black man who taught history at the school, and won approval from the **National Association for the Advancement of Colored People** (NAACP). Still, the show tended to idealize the two for their ability to assimilate mainstream white values rather than challenge them.

By the mid-1970s, such experimentation was largely abandoned. Idealistic hope for the racially harmonious world of *Room 222* seemed naive in the light of continued racial tension in America. *East Side/West Side* was too hot to handle. Instead, television producers turned to black sitcoms.

Almost without exception, the comedies played into stereotypes of both black men and black women. The father of the family was a buffoon whose scheming resulted in a series of comic scrapes. His family tirelessly

In 1972, two black women were nominated for Academy Awards in the Best Actress category: Cicely Tyson, for her stunning performance as the sharecropping mother in Sounder *(shown here with Kevin Hooks, the actor who played her son), and Diana Ross, for her depiction of Billie Holiday in* Lady Sings the Blues. (PRIVATE COLLECTION)

bailed him out of trouble. Particularly long suffering was the family's matriarch, who was usually either his wife or his mother. Invariably large, the matriarch did little more than endlessly fret about the house. She was either a sharp-tongued, explosive personality such as La Wanda Page's Aunt Esther in *Sanford and Son,* or a long-suffering comic foil such as Esther Rolle's Florida Evans of *Good Times,* Mabel King's Mama Thomas of *What's Happening!* and Isabel Sanford's Louise Jefferson from *The Jeffersons.*

The women who acted in these shows, for the most part, continued the tradition of working as well and as humanely inside the stereotypes as possible. Several of them used the sitcoms as springboards for serious careers. Esther Rolle, for example, had come to television from a distinguished career in black theater. She won one Emmy and five nominations for her role as Louise Jefferson. Then she went on to do a number of dramatic roles in such television movies as *I Know Why the Caged Bird Sings* in 1979. She has also appeared in films such as *Driving Miss Daisy* and on the dramatic stage.

As for film, the situation was more confused. There were signs of hope, with more black women onscreen, even in starring roles. But the search for "the new black woman" was turning up some odd and contradictory images.

In 1972, two black women were nominated for Academy Awards in the Best Actress category: Cicely Tyson for her stunning performance as the sharecropping mother in *Sounder* and **Diana Ross** in *Lady Sings the Blues.* It's difficult to imagine two women who were more different in background, experience, and style.

While Tyson was working in small theaters, developing her gift for acting, Diana Ross was singing in wigs and sequins as part of the most popular female group in the history of Motown, The Supremes. When it was announced that she would play the role of **Billie Holiday** in *Lady Sings the Blues,* few people thought she would be up to it, but for the glamorized, romanticized Lady Day of this 1970s melodrama, she was perfect and full of life, energy, vulnerability, and glamour. In her drug-addiction scenes, Ross' performance was harrowing.

There were other women who came from off-Broadway to Hollywood about this time. Rosalind Cash, an actor of great intelligence and intensity, had established herself in New York as a member of the Negro Ensemble Company. She was mostly wasted in such films as *The New Centurions* in 1972 and *Uptown Saturday Night* in 1974 and returned to the NEC in 1980. In the nineties, television viewers have been privileged to see her portraying women with strength and edge in a number of different series and dramas.

Gloria Foster started her career at Chicago's Goodman School of Drama before moving to New York, where she stunned critics in her debut performance in *In White America* in 1963. Her power and the magnitude of her talent were revealed when she played the title role in the Greek tragedy *Medea* a couple of years later. In Hollywood, that same power would cause problems. Most of the roles she was offered in films and on television were too small for her talent. She was excellent in *The Comedians* in 1967, for example, but not so well suited to clowning around with Bill Cosby in *Man and Boy* in 1972. She eventually went back to the stage, where she seems to belong. Her performances have been remarkable in such plays as *Sister Son/ji*, written by **Sonia Sanchez** and directed by **Novella Nelson** in 1972; Ntozake Shange's adaptation of Bertolt Brecht's *Mother Courage and Her Children* in 1980; and *Having Our Say*, based on the book by the Delaney sisters in 1995.

There was yet another sort of black star at about this time. The first of them were men in such movies as *Sweet Sweetback's Baadasssss Song*, *Shaft*, and *Superfly*. These films, according to Shirley E. Thompson in *Black Women in America*, "featured tough black male heroes who defied whitey at every turn. To compensate for years of silly and asexual black male characters, these 'blaxploitation' pictures celebrated the strong sexuality of black men. Not surprisingly, women, black as well as white, were merely trophies for the new black male hero as they had been for white male heroes."

There was no room in this genre for an interesting, intelligent woman in the life of the *baaaad* male star. However, there was room for a *baaaad* female star. The most successful of these was **Pam Grier** in such films as *Coffy*, *Foxy Brown*, and *Black Mama, White Mama*. Grier didn't come from either the stage, like Tyson, or the music industry, like Ross, but from the switchboard at American International Pictures, the company that produced her films. Her career in movies didn't last beyond the vogue for astonishingly tough black women who carried guns and cast a mighty, curvaceous shadow (although she did later become active in theater). Tamara Dobson, too, played the queen of macho in seventies movies such as *Cleopatra Jones*, after a career in modeling.

The 1970s were, in a sense, the first heyday of black movies and television shows, and the height of the heyday was *Roots*. The story of *Roots* actually began two years before it reached the airwaves, with another television film. Until Cicely Tyson walked onto the screen as a 110-year-old woman in *The Autobiography of Miss Jane Pittman*, the decision makers at the networks would never have believed that black history could sell soap. But America watched enthralled as one of its finest actors showed how stirring, even exciting, the story of a courageous African American could be. That drama, and Tyson's remarkable performance in it, paved the way for the miniseries that changed the image of African Americans on television.

The other roots of *Roots* lie in the black theater movement. When Alex Haley's producers began to cast, they had to go no further than the talented, committed actors working with the New Federal Theater or with the Negro Ensemble Company in New York.

Tyson herself came to film and television from the black theater movement. For 15 years, she worked in the theater on and off Broadway and in small parts in films and television. She became one of the New York's most admired and celebrated young actors, winning the Drama Desk Award as outstanding off-Broadway performer two years in a row, in 1961 and 1962.

Tyson appeared in the television series, *East Side/West Side* for the 1963–64 season, but did not have much opportunity to show what she could do. In 1968, she was cast in a role specially tailored for her in the film *The Heart Is a Lonely Hunter*. Her performance was wonderful, as usual, but she didn't appear in another film for four years. She

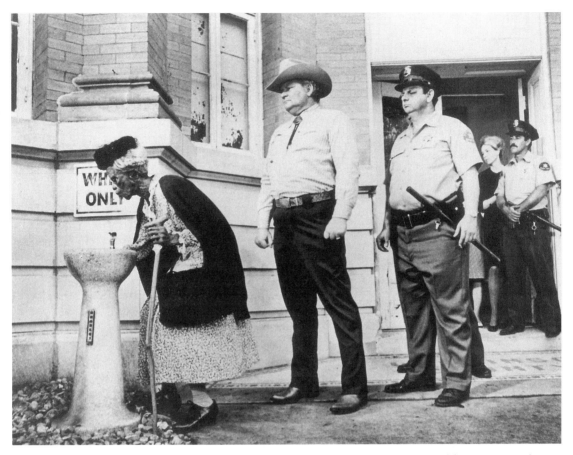

Until Cicely Tyson walked onto the television screen in 1974 as a 110-year-old-woman in The Autobiography of Miss Jane Pittman, *network decision makers never believed that black history would attract an audience. The TV movie won Tyson two Emmy Awards.* (DONALD BOGLE)

had made a decision not to appear in any movie that used stereotypical images based on race.

Then, in 1972, Tyson appeared as the strong young mother in *Sounder*. She was splendid in a part that fell into none of the old stereotypes but was clearly that of a black woman struggling to survive and keep her family intact in white America. She followed that success two years later with *The Autobiography of Miss Jane Pittman*, for which she won two Emmy awards. In 1976,

she was nominated again for her role as Kunta Kinte's mother in *Roots*.

It would be difficult to overestimate the importance of the miniseries based on Alex Haley's best-selling novel, *Roots*. Although it was eagerly awaited, no one could have foreseen the tremendous audience response the series of programs elicited. What *Jane Pittman* had foreshadowed, *Roots* brought to a spectacular fulfillment. African-American history was compelling, dramatic, and moving, and people of every race responded positively to it, African Americans in particular.

In the cast of *Roots* and its sequel, *Roots: The Next Generation* (1979), were some of the most distinguished black actors in the United States, including Ruby Dee, **Olivia Cole, Debbie Allen**, Diahann Carroll, Leslie Uggams, Helen Martin, and **Madge Sinclair**. Writer **Maya Angelou** also played a role.

From the end of the 1970s until the mid-1980s, black women again became scarce. There was one film, however, that was important enough—and controversial enough—for ten. It resonates through the decade that followed it as *A Raisin in the Sun* did thirty years before.

Maya Angelou's Georgia, Georgia *(1971) was the first original screenplay by a black woman that was ever made into a film.* (SCHOMBURG CENTER)

THE COLOR PURPLE

During the twentieth century, black women have written of their lives in novels, poems, and plays with such skill and truthfulness that they have become perhaps the most extraordinary voice in the American chorus. That voice, sometimes heard onstage, was virtually silent in films and television until 1985. Before that, there had been *A Raisin in the Sun*, and Maya Angelou's *Georgia, Georgia*. Produced in 1971, the latter was the first original screenplay by a black woman that was ever made into a film. These, though, were isolated examples. For the most part, black women in films and television were asked to perform in roles crafted by others to deliver truths that were not their own.

Then **Alice Walker**'s extraordinary novel *The Color Purple* came to the attention of Hollywood's hottest director, Steven Spielberg, and he decided to film it. Here on the screen was a black woman's life, written by a black woman. A story of love, abuse, sisterhood, support, anger, and survival, this tremendous film was a tremendous success.

Spielberg cast, in the central role of Celie, a young comic named **Whoopi Goldberg** who had been performing in a one-woman show in theaters around the country. For another principal role, he cast Oprah Winfrey, the highly successful talk-show host. Both received Academy Award nominations.

There was a strong reaction to both the book and the film in the black community because of their stark depiction of the men in Celie's life. People always react strongly when rage is a significant element of art, and when so few portraits of black men are on the screen, it is difficult to look at one painted by a black woman that is not favor-

Whoopi Goldberg's first film performance, as Celie in Steven Spielberg's adaptation of Alice Walker's Pulitzer Prize–winning novel The Color Purple, *earned her an Academy Award nomination as Best Actress of 1985.* (DONALD BOGLE)

able, even when it is true to her own experience and vision.

As a result of this film, Winfrey moved into the superstar category. She had first broken into the limelight in 1984 when she moved to Chicago to take over the wilting morning show *A.M. Chicago*. Within a month she had equaled the ratings of Phil Donahue; in three months, she had surpassed the white-haired talk-show star; in only a year and half, the show had been expanded to an hour and renamed *The Oprah Winfrey Show*. Winfrey was on her way.

After *The Color Purple*, Winfrey expanded her activities to include producing: In 1989, she made a television movie version of **Gloria Naylor**'s novel *The Women of Brewster Place*, which led to a short-lived dramatic series. Again, the voice of a black woman was heard, and again, fine actors were brought to the attention of the viewing public. Both of these are crucial steps in securing a place for black women in film and television

Whoopi Goldberg went from *The Color Purple* to become the first truly "bankable" black woman in movies—the only black woman who could—in the opinion of Hollywood and its financial backers—bring 'em in at the box office without a white and/or male costar. In the ten years since *The Color Purple*, she starred or costarred in more than a dozen films. For one, *Ghost*, she received an Academy Award as Best Supporting Actress; *Sister Act*, in 1992, was a huge box-office success; *Made In America*, in 1994, established Goldberg as a romantic lead.

Goldberg's success raised the possibility that there were other black women who could bring in audiences. One contender is **Angela Bassett**. After receiving both a bachelor's and master's degree at the Yale School of Drama, she began working fairly regularly in commercials and on television in Hollywood. After she appeared in John Singleton's *Boyz N the Hood*, Spike Lee cast her as **Betty Shabazz** in *Malcom X*. Shortly thereafter, she played the mother of the famous Jackson family in a television miniseries. But her most spectacular role to date is **Tina Turner** in the film biography *What's Love Got to Do with It?* Like Cicely Tyson's early career, Bassett's makes you wonder when someone will write fictional black women for films who begin to compare with the ones borrowed from life.

Singer **Whitney Houston** made her film debut in 1992 in *The Bodyguard* with Kevin Costner. The movie was extremely successful and reinforced the idea that black women had box office appeal.

In 1996, Bassett and Houston were teamed in the first big studio movie made especially to appeal to black women, *Waiting to Exhale*. Based on **Terry McMillan**'s best-selling novel, the film presented four black women in search of love in the modern world. Like traditional Hollywood "women's movies," it featured beautiful women in chic clothes having trouble with men. There could be no clearer sign of the times.

Black women have moved into the mainstream in television as well, thanks in large part to two sisters from Texas, **Debbie Allen** and **Phylicia Ayers-Allen Rashad**.

Debbie Allen got her entertainment start signing, dancing, and acting on Broadway in 1971. She made two highly praised appearances on TV in the late 1970s in *Roots: The Next Generation* and in a starring role in the short-lived 1977 variety show *3 Girls*

The Cosby Show spinoff, A Different World, *consolidated Debbie Allen's position as one of the most powerful women in the industry. She eventually became both the director and the producer of the show.* (DONALD BOGLE)

In the mid-1980s, the women of the Huxtable family, on NBC's The Cosby Show, *were the most-watched black women in the history of prime-time television (clockwise, from top left: Sabrina Le Beauf, Tempestt Bledsoe, Lisa Bonet, Keshia Knight Pulliam, and Phylicia Rashad).* (PRIVATE COLLECTION)

3. It was Allen's involvement with the dramatic series *Fame* that secured her high television status.

Allen's performance as dance teacher Lydia Grant was strong and complex, but the show also launched her career behind the scenes. She won two Emmys for her choreography and also began to direct, beginning with a few *Fame* episodes and then branching out to other shows. In 1989, she won Emmy nominations for both choreographing and directing *The Debbie Allen Special.*

Meanwhile, in 1984, *The Cosby Show* premiered. The Huxtables were a solid, upper-middle-class family. Cliff Huxtable (Bill Cosby) was a doctor. Claire Huxtable (Allen's sister Phylicia Rashad) was a lawyer. Lovely to look at, complex, and professional, she was a black woman to be proud of and to enjoy. The show was one of the most successful of all time, and the women in the cast were repeatedly nominated for Emmys. Many talented black actresses were also featured in guest appearances.

The *Cosby Show* spinoff, *A Different World,* consolidated Debbie Allen's position as one of the most powerful women on television. She took over direction of the show when it was not doing well, turned it around and eventually became the show's producer. Like its parent show, *A Different World* used a multitude of established black actors as regulars, semiregulars, and guests: The formidable Rosalind Cash turned up as a college administrator, and Diahann Carroll appeared as the mother of a spoiled, upper-class student, played by Jasmine Guy.

In 1989, Allen appeared in and choreographed a black adaptation of *Pollyanna* that starred her sister in the role of the aunt. In 1992 she directed the television movie *Stompin' at the Savoy.*

The success of *The Cosby Show* gave rise to a host of sitcoms depicting black families. They were, on the whole, less stereotyped than the sitcoms of the 1970s, but none offered really fine roles for women. Still, the number of black women on television was increasing tremendously.

Marla Gibbs appeared in *227* as an urban lower-middle-class, wisecracking wife and mother. Gibbs was also named creative consultant for *227,* which gave her some artistic control over the show. *Head of the Class* featured among its class of gifted students, three black women played by Robin Givens, Kimberly Russell, and Rain Pryor. The Fox network's *21 Jump Street* featured Holly Robinson as Hoffs, an intelligent and complex character.

Beginning in 1991, the dramatic series *I'll Fly Away* featured a remarkable performance by **Regina Taylor** as a single black mother in the South during the early days of the civil rights movement. The quality of the series was so high that, when it was dropped by a major network, it was picked up by PBS.

Even daytime soap operas jumped on the bandwagon, an unprecedented move in a genre that traditionally excluded black characters. By the late 1980s, virtually every soap featured black women in a wide range of roles. In 1989, Debbi Morgan won an Emmy for her good-hearted character Angie Hubbard on *All My Children,* a sure sign that black women had gained respect in the world of soaps.

In 1990, for the first time, black women were given the opportunity to engage in the kind of parodic social criticism and political satire that *Saturday Night Live* allowed its ever changing cast of predominantly white men, white women, and black men from

1975 onward. (It should be noted that remarkable comic Danitra Vance did appear on *SNL* for the 1985–86 season.) Kim Coles, T'Keyah "Crystal" Keymah, and Kim Wayans were regulars on *In Living Color*. However, some critics charged the show with perpetuating some unfavorable black stereotypes and also pointed to the high number of white writers on the show.

Begun in the 1950s, the Public Broadcasting System (PBS) was always a step ahead of the commercial networks in its positive attention to black women. Its series, movies, documentaries, and specials frequently featured black women from very early on in its history.

PBS also led the way in giving black women other important creative opportunities: The first black woman with the executive power to develop programs from their inception to the on-screen product was Jennifer Lawson, executive vice president of national programming and promotion services for PBS. The executive position is where an authentic voice for black women in entertainment has to begin. There is ample evidence for this in the history of radio: Black women have often found their way onto the air by buying a station—lock, stock, and barrel. However, in television and film, black women are only now coming into the positions of power, where the ideas are conceived and the lines are written before the curtain goes up or the cameras begin to roll.

TAKING CHARGE

If you had no money, no strings to pull, and no reason to think anyone was going to help you, would you write a play, a television script, or a screenplay? Which one of these could you produce in a parlor or a storefront on a budget of $25?

Black women have been writing plays for almost as long as there has been an American theater. Today's playwrights build on the achievements of the women of the past. Following in the footsteps of Zora Neale Hurston, Georgia Douglas Johnson, Alice Childress, Lorraine Hansberry, Adrienne Kennedy, and J. E. Franklin, they are writing plays that illuminate the lives of black women, even if they are sometimes still presenting them in storefront theaters. **Anna Deavere Smith, Endesha Ida Mae Holland, J. California Cooper** and **Pearl Cleage** are among the produced playwrights of the nineties.

One important reason why black women have fared considerably better in the theater than in either film or television and why the acting roles are more significant and honest and the portrayals are fuller is because black women have more control in the theater than in other media; their voice is heard.

The situation in film has been more complex. It has been almost a hundred years since the first short, silent films were shown in nickelodeons. For most of those years, production costs would have made it unrealistic to the point of foolishness for a black woman to try to make films. Then, in the past two decades, things have begun to change.

Young filmmakers often start with documentaries. These are in some ways less difficult for a creative newcomer to make than films that require screenplays and actors, costumes and sets. They are also less expensive and sometimes easier to finance. Madeleine Harris made this choice in the early seventies with her film *I Am Some-*

body, one of the first known works by a black woman filmmaker.

In 1982, Kathleen Collins became the first African-American woman to direct a feature-length film, *Losing Ground*. It was also the first black independent film to show the life of a young black woman professional.

Julie Dash began a series of films about black women in the United States in 1983; for the first, a short film called *Illusions*, she was awarded the Black American Film Society award. In 1989, it was named Best Film of the Decade by the Black Filmmaker's Foundation. With this promising start, Dash went on to make *Daughters of the Dust*, set in 1902 on an island off South Carolina.

In 1989, Euzhan Palcy, from Martinique, became the first black woman to direct a film that was distributed by a major studio. The film, *A Dry White Season*, starred Donald Sutherland, and was based on Palcy's own screenplay. The first black woman from the United States to get a major commercial film release was Leslie Harris. Her *Just another Girl on the I.R.T.* opened in 1993. Darnell Martin is the first African American woman to make a film through a major studio, *I Like It Like That* (1994).

In television, the path to positions of genuine creative power has been just as difficult to travel as in film, but black women are beginning to complete the journey. A prime example is **Yvette Lee Bowser**: At the age of twenty-nine, she became the first black woman to develop her own prime-time series, *Living Single*. The story of four black women, it is based on Bowser's own experience and view of life. The surprise hit of its premier season, the situation comedy stars rapper **Queen Latifah** and Kim Fields, formerly of *The Facts of Life*.

Winifred Hervey-Stallworth is the executive producer of *The Fresh Prince of Bel-Air*. When she took over the show from its original producer, many noticed the increasing honesty of the scripts and sensitivity in dealing with the women on the show.

It has been a long road from the Hyers Sisters and their Coloured Operatic and Dramatic Company, the Anita Bush Players, Florence Mills, and Ethel Waters. There will be, in the future, more struggles with stereotypes and more moments of invisibility, but black women have moved into positions of control in theater and entertainment, and that should help ensure that the voices of black women will be heard, telling their own stories and giving us one more way to know the world.

[The material on television in this introduction is adapted from the article "Television," by Sarah P. Morris, in *Black Women in America: An Historical Encyclopedia*.]

A

Alice, Mary (1941–)

Two aspects of the life of formidable stage and screen actress Mary Alice seem both related and revealing: She has never had a hobby and she has never been married. "Most everything she does," an interviewer observed, "is in some way related to the theater."

Born Mary Alice Smith into a strict Baptist family on December 3, 1941, in Indianola, Mississippi, the actress's family moved from Indianola to the Rush Street area on Chicago's near north side when Mary was two years old. Too young to play with her brothers and sisters, she became a loner, a bookworm, and a good student with a love for math. So remarkable were her teachers's examples that she remembered their names decades later and, before turning to acting, was herself resolved to teach. She attended Chicago Teachers College (now Chicago State University), and for several years after graduating she taught the third, fourth, and fifth grades. "The only theater I remember then," she has said, "was a speech class where we did skits, but not much else."

Later in her acting career she spoke often of hopes to return to teaching, referred to her Chicago teaching years as the most meaningful in her accomplished life, has had a New York State substitute-teacher's license and, indeed, done a few classroom stints, including drama in Brooklyn's High School Redirection program.

Mary Alice took up acting and New York for two reasons. In 1966, she fell in love with a man who drew her to a community theater before he moved to New York. She shrank from an offered role in *A Raisin in the Sun*, but she became a part-time secretary for the theater company and finally submitted to her first acting ordeal as Big Mama in *Cat on a Hot Tin Roof*.

That same year, playwright-director-actor Douglas Turner Ward, soon to form New York's **Negro Ensemble Company**, brought a troupe to Chicago to perform his plays *Days of Absence* and *Happy Ending*. Chicago Actors' Equity stipulated that Ward hire one local woman, and Mary Alice Smith was chosen. For $20 a week, she played three roles and twice weekly washed and ironed the cast's laundry, but Ward told her that if she ever went to New York, he would discuss NEC work with her.

The next year, she did go to New York, following her love interest and having friends there who were actors. Still, she was in pursuit of a teaching career or thought she was. She auditioned for Ward and the NEC, "and they turned me down! But they did one good thing for me—they put me into an acting class taught by Lloyd Richards. I'm an actor today because of that." Never asked to join the company, she eventually performed in its productions, including *In the Deepest Part of Sleep* (1974) and *Zooman and the Sign* (1980), both by Charles Fuller.

Her mentors would include Ward, Joseph Papp, Uta Hagen, Kristin Linklater, Louis Johnson, and the founder of Off-off-Broadway's Cafe LaMama, Ellen Stewart. But it was Richards, later Yale Drama School dean, who "taught me how to use myself" and helped her "add layers, and layers, and layers, and layers." He taught "that you must always have secrets on stage because that's the resource you draw from every night."

She was in her first off-Broadway show at the Greenwich Mews—the Cynthia Belgrave production of Wole Soyinka's *The Trials of Brother Jero* and *The Strong Breed*—in October 1967 and joined Equity in January. "That's how I started this career." *A Rat's Mass* and *Street Sounds* at LaMama, Genet's *The Blacks* at The Theater Company in Boston and shows at Arena Stage in Washington, D.C., followed. In 1969 came her Broadway debut as Cora in Charles Gordone's *No Place to Be Somebody*, which enjoyed a national tour. She began doing regional theater, had some television work, and once did a Grape Nuts commercial.

West Coast television work, and a turning point, came in early 1974 with the lead in Phillip Hayes Dean's *The Sty of the Blind Pig*, directed by Ivan Dixon for Hollywood Showcase Theater. "I can bring some dignity to this even though there may be little there," she said. A casting director who saw it and had actually seen her act in the Chicago community theater asked her to read for the role of Frances, Fred Sanford's kid sister, in the half-hour Norman Lear sitcom *Sanford and Son* starring Redd Foxx as Sanford.

The role won, she went on to guest spots on television's *Good Times* and *Doctor's Hospital* and starred again for Hollywood Showcase in *Requiem for a Nun*. This led to her first good film role, as the mother of three Supremes-like sisters in Warner Brothers' *Dreamgirls*-precursor, *Sparkle*, a 1976 release.

Papp cast her in his New York Shakespeare Festival's Public Theater production of *Man-woman*, then as Portia in *Merchant of Venice* for his short-lived Black and Hispanic Repertory Company, then in Ntozake Shange's poetic sketches titled *Spell #7*. Alice appeared in *Second Thoughts*, a Black Theater Festival production at Lincoln Center. Her performances in *Julius Caesar* and in Athol Fugard's *Nongogo* at the Manhattan Theater Club won her the 1979 Obie. Of *Spell #7* and her 1980 performance of Judy Grahn's long poem, *A Woman Is Talking to Death*, at the Public, a journalist wrote, "her work was so intense it was literally frightening. . . . She seemed like a human bomb that could go off any minute."

One of Mary Alice's most impressive roles was that of Rose, who is betrayed by her husband Troy (played by James Earl Jones), in the 1987 Broadway run of August Wilson's Pulitzer Prize–winning *Fences*, for which she won a Tony. Explaining the power she brought to the role, she said, "I based her not only on myself but on my mother, my aunts, my grandmother, and other women I knew growing up in the 1950s. . . . These were women who were not educated, living in a time before women's liberation, and their identities were tied up in their husbands. They put up with a lot of indignities and humiliations because they were women and were attached to men, and their life outside the house was very limited."

She was surprised when, during *Fences*, her mother told her she had never been able to fulfill her dream of being a nurse. Ozelar Jurnakin Smith brought up two sons and two twin daughters as well as Mary, the youngest, while working in a Chicago factory. She "had never had the experience of living alone, of being an individual, or of being responsible for herself."

Alice's involvement with *Fences* began in 1983 when she was invited to be in a staged reading of it for the Eugene O'Neill Theater Center's National Playwrights' Conference. It was first mounted at Yale and then moved to the Goodman Theater in Chicago, where she looked out her hotel window upon her old neighborhood. "I pulled the blinds on that window and never raised them again, all the time we were in Chicago." She persuaded her mother to see the show because James Earl Jones was in it.

Alice broke from the *Fences* Broadway run after her mother's death, feeling that it signified change, and played a black college women's dorm house mother in the NBC *Cosby Show* spinoff *A Different World* for a season and a half. But "I felt like I had sold out."

In the role of Suzie in the 1990 feature *To Sleep With Anger*, she did find "a great deal of complexity and truth," and she had early learned to love the camera, finding that film work improved her acting. On television, she appeared in *Police Woman*, the daytime soap *All My Children* (in a continuing role), *L.A. Law*, and in numerous television dramas and specials, including *Denmark Vesey*, *Charlie Smith and the Fritter Tree*, *Monkey in the Middle*, *The Resurrection of Lady Lester,* and *Joshua's World.* Her feature roles got better as did the features, some for television—*Teachers*, *Beat Street*, *The*

Women of Brewster Place, *The Brass Ring*, *The Killing Floor*—and some for film —*Bonfire of the Vanities* and *Awakenings.*

Her Shakespearean roles up to Queen Margaret in Papp's production of *Richard III* (1990) had been two and far between—Cordelia in Arena Stage's *King Lear* (1968) and Portia in a Papp production of *Merchant of Venice*. Although the Obie she won for the latter was when "I finally accepted the fact I was an actress," she was unhappy with her art in both. But as Margaret she garnered great press plaudits with a single scene—Margaret's cursing of her enemies, especially Richard, played by Denzel Washington.

In 1995, Alice and **Gloria Foster** portrayed real-life sisters **Bessie and Sadie Delaney,** in the hugely successful *Having Our Say,* directed by Emily Mann for Princeton's McCarter Theater and then transferred to the Booth on Broadway. For other actresses, to have played the 101-year-old Bessie might have been a final validation and valediction; for Mary Alice, whose self-knowledge has come slowly but in giant strides, it was simply another beginning.

GARY HOUSTON

Allen, Billie (1927–)

One of the most shocking, insightful, and historically important plays in the history of black theater was **Adrienne Kennedy**'s *Funnyhouse of a Negro*, which premiered in 1964. Billie Allen's performance as Sarah in that play established her as one of the most important black actors of her generation.

Billie Allen was born in Richmond, Virginia. After attending Hampton College, she began her career as a dancer in ballet and then in musical theater. She also toured as a concert soloist in the United States and Europe. While dancing in Boston in a production of *Four Saints in Three Acts*, she was noticed by director Elia Kazan, who asked her to audition for his upcoming production of *Camino Real*. The audition consisted of improvisations with Eli Wallach. Though she didn't get the role, Wallach suggested her for a scholarship to Lee Strasburg's Actors Studio.

Allen's first dramatic role was in a revival of *Mamba's Daughters* with the original star, **Ethel Waters**. There followed roles on Broadway in **Lorraine Hansberry**'s *A Raisin in the Sun;* off-Broadway in *This Property Is Condemned, Take a Giant Step,* and *Black Monday;* and at the Berlin Festival in *This Property Is Condemned* and *The Happy Journey* (in which she performed with the play's author Thornton Wilder). She was also a regular on *The Phil Silvers Show* on television. During this time, she married engineer Duane Grant and had two children, Duane and Carolyn.

In the years that have followed her stunning performance in *Funnyhouse*, she has appeared often on Broadway and off in such shows as *Blues for Mr. Charlie, Bohikee Creek, A Teaspoon Every Four Hours,* and *Every Night When the Sun Goes Down*. She has also appeared often on television and was featured in the film *Black Like Me*.

Allen was a founding member of the Frank Silvera Writers' Workshop, where she directed the Marcus Hemphill play *Inacent Black* in 1981. That same year she directed and co-authored a documentary on Romare Bearden that was shown on PBS, and married composer Luther Henderson. Since that time, she has acted in *The Vernon Johns Story* with James Earl Jones, developed a

musical version of Langston Hughes' *Little Ham* for the St. George Playhouse in New Brunswick and directed *Funnyhouse of a Negro* at the Tisch School in New York. Working with her husband, Luther, she has also developed two plays at **Rosetta LeNoire**'s AMAS theater, *The Crystal Tree* and *Miss Waters*.

"As a Black woman growing up in an institutionalized racist society, theater saved my life," Billie Allen says. An actor of power, wit, and grace, she has helped to ensure that America has less racist examples of black women in its theater.

HILARY MAC AUSTIN

Allen, Debbie (1950–)

She directed a successful, long-running television series, and that achievement, which would mark a career high for almost any black woman in show business today, is just something she has done by the way.

Debbie Allen was born into a remarkable family on January 16, 1950, in Houston, Texas: Her father, Andrew Allen, was a dentist, and her mother, Vivian Ayers Allen, a poet who was nominated for the Pulitzer Prize. Her sister, **Phylicia Rashad**, has become a well-known actress, and one of her brothers is Andrew "Tex" Allen, a jazz musician.

Allen decided early that she wanted to be a dancer. She began her training when she was three, and by the time she was eight, she had decided to go into musical theater. When she tried to enroll in the school of the Houston Foundation for Ballet, she was rejected for reasons that her mother considered discriminatory. As a result, her family first hired a former dancer in the Ballets Russes to give Allen private lessons, and then her mother took the three oldest children to Mexico City so that Allen could train with the Ballet Naçional de Mexico. At fourteen, she went back to the Houston Foundation for Ballet and was admitted on a full scholarship.

Allen hoped, after graduation from high school, to attend the North Carolina School of the Arts, but again she was rejected. This time, discouraged, she abandoned her dance training and went to **Howard University** to study speech and theater. She was not there long, however, before choreographer Mike Malone drew her back into the dance world. She joined his dance troupe, began to perform with other students at the university, and studied at the National Ballet School. She also became head of the dance department of the Duke Ellington School of the Performing Arts and graduated cum laude from Howard in 1971. She left immediately for New York City.

Allen was soon hired to appear in the chorus of *Purlie*, a musical version of Ossie Davis' *Purlie Victorious*. In 1973, after a stint as a principal dancer in the Universal Dance Experience with George Faison, she went back to Broadway for *Raisin*, a musical adaptation of Lorraine Hansberry's *A Raisin in the Sun*, in which she played Beneatha and received excellent reviews. She remained with the show for almost two years. When it closed in 1975, Allen made individual appearances on a variety of TV shows such as *The Love Boat* and *Good Times* and worked as choreographer on others. She also made a pilot for NBC called *3 Girls 3*, which was not successful, worked on a Ben Vereen special, and appeared with Jimmy Walker in a made-for-television movie called *The Greatest Thing That Almost Happened*. Three more Broadway ap-

In show business, Debbie Allen is the contemporary equivalent of a Renaissance woman—a singer, dancer, actor, choreographer, director, and producer. (DONALD BOGLE)

pearances—in *Guys and Dolls*, a disco version of *Alice in Wonderland*, and *Ain't Misbehavin'*, failed to put Allen on top, as did her role as Alex Haley's wife in *Roots: The Next Generation*.

Then, in 1980, Allen went back to Broadway for a revival of *West Side Story*. This time she received critical and popular acclaim. In that same year, she appeared in the tiny role in the movie *Fame* that would change her life. The tough dance teacher Lydia spoke only two lines, but she made an impact. When the movie became a television series, Allen was there as actress and eventually as choreographer, director, and producer.

In 1981, Allen appeared in the film *Ragtime* and in 1986 was Richard Pryor's bitter, disappointed wife in *Jo Jo Dancer, Your Life Is Calling;* that same year, she appeared in Bob Fosse's Broadway revival of *Sweet Charity.* In the meantime, she continued to work on *Fame* and direct episodes of other television series, including *Family Ties* and *Bronx Zoo;* her directing of the flagging series *A Different World* in 1988 turned it around.

The following season, Allen appeared in her first television special and choreographed a black adaptation of the Pollyanna stories, in which she worked with her sister, Phylicia Rashad. In 1992 she directed the made–for–television movie *Stompin' at the Savoy.*

Debbie Allen married Winfred Wilford in 1975, and the couple was divorced in 1983. In 1984, she married Norman Nixon. They have two children, Vivian Nichole and Norman Nixon, Jr.

KATHLEEN THOMPSON

American Negro Theater (1940–1949)

The American Negro Theater (ANT) started in the basement of Harlem's Schomburg Library on 135th Street and produced 18 plays between its June 1940 onset and its closing in 1949, when a Rockefeller Foundation grant ran out. Its mission—to train and give an outlet to black theater artists in a scene that generally restricted them—foreshadowed the later, more lasting **Negro Ensemble Company** (NEC), but highly talented women were part of ANT's history, as they would be of NEC's.

Helen Martin, destined for a stage, screen and television career, was an ANT founder along with actors Frederick O'Neal, Sidney Poitier, and Harry Belafonte and playwright Abram Hill. *Hits, Bits, and Skits*, ANT's premiere show, opened July 17, 1940, with Martin. She acted in ANT's *Three's a Family* (1943) and its revival of Hill's *On Strivers Row* (1946).

Alice Childress, who became a famed playwright, joined ANT after two years of high school and appeared in its 1941 production of *Natural Man*. She played several leads for the company and in 1944 was in the cast of its biggest hit, *Anna Lucasta*, which starred Hilda Simms as Anna and moved to Broadway.

Simms was replaced by Ruby Dee, whose career began at ANT. In *Anna Lucasta*, Dee met her future husband, Ossie Davis, also an ANT member. She became one of the most respected actors of her generation, active in films, television, radio, and onstage.

Clarice Taylor, later in the NEC ensemble, was an early ANT member and acted in *On Strivers Row* and *Home Is the Hunter* (1945). She went on to a career in television and film. She played Bill Cosby's mother in *The Cosby Show* and Moms Mabley in a recreation of that comedienne's act that played on Broadway.

Frances Foster, so instrumental in NEC's founding, was not in ANT but was still much affected by it. O'Neal saw her performance in the title role of *Salome* in a YMCA across the street from ANT and encouraged her to get an American Theater Wing scholarship. She did, and in the years to follow, the career that resulted often intersected with the many others helped during American Negro Theater's brief span.

GARY HOUSTON

Andrews, Regina M. Anderson
(c. 1900–1993)

"All ethnic groups and peoples need the dramatic forms of cultural expression." In the 1920s, this was how Regina Andrews answered the question, "Does Harlem need its own theater?" She has lived her answer as a founder and promoter of, and playwright for, the Harlem little-theater movement.

Although she was born in Chicago around the turn of the century, Andrews has spent most of her adult life in New York City. Before she married New York Assemblyman William T. Andrews, the apartment she shared with Ethel Ray Nance was always filled with aspiring artists who came to discuss their creations and to receive the encouragement they needed. Later, Andrews and her husband were very much involved in the social, political, and cultural affairs of the city. They had one daughter, Regina Ann.

As assistant to Ernestine Rose at the 135th Street Branch of the New York Public Library and later as head librarian, Andrews helped set up a theater in the basement where various drama groups and street corner orators could perform. One of the drama groups with which she was actively associated was W. E. B. DuBois' Krigwa Players, which emphasized black theater about, by, for, and *near* black people. In February 1929, after the Krigwa Players had disbanded, Andrews and Dorothy Peterson, aided by such community leaders as Theophilus Lewis, Ira De Augustine Reid, **Jessie Fauset**, and Harold Jackman, established the Negro (Harlem) Experimental Theater in the basement of the library.

Because of her professional association with the library, Andrews wrote numerous dramas for the group under the pseudonym Ursala Trelling. Her most popular play was *Climbing Jacob's Ladder*, which was performed in 1931 after the group had moved to the Saint Philips Protestant Episcopal Church parish house on 133rd Street. Andrews had been inspired to write this drama about a late-nineteenth-century lynching in the United States by the great journalist and humanitarian, Ida B. Wells-Barnett. Other plays by Andrews include *The Man Who Passed*, *Matilda*, and *Underground*.

Andrews served the New York Public Library in both the 115th Street and the Washington Heights branches and was famous for the forums she held, which included such luminaries as Eleanor Roosevelt. She retired from the New York Public Library in 1969. She died on February 5, 1993.

ANNETTA JEFFERSON

Archer, Osceola (1890–1977)

"I know one race—the human race," Osceola Archer said once. "We are becoming more and more fragmented . . . in every direction. We are creating our own destruction." She was comparing the **Negro Ensemble Company**, a product of the 1960s, with the **American Negro Theater** where, during the 1940s, she had directed plays and taught Sidney Poitier, Harry Belafonte, and Ossie Davis, among others.

Osceola Macarthy was born in Georgia in 1890. Of black, white, and Indian ancestry, she fit into an elusive racial category. She told a *New York Times* reporter in 1968 that she was often turned down for jobs with the comment, "You're not Negroid enough, you're too light, you will photograph too white, your speech is too perfect."

Macarthy graduated from **Howard University** in Washington, D.C., in 1913. At Howard, she studied with renowned Rhodes scholar Alain Locke and sociologist Kelly Miller. She also studied classical Greek and was a member of the Howard Players. Delta Sigma Theta, the sorority she cofounded with twenty-one other women, was at the time of her death on November 20, 1983, the largest sorority in the country, with more than 713 chapters.

Osceola Macarthy became Osceola Adams in 1915 when she married Numa P. G. Adams, first dean of Howard University's medical school. The family lived in Chicago for ten years, from 1919 to 1929, where Numa Adams attended medical school. While there, Osceola Adams worked as a dress designer under the name of Mrs. Adams and attended the University of Chicago. Her artistic bent also expressed itself in painting, which she did on Sundays. Once their only son finished high school, Dr. Adams encouraged his wife to return to school for her master's degree so that she could ensure her own future. She earned a graduate degree in drama from New York University in 1936, by then adopting the stage name of Osceola Archer.

Osceola Archer debuted on Broadway in *Between Two Worlds*, the Elmer Rice play that opened at the Belasco Theater in October 1934. She played Rose Henneford, a maid with exquisite taste and manners, more refined in fact than the woman for whom she worked. Henneford, trained as a librarian, was married to a doctor whose career was hurt by discrimination. The role was not terribly far from Archer's own life.

Osceola Archer in 1935 appeared, along with **Rose McClendon** and Orson Welles, in Archibald MacLeish's short-lived *Panic*, which Martha Graham choreographed and for which Virgil Thomson supplied music. Her husband advised her that she had entered a precarious profession and should consider teaching for a while. She taught at Bennett College in North Carolina, but the professional stage was a much stronger magnet than academia. Her husband died in 1940 while she was on tour with *The Emperor Jones*. At that point, she moved to New York permanently. From 1946 to 1956, she became resident director at Putnam County Playhouse in Mahopac.

Osceola Archer performed almost exclusively in classics of the modern stage, among them *Riders to the Sea*, *The Skin of Our Teeth*, *The Crucible*, *The Sea Gull*, *Ring Around the Moon*, and *Blood Wedding*. She performed with the New York Shakespearean Festival in 1960 and also appeared on television in the 1950s and 1960s in such productions as *Teahouse of the August Moon*, *Rashomon*, *The Power and the Glory*, and *Pygmalion*. She filmed *An Affair of the Skin* in 1963, appearing with **Diana Sands**, Viveca Lindfors, and Herbert Berghof.

Osceola Archer was a pioneering black director and actress who fought relentlessly against racial barriers, participating on a panel against bias in the entertainment industry when she was nearing eighty. She belonged to the Actors' Equity Committee for Minority Affairs and was also a member of the executive committee of the Stage Door Canteen. Playwright Philip Hayes Dean remembers her as an elegant and eloquent woman. Paul Robeson always greeted Osceola Archer with "Hello, Lady": Archer and Robeson toured together in *The Emperor Jones* during the summer of 1935. Osceola Archer died in New York at the age of ninety-three.

BARBARA LEWIS

Avery, Margaret (19??–)

As the survivor Shug in *The Color Purple*, Margaret Avery riveted audiences and walked away with an Academy Award nomination as Best Supporting Actress. It was not an overnight success.

Born in Mangum, Oklahoma, Avery moved to San Diego, with her family when she was two years old. She was an only child. Avery's father was in the navy, and she spent her childhood in a kind of navy cocoon. Her mother worked as a nurse at a nearby hospital and, as a teenager, Avery was a candy striper and a member of the Future Nurses club. A future as a nurse, however, was not in the cards.

Already interested in acting while in high school, Avery was discouraged by the kinds of roles she was given, so she decided to become a teacher. She attended the University of California at Berkeley for five years, graduated, and received her teaching credentials.

Avery then taught in a small private school for a year, but in her heart she was preparing for a career in acting. She worked at night as a singing waitress to pay for private lessons in voice, dance, and acting; at the end of the year, she took her savings and went to New York. Two months later, she headed back to Los Angeles, California, having disliked the East Coast pace, and worked as a singer with the Nicholas Brothers in Las Vegas. She stayed on after the gig was over, working first as a lounge singer and then as a substitute teacher. After six months, it was back to Los Angeles.

Unable to get an appointment, she showed up at a film audition anyway and bluffed her way in. She got the role and, a few years later, was costarring with Clint Eastwood and Hal Holbrook in *Cool Breeze*. Many other films followed, including *Which Way Is Up?*, *Magnum Force*, and *The Fish That Saved Pittsburgh*, but Avery was given little opportunity to realize her potential as an actor. She seemed to be valued more for her beauty than her talent—not an unusual situation for women in American film.

A number of appearances in such television series as *Kojak*, *Sanford and Son*, *Night Stalker*, and *The Rookies* followed. She was also featured in the specials *Louis Armstrong Chicago Style* and *Scott Joplin*. By the early 1980s, she had done fourteen years of hard and insufficiently recognized work and then four years without a Hollywood job. While studying to be a court reporter, Avery decided to rebuild her singing career. She got jobs in Las Vegas and then toured the Far East with considerable success. Then Stephen Spielberg cast her in what turned out to be one of the most important films of the 1980s.

Since her performance in *The Color Purple*, Avery has appeared in the films *Blueberry Hill*, *Riverbend*, and *The Return of Superfly;* her schedule also included an appearance with Lillian Lehman and John Amos in *Mardi Gras for the Devil*. On television she acted in *Murder She Wrote* and *Spenser: For Hire*. Avery works continuously with the Inner City Cultural Center in Los Angeles.

KATHLEEN THOMPSON

B

Bassett, Angela (1958–)

"She stressed hard work and college," Angela Bassett once said of her mother, "insisting that we didn't become products of our environment."

The mother was Betty Bassett, a lone parent whose marriage to Angela's father had been annulled a little more than a week after they married. Bringing up the film-star-

A graduate of the Yale School of Drama, Angela Bassett reached fame playing Tina Turner in the movie biography What's Love Got to Do With It. *(PRIVATE COLLECTION)*

to-be and her sister through high school, Betty Bassett worked for Florida's Health and Human Services Agency.

In their environment—the Jordan Park public housing complex in St. Petersburg, Florida—"the big thing was heroin." Without her mother's influence, as well as that of her grandfather and great-grandfather, Angela has said, "the neighborhood would have raised me the way it wanted to raise me, which meant having sex at a young age, doing drugs, smoking in the bathroom, hanging out, and defying parental guidance."

She was born in Manhattan's Harlem in 1958 and reared there by her aunt, the family's first Ph.D., until she was five. Then she was sent to Florida to live with her mother. While growing up, she delivered monologues and gave poetry readings at church conventions, but it was at sixteen, as a high school senior, that she knew her destiny lay in acting. A class trip took her to Washington, D.C., where she saw James Earl Jones in a stage adaptation of John Steinbeck's *Of Mice and Men* at the John F. Kennedy Center for the Performing Arts. "I sat there weeping in the theater," she would remember. "I thought, 'If *I* could only make people feel this bad' . . ."

Betty Bassett typed her daughter's application to Yale University and fully supported Angela's switch of majors from business to acting. Angela studied there on a scholarship and, after six years, received her B.A. and from the prestigious Yale School of Drama an M.A.

Moving to New York, she worked in a beauty salon and in the *U.S. News and World Report* photo department before winning roles both on and off Broadway, most notably in two August Wilson plays, *Ma Rainey's Black Bottom* and *Joe Turner's Come and Gone.*

In 1988 she settled in Los Angeles, where work in commercials and appearances on such television shows as *Equal Justice*, *Tour of Duty*, *thirtysomething*, and *The Cosby Show* quickly led to roles in the feature films *F/X*, *Kindergarten Cop*, *Innocent Blood*, and *City of Hope.*

But it was in the meatier, strong-mother parts, starting with the single mother in director John Singleton's *Boyz 'N The Hood* (1991), that she evidenced a debt to the example of her own mother. That feature caught the notice of Spike Lee, who cast her as **Betty Shabazz**, Malcolm X's wife and herself a mother of six, in the $34 million biopic *Malcolm X*. By the end of 1992, she was playing Katherine Jackson, matriarch of the Jackson Five (whom she had idolized as a teen) in the ABC-TV miniseries *The Jacksons: An American Dream.*

Perhaps her most applauded portrayal, again of a real-life figure, is in the movie biography of **Tina Turner**, *What's Love Got to Do With It*. For the month before its filming, Bassett studied Turner videos, read the rock star's autobiography *I, Tina* several times, twice was rehearsed by Turner herself, exercised with free weights and dieted on skinned chicken breasts, broccoli, brown rice, oatmeal, and "some kind of alternative cheesecake you wouldn't recognize." Her fine performance came once more from a connection to

her own life: "Tina's a black woman from the South, and so am I. Tina went through abuse, and I've seen it. I know it." Just as Tina Turner triumphed, so has Angela Bassett.

She got "above-the-title" billing for her part in the 1995 film version of **Terry McMillan**'s novel *Waiting to Exhale*, in which she costarred with Whitney Houston.

GARY HOUSTON

Baxter, Karen (19??–)

Some people see artists and the work they produce as treasures. Their eyes light up at the sight of talent, and their voices warm when they speak of art. They also know how to put together a budget, write a press release, and talk grants with foundations. They are called arts administrators, and Karen Baxter is one of the best.

Baxter was born in Los Angeles, California, the daughter of Roy Allen, a producer and director for CBS-TV, New York, and Margaret Peal Allen, an educator with the New York City Board of Education. Baxter began to work in the theater in 1967 as an administrative assistant at the New Lafayette Theater, a black theater in New York.

She received her bachelor's degree in sociology from City College of New York in 1971. While she was still in college, Baxter was personal secretary to singer Nina Simone. The year after her graduation, she became literary manager at the New Lafayette.

In 1973, Baxter launched two enterprises. With actor Beverly Todd, she founded the Sunshine Circle Montessori School in New York, which emphasized learning through the arts. She also cofounded Nasaba Artist Management with actor Whitman Mayo. The group produced radio soap operas and handled a number of concerts. It was while working with Nasaba that Baxter first met reggae artist Bob Marley, whom she later managed.

In 1976, Baxter became administrative director at the Frank Silvera Writers' Workshop, another historic institution in the black arts movement. It was after her two-year stint there that she joined Don Taylor Artist Management and managed Marley, Jimmy Cliff, Burning Spear, and others. She was also assistant to the producer of the Broadway musical *Reggae* and worked with the Reggae Tribute Company to produce the film *Reggae Sunsplash—A Tribute to Bob Marley.*

From 1983 to 1988, Baxter worked in a production capacity on a number of feature films. In 1988, she was named managing director of the Rites and Reasons Theater, a part of the Afro-American Studies Program at Brown University in Rhode Island. Rites and Reasons is a crucial resource for contemporary African-American theater and theater artists: Involving such writers as Ossie Davis, Sherley Anne Williams, and Rosa Guy, the theater offers a place for original scripts to be developed and produced.

At the same time, Baxter produces the AUDELCO (Audience Development Committee) Awards, which honor excellence in black theater. Hosts for the awards have included Morgan Freeman, Avery Brooks, **Phylicia Rashad**, and others.

Over the years, Baxter's contribution to nurturing and promoting black artists has been invaluable.

KATHLEEN THOMPSON

Best known as "Aunt Delilah" in the 1934 film Imitation of Life, *Louise Beavers made it a point throughout her life to play a diversity of roles.* (SCHOMBURG CENTER)

Beavers, Louise (1908–1962)

Film character-actress Louise Beavers was born on March 8, 1908, in Cincinnati, Ohio. In 1913, her family moved to Pasadena, where Beavers spent the rest of her youth.

After graduation from Pasadena High School, she worked in the early 1920s as a maid for silent screen actress Leatrice Joy, a star of many Cecil B. DeMille epics. While working for Joy, Beavers pursued her own dreams of stardom: She appeared briefly as a maid in the 1923 silent *Golddiggers;* during 1923–26, she performed amateur plays with sixteen other young women in a troupe called The Lady Minstrels. Exactly how she got her "big break" in Hollywood remains unclear. She herself gave two different accounts. In one interview, she claimed that an agent from Universal Studios approached her after seeing a Lady Minstrels production. Much later, Beavers wrote in a December 1949 *Negro Digest* article that she was spotted by a representative from Central Casting when she sang solo in an amateur talent show.

However mysterious, Beavers' launch into a movie career was far from glamorous. Her first big role, as a slave in the 1927 silent *Uncle Tom's Cabin*, paved the way for a lifetime of playing mammies, cooks, and maids in more than 100 (mostly forgotten) movies. For most of Beavers's professional life, there were simply no other roles offered to black actresses. In order to land even these stereotyped parts, Beavers was often forced to speak in unfamiliar southern dialect and to overeat so that she would maintain a mammylike plumpness.

Even though relegated to the periphery of the screen, Beavers managed to establish a comic presence that became her signature. A famous example of her talent is her portrayal of Pearl, Mae West's sassy maid, in Paramount's 1933 *She Done Him Wrong*. In their scenes together, Beavers provided a sharp foil to West's sultry humor. (In an interesting postscript to the film, the two actresses remained close friends throughout Beavers' life.) Such comedic talent won for Beavers maid roles in such comedies as the Jean Harlow vehicle *Bombshell* (1933) and the musical *Holiday Inn* (1942).

As an alternative to "sassy Pearl" roles, Beavers often played earnest, God-fearing maids in domestic dramas or tearjerkers, in which Beavers' characters proved their absolute devotion to white employers by providing much-needed miracle cures or wads of money. In *Made for Each Other* (1939), she rescues destitute Carole Lombard and James Stewart. In *The Big Street* (1942), the lucky couple is Lucille Ball and Henry Fonda.

Perhaps the most important of these helpful-maid roles was Beavers' Delilah in the very popular 1934 Universal picture *Imitation of Life*. In the film's plot, single white mother Bea (Claudette Colbert) sells her maid Delilah's pancake recipe and becomes a millionaire. The film received glowing reviews for its sensitive treatment of "race" —meaning that the film portrayed two women of different colors going into business together. The film's critics pointed out that Delilah was, in fact, just a glorified mammy figure. Nevertheless, one of the film's central images, that of Delilah grinningly holding a griddle, had already firmly entrenched itself in the American cultural psyche. Beavers, who hated pancakes, had finally reached stardom.

Beavers remained active in show business throughout her life. When she could, she diversified her characters. She played a Harlem numbers queen in *Bullets or Ballots* (1936) and acted in two films with all-black casts (*Life Goes On* [1938] and *Reform School* [1939]). She also experimented with different media: In 1935, she appeared in a one-woman show at the Roxy Theater in New York; in the 1952–53 television season, she played the title role in *Beulah*, a popular ABC series about a sassy maid and made many TV appearances in various variety shows; and in 1957, she traveled to San Francisco to make her dramatic theater debut in *Praise House*. Her last film, *The Facts of Life*, was released in 1961.

Louise Beavers died of diabetes on October 26, 1962, at Cedars of Lebanon Hospital in Los Angeles. She was survived by her husband LeRoy Moore, whom she married in the late 1950s. She was inducted into the Black Filmmakers Hall of Fame in 1976.

SARAH P. MORRIS

Belgrave, Cynthia (19??–)

There are some actors who illuminate a role, and some who illuminate the communities in which they live and work. Cynthia Belgrave is one who does both.

Born in Boston, Belgrave began to act in church plays at the age of four, she later joined a community theater, and then received a degree in graphic arts from the Massachusetts College of Arts before moving to New York in 1957 to pursue her acting career. She quickly became involved in the black theater movement.

She played the role of Mrs. Johnson in the original Broadway cast of *A Raisin in the Sun* but appeared more often off-Broadway in black and other experimental theaters. She acted in landmark plays such as *The Blacks* (in which she created the role of Adelaide Bobo), *Take a Giant Step, Simply Heavenly, Funnyhouse of a Negro,* and *The Amen Corner.* In later years, Belgrave performed at the Cleveland Playhouse in the first interracial production of *Harvey.*

While she appeared in a number of films, including *Requiem for a Heavyweight, Black Like Me,* and, later, Robert Townsend's *Meteor Man,* and continued to appear onstage, Cynthia Belgrave's interests turned more and more to her community. "I don't work as often as it's offered to me," she said in a *Christian Science Monitor* interview in 1968. "Things offered to a black

actress often fall into categories of allowing yourself to be burlesqued or plac[ing] yourself in a position of caricaturing or demeaning whole groups of people."

Instead, Belgrave created Farris-Belgrave Productions with her husband Kenneth Farris and began to produce the kind of theater she could believe in. One of the first of these productions was two short plays by Nigerian playwright Wole Soyinka, *The Trials of Brother Jero* and *The Strong Breed,* at the Greenwich Mews Theater in 1967. Belgrave directed the production.

In 1977, Belgrave and Farris founded the Cynthia Belgrave Artist Theater Workshop (CBATW) (later the Community-Based Arts and Theater Workshop). CBATW's productions involve both the community and its audience: *Sweet Stuff,* with music by Danny Holgate and book and lyrics by Belgrave, was presented to schools in Brooklyn and, for one summer, in New York City parks. Dealing with issues of concern to young people, it remained unfinished until each audience provided its own ending. *Baby Dearest,* by Belgrave, was about teen pregnancy and was also taken to the schools.

Belgrave and CBATW also work with senior citizens. This part of their mission began when St. Ann and the Holy Trinity Church commissioned a piece called *Passage.*

Talking about Belgrave as a director, actor Barbara Wise said, "She is warm and generous. Cynthia is always taking things a step further. Her directing always involves reaching a higher level."

Of her work as a teacher, Belgrave herself says, "I try to create an environment for the people in my workshop where they'll feel safe to create, to make mistakes, and to experiment. They know that I will not hurt their feelings. I will not make them feel foolish. I will not injure them in any conscious way because I have found that the creative person is very fragile." This gentle and generous approach to teaching is in striking contrast to that of many acting teachers.

Belgrave believes very strongly that "live theater is life-enhancing, a celebration." To young people considering work in the theater she says, "Do your best. Then, if you're a star, it'll be great. And if you're an unknown, well, it'll still be great."

KATHLEEN THOMPSON

Bentley, Gladys (1907–1960)

Entertainer Gladys Bentley was born in Philadelphia in 1907. When she was a teenager, she ran away from home, as have many gay adolescents who were looking for a world in which they could be themselves. Bentley, a lesbian, found her world in the clubs of Harlem. She supported herself by playing the piano and soon developed a reputation for improvising risqué lyrics to the melodies of popular songs. During the 1920s, Bentley adopted her characteristic costume, a white tuxedo and top hat, and headlined at Harry Hansberry's Clam House. The entertainer soon became a cult star. The intellectual and artistic set of New York—including Langston Hughes and sculptor Isamu Noguchi, who did a bronze head of Bentley in 1929—found her nightclub act fascinating. Offstage, Bentley maintained this image, almost always wearing men's clothing. She was once described as the person for whom the term cross-dressing was invented (though George Sand might have disputed this).

Flamboyant singer Gladys Bentley was once described as the person the term cross-dressing was invented for. (MOORLAND-SPINGARN)

When American society moved into a repressive phase in the late 1940s and the 1950s, Bentley was forced to deny her sexual orientation in order to get work, and she never regained the success she had had earlier in her career. She died in 1960.

KATHLEEN THOMPSON

Berry, Halle (1968–)

Halle Berry's story might be said to run from Bedford to Bedrock. Bedford is the south-east Cleveland suburb whose Bedford High School she attended while imagining a high-fashion modeling career. Bedrock is the environs of those prehistoric, once-TV-series cartoon characters depicted in the 1994 comedy feature *The Flintstones*. Her role in the film had been written for Sharon Stone, but "It's 1994," Berry said. "Isn't it about time we integrated Bedrock?"

One of two daughters, Halle Berry was born in Cleveland in 1968 and has lamented, since becoming the subject of interviews, the persistence of queries about her interracial parentage. Her father, an alcoholic and wife-abuser, quit the marriage when Berry was four. It was her white mother Judith who placed her daughters before a mirror and said, "Even though I am your mother and I'm white, you are still black. In this mirror you see black, and that's what the world is going to see."

Judith knew little of African-American history, but in the fifth grade, Berry had a teacher named Mrs. Sims who was black and "became a fairy godmother of sorts while I was attending an all-white school. Because of her, I never questioned who I am too deeply."

By 1986, Berry had become Miss Teen Ohio and the Miss USA first runner-up. After acquiring a manager, Vincent Cirrincione, and moving to New York, Berry was cast as the model Emily in the briefly aired ABC series *Living Dolls*. That led to her 1991 film debut in the Spike Lee–directed *Jungle Fever*. She prepared her role as a crack cocaine addict by remaining slovenly for days. The portrayal allowed her to shed the model image that until then had stuck to her. Commuting between New York and Los Angeles, she then acted in the films *Strictly Business* (as a club girl) and *The Last Boy Scout*.

She lived not quite happily in a duplex in Los Angeles for three and a half years. In 1992 Berry appeared as an art teacher and Eddie Murphy's love interest in *Boomerang* and, as the late Alex Haley's great-grandmother, she aged from fifteeen to sixty-five in the South Carolina-shot television miniseries *Queen*. After her New Year's Day, 1993, wedding to Atlanta Braves right fielder David Justice, also from Ohio, she and her husband settled in Atlanta. By the next year, however, busy careers mandated they have homes in both places.

In Paramount's 1994 release, *Losing Isaiah*, Berry played a onetime addict of, again, crack. She attempts to regain custody of the child she had abandoned; the child's adoptive mother was played by Jessica Lange. Following the filming, Berry spent three months in Morocco as Sheba for Showtime's *Solomon and Sheba*. When told that a movie actress doesn't do television work, she said, "Black actresses don't have the same choices as white actresses have." About playing the Ethiopian queen, she said, "When [Italian] Gina Lollobrigida did the movie the first time, it was an injustice."

By late 1994, Berry had formed her own production company and agreed to star in Disney's *Eden Close* as well as a film biography of **Dorothy Dandridge**. Hoping once to play black Communist **Angela Davis** and at another time Black Panther leader **Elaine Brown**, the former beauty queen acknowledges the outspokenness of her public criticisms, whose targets have ranged from violent "blaxploitation" movies to Hollywood's racial stereotypes to **Whoopi Goldberg**.

Her strongest opinions, however, are positive and constructive. "We have to make meaningful films with all-Black casts that do well at the box office," she says. ". . . We have to put our money where our visions are."

GARY HOUSTON

Bowman, Laura (1881–1957)

No history of the Negro in the twentieth-century theater can be complete without the name of Laura Bowman, whose 50-year career spanned stage, screen, and radio. The daughter of a Dutch mother and a mulatto father, Laura Bradford was born on October 3, 1881, in Quincy, Illinois, but was raised in Cincinnati, Ohio. She began singing as a youngster in church choirs, but her professional career began as a chorus girl in *In Dahomey* (1902), starring the legendary comic team of Bert Williams and George Walker. Bowman had married Henry Ward Bowman, a railroad porter in 1898 but had left him after only a few years of marriage.

In 1903, the cast of *In Dahomey* sailed from New York to London where they gave a command performance at Buckingham Palace at the ninth-birthday party for the Prince of Wales. After the first company of *In Dahomey* broke up in London, Bowman and Pete Hampton, an executive and star of *In Dahomey* who had fallen in love with her, formed a quartet called the Darktown Entertainers, featuring William Garland, tenor; Fred Douglas, bass; Pete Hampton, baritone; and Bowman, soprano. Bowman and Hampton had a common-law marriage. The Darktown Entertainers sang a variety of songs, and Bowman performed several character sketches in costume. These char-

acterizations proved to be good training for her later work on the dramatic stage.

After the Darktown Entertainers disbanded, Bowman and Hampton performed as a duo in Switzerland, Moscow, Budapest, and England. At the start of World War I, when the English government ordered all foreigners home, the couple returned to New York, and Hampton and Bowman toured the East Coast performing their act. Shortly afterward, however, Hampton died.

In 1916, Bowman joined the celebrated **Lafayette Players**, Harlem's most successful stock acting troupe. At her first rehearsal she met Sidney Kirkpatrick. After appearing in numerous shows at the Lafayette, Bowman and Kirkpatrick left the company, married, and formed an act. They played along the East Coast before moving to Indianapolis, Kirkpatrick's hometown. Racial restrictions were so severe for black performers in Indianapolis that they billed themselves as a modern Hawaiian duet in order to work. Because the couple was fair skinned, they were able to play in theaters where neither black performers nor patrons were allowed.

In 1923, Bowman and Kirkpatrick returned to New York, where she played the part of Aunt Nancy in Willis Richardson's *The Chip Woman's Fortune*, the first drama by a black author to reach Broadway. After *Chip Woman* closed, the couple worked in the Indianapolis area again before rejoining the Lafayette Players. In February 1928, Bowman played Josephine, Mose's wife, in *Meek Mose*, written by actor Frank Wilson (who had played the title role in *Porgy*). The show ran for thirty-two performances at the Princess Theater in New York. *Meek Mose* received mixed reviews, but Bowman's acting was praised.

Bowman and Kirkpatrick moved to Los Angeles in August 1928 with the Lafayette Players. After the group disbanded in 1930 (they later reunited in 1932 before disbanding permanently), they became members of the Hall Singers and sang in the films *Check and Double Check* with Amos and Andy and *Dixiana* with Bebe Daniels (both 1930).

Bowman returned to New York, where she appeared as a servant in *Sentinels* (1931). Virtually all the critics panned the play but cited Bowman as giving an excellent performance. Four months later, Bowman was back on Broadway in *The Tree* (1932). This drama about lynching in the North also was panned by the critics, but Bowman's work was again enthusiastically received. After more than twenty-five years in show business, Bowman had finally begun to establish herself as a dramatic actress on the professional stage. Although the shows were short lived and her roles were stereotyped, she had had two Broadway openings within six months, quite an accomplishment at the time.

In 1932, Bowman appeared on the screen in *Ten Minutes to Live*, produced by Oscar Micheaux, a black film pioneer. She and Kirkpatrick then went back to performing their act, but shortly thereafter, her husband died in Harlem Hospital of a heart attack, and Bowman was once again left a widow. A few weeks later, however, in February 1933, she appeared in *Louisiana*. Written by black author Augustus Smith, *Louisiana* opened at the Majestic Theater in Brooklyn before moving to the 48th Street Theater. For the most part the reviews were unfavorable, except for Bowman's.

After Kirkpatrick's death, Bowman began to drink heavily at a bar in Harlem frequented by theater people. While there, she met her fourth husband, LeRoi Antoine. Antoine, a Haitian who had aspirations of becoming an opera singer, was twenty-three years her junior. She called him "my boy," and many of her friends called her a "cradle snatcher." Nonetheless, after knowing each other for only a short time, Bowman and Antoine were married, and Bowman became a recovering alcoholic.

At the end of 1933, Bowman returned to Broadway in *Jezebel*, with film star Miriam Hopkins playing the title role, and Bowman playing Mammy Winnie to good notices. During the 1930s, Bowman worked with Helen Hayes on the radio program *New Penny Show* and acted on other radio programs including *Stella Dallas, John's Other Wife, Pepper Young's Family, The O'Neills, Pretty Kitty Kelly,* and *The Southernaires.* During that time, she could be heard on some radio show nearly every day. Also, in 1934 Bowman recreated the role of Aunt Hagar in *Drums of Voodoo,* the film version of *Louisiana;* the following year, she was seen in Oscar Micheaux's *Lem Hawkin's Confession* (1935).

Returning to drama, Bowman played Miranda, a servant, in Sophie Treadwell's *Plumes in the Dust* (1936) at the 46th Street Theater in New York. Pauline Myers, one of Bowman's students, played Lou, another servant. In 1938, she appeared in the landmark production of *Conjur* at the Saint Felix Street Theater in Brooklyn playing Parthenia, the Conjur Woman. A new play about religion and superstition, *Conjur* featured an all-black cast, which was considered bold in Brooklyn theatrical circles. That same year, Bowman was seen in Oscar Micheaux's *God's Stepchildren.*

During the early part of 1939, Bowman was in Broadway's *Please, Mrs. Garibaldi* playing Endora, servant to an Italian-American family; the show closed after only four performances. Antoine had costarred in *Voodoo Fire*, produced by Warner Brothers and starring Floyd Gibbons, and when he decided to pursue a film career, the couple moved to Los Angeles. They were disappointed by Hollywood, but fortunately Bowman still had a film contract, and in 1940 she appeared as Dr. Helen Jackson in *Son of Ingagi*. Written by Spencer Williams, this film is significant as the first all-black horror film. Also in 1940, she was seen on the screen in *The Notorious Elinor Lee* with Edna Mae Harris and Robert Earl Jones. In order to make ends meet, Bowman organized an amateur theater troupe and taught acting. Earlier, in Harlem, she had opened the National Art School, where she taught acting.

Bowman returned to New York in 1946 to perform in *Jeb*, a play about a World War II veteran, starring Ossie Davis; Ruby Dee played his sweetheart, and Bowman played his mother and was paid a weekly salary of $250. *Jeb* received mixed reviews, and the show ran for only nine performances. Immediately following the closing of *Jeb*, Bowman, Davis, and Dee were cast in one of the touring companies of *Anna Lucasta*, Abram Hill's adaptation of Philip Yordan's play about a Polish family. Bowman played Theresa, the role created by **Georgia Burke** on Broadway; she also performed with the Broadway cast.

Theresa was Bowman's last role. After a paralyzing stroke, she retired from the stage. For seven years, she had been Antoine's benefactor; now he took care of her. Although she had earned a considerable amount of money, she now was destitute. Confined to her bed, Bowman expressed bittersweet feelings about her life in show business: "I must say that my 50 years in the theater have been most colorful . . . but, nevertheless, I have paid a price for my fifty years."

On March 29, 1957, at the age of seventy-six, Bowman died in Los Angeles. Her obituary in the *New York Times* on March 31, 1957, is a testament to her determination and talent: "It was said of Miss Bowman that she had played in about every country that had a theater."

By performing on the stage, in film, and on radio, Bowman was able to sustain a career that lasted a half-century. It was her flexibility, the ability to move from one area of show business to another, that enabled her to keep working. The problems of race relations in America during the period were reflected in the roles she was permitted to play. When she made the transition from a very successful career on the musical stage to drama, the majority of her roles, which were written by white authors, were as servants. Despite the negative implications, however, both black and white critics agree that Bowman brought a certain dignity to every role she played.

A charter member of the Negro Actors Guild, Bowman often spoke out against the ill treatment of black characters and black performers; yet in order to earn a living, she, like some of her contemporaries, continued to play the parts that were available to her. In so doing she helped keep a black presence on Broadway. Moreover, by utilizing the paths open to her, she helped find new gateways through which other black women have since entered. Because of her perseverance, Bowman was among the first group of black women to become respected dramatic actors on the Broadway stage, establishing herself as a role model for the contemporary black dramatic actor.

Through her association with the Lafayette Players and her own shows (she hired other black actors, singers, and dancers), Bowman also helped foster and develop black theater. In addition to organizing amateur acting troupes, she taught some of the black actors of the 1930s and 1940s, and by helping to provide trained talent, she made a contribution to mainstream American theater. Thus, although she never had the opportunity to reach her full potential, Bowman, like some of her contemporaries, not only survived, but flourished.

JO A. TANNER

Burke, Georgia (1894–1986)

"I don't act. I just talk and mean it, like I'm talking to you now." That was the style of Georgia Burke, an enduring character actress on Broadway and radio. Working during the 1930s and 1940s, when black actresses could get little more than roles as servants, Burke used that straightforward philosophy to transform these stereotyped roles into statements of power, hope and conviction.

Born the daughter of a Methodist minister and a nurse in LaGrange, Georgia, Burke was raised one of eight children. While the New York Times and Variety give her birth date as February 28, 1878, the Amsterdam News lists her birth date as 1894. Given the facts of her life and career, the 1894 date seems to be more likely.

Educated in the Atlanta public schools, she went on to Clark University and Claflin University in Orangeburg, South Carolina. After graduating, she taught grade school in

Wilson, North Carolina, for six years. She considered herself set for life.

A trip to New York in 1928 changed all that. She was taking a summer course at Columbia University when a friend talked her into auditioning for Blackbirds, which would become a Broadway hit. She sang "St. Louis Blues" and was hired on the spot.

Burke went on to supporting roles in numerous Broadway shows, including The Grass Harp, The Wisteria Tree, No Time for Comedy, Mamba's Daughters, They Shall Not Die, Five Star Final, Savage Rhythm, Anna Lucasta, Cabin in the Sky, Mandingo, and James Baldwin's The Amen Corner. She toured Europe and Russia as part of the original cast of Porgy and Bess. In 1944, she received a Donaldson-Billboard award as Best Supporting Actress in Decision.

In that play, Burke played Virgie, a cook who left her job in a white household to go to work in a war plant. Though much of her role was comedy, the New York Times stated that "she keynotes the play." The same article reported that "Edward Chodrov, the author, originally had **Hattie MacDaniels** [sic] in mind for Virgie, but he was unable to get her. He went to Paul Robeson in despair; asked what he should do. Robeson recommended Georgia Burke. After Chodorov saw her in the role he said, 'I was very fortunate to be unfortunate in not getting Miss MacDaniels.' "

While typecasting limited the nature of Burke's roles, she shared the stage with many of the great stars of Broadway. Famous headliners included Eubie Blake, Noble Sissle, **Ethel Waters**, Canada Lee, Helen Hayes, Katherine Cornell, Jane Cowell, Bill "Bojangles" Robinson, Jose Ferrer, and James Earl Jones.

In spite of her busy Broadway schedule, Burke maintained a five-day-per-week job in radio serials. Sometimes, she played two live radio roles during the day and then played on Broadway at night. There were times when she had to be written out of her radio roles for weeks at a time so that she could join the road production of her Broadway shows. Her radio work included fourteen years as a nurse in the soap opera *When a Girl Marries* and extended to many popular radio serials of the day, such as *Ma Perkins, True Story, Whispering Street, Show Boat, Bright Horizon, Rosemary*, and *Hill Top House*.

Burke continued her work into the early years of television. Among many appearances, she reprised her stage role in the television version of *The Grass Harp*. She was active in the NAACP, and despite her many servant roles, she never learned to cook.

ANDRA MEDEA

Burrill, Mary P.   (c. 1884–1946)

The September 1919 issue of *Birth Control Review*, a monthly periodical that agitated for the birth-control rights of women, was a special issue on "The Negroes' Need for Birth Control, as Seen by Themselves." To this issue, Mary Burrill contributed *They That Sit in Darkness*, one of her two known published plays. Possibly the first feminist play written by a black woman, *They That Sit in Darkness* informs us that every woman should have access to birth control. The play also emphasizes the importance of acquiring an education to improve black America. Burrill's other work, *Aftermath*, was published the same year in another periodical, the *Liberator*, and was produced

during the 1920s by the Krigwa Players of New York City. *Aftermath* focuses on a decorated black soldier returning home from World War I, only to discover that his father has been lynched and burned. Although these are her only two available plays, she was known to have written others.

Burrill holds an important place in theater history because she was one of the earliest black women to promote social change through plays that chronicle the plight of black Americans realistically.

The daughter of John H. and Clara E. Burrill, Mary P. Burrill was born and raised in Washington, D.C., where she graduated in 1901 from the famous M Street School (later Dunbar High School). Burrill attended Emerson College of Oratory (later Emerson University) and received a diploma in 1904. She returned to Emerson in 1929 and earned a Bachelor of Literary Interpretation degree. While at Emerson, she revised *They That Sit in Darkness* and renamed it *Unto the Third and Fourth Generation*.

Burrill had a reputation as an outstanding teacher and directed numerous productions throughout Washington, D.C. She spent most of her career at Dunbar High School, where she taught English, speech, and dramatics. During Burrill's years at Dunbar High School, she inspired many students, among them Willis Richardson, who became the first black dramatist on Broadway, and **May Miller,** who became the most published black female playwright of the 1920s and 1930s.

During the 1920s, Burrill was well known throughout the District for her directing of classical plays. She served as director of the Washington, D.C., Conservatory of Music School of Expression from 1907 to 1911 and taught elocution, public speaking, and dramatics there. Upon her retirement from Dunbar High in 1944, Burrill moved to New England. She died on March 13, 1946.

KATHY A. PERKINS

Burrows, Vinie (1928–)

The career of Vinie Burrows started very near the top of the American theater establishment. She debuted, while still in college, on Broadway with Helen Hayes. Yet, in the years that have followed, established theater has provided her with so little satisfaction, challenge, and opportunity to fulfill her potential that she has created her own, culturally rich form of dramatic expression.

Vinie Burrows was born on November 15, 1928, in the city of New York. She went to New York University, from which she earned a B.A., but only after she appeared in *The Wisteria Trees* in 1950. The next year, Burrows was in the cast of a revival of *The Green Pastures*. She continued to have an unusually successful theater career, especially for a young black woman. The year 1954 brought *Mrs. Patterson* at the National Theater and, in 1955, Burrows appeared in Thornton Wilder's classic, *The Skin of Our Teeth*. Also in the 1950s, she appeared in *Ponder Heart*, *Jezebel's Husband*, and *Mandingo*.

In the 1960s, however, Burrows found that work in the theater was neither as frequent nor as satisfying as she had hoped. She took the situation into her own hands, creating a series of remarkable one-woman shows. *Shout Freedom*, in 1965, celebrated liberation for women and children. *Dark Fire* was a dramatic presentation of African legends and other folklore. *Sister! Sister!*, in the words of the *New York Times*, "sets

itself the daunting task of evoking the very essence of womanhood by interweaving the voices of 19 women of diverse race and culture." That piece was presented in Los Angeles and Martha's Vineyard in the early 1970s and revived at American Place Theater in 1992.

Perhaps Burrows most famous piece is called *Walk Together, Children*. The combination of poetry, prose and, songs by black authors tells the story of the black experience in America. It was produced off-Broadway at the Greenwich Mews Theater in November 1968 by Robert Hooks to enthusiastic reviews. Clive Barnes called her "a magnificent performer," and the *Post* called her "funny, gutsy, diverse, and colorful, ironic, apocalyptic." From New York, the show went on tour, eventually being performed thousands of times at colleges and universities around the United States and in a number of other countries.

Burrows had, in her words, "tapped a rich vein from my own black culture and heritage." She would mine that vein again in 1973 in *Phillis Wheatley, Gentle Poet, Child of Africa* about the slave poet who lived before the Revolutionary War. This dramatic presentation of Wheatley's poems and letters was prepared with dancer Pearl Primus.

Burrows' piece for three black women, *Her Talking Drum*, was performed in 1989 at the American Place Theater. Burrows' performance in the piece was called "passionate and commanding" by the *New Yorker*. In 1991, she appeared off-Broadway in the play *Homemade Love*. The 1992 revival of *Sister! Sister!* at American Place was enthusiastically received. In 1993, Burrows appeared in **Sonia Sanchez**'s *Sister Son/ji* and, in 1994, was given the

AUDELCO Award as Best Actress for her performance as Obatala in *Shango De Ima*.

In keeping with her activist approach to theater is Burrows participation in political movements. She is a prominent advocate of black and women's rights, disarmament, and the destruction of apartheid. She served as a member of a United Nations fact-finding mission, visiting African states to investigate the condition of women and children as victims of apartheid. She is a permanent NGO (Nongovernmental Organization) representative to the United Nations from the Women's International Democratic Federation. She has addressed the United Nations Commission on the Status of Women.

Vinie Burrows, with extraordinary talent, passion, and creativity, has helped to shape the American theater and the American consciousness.

KATHLEEN THOMPSON

Bush, Anita (c. 1883–1974)

Speaking in an interview about the opening of the Lafayette Players, Anita Bush once said, "I laugh whenever I hear myself called 'The Little Mother of Drama.' No one will ever know what labor pains were borne by me the week before the first show opened." It was in November 1915 that this young, determined black performer finally brought her long-held dream to reality: a black dramatic stock company that would perform serious, nonmusical theater for black audiences. Bush was convinced that black performers could be just as good at legitimate drama as their white counterparts, that singing and dancing were not the only threatical realms in which black people could excel. Except for the short-lived African Grove Theater, founded in 1820, few black performers had ventured into the domain of serious acting. Anita Bush was to change the face of legitimate theater in America.

Brought up in New York, the daughter of a popular tailor who catered to show-business folk, black and white, Bush came into contact early with the profession that was to shape her life and the lives of so many other black performers. In a 1969 interview, she spoke of "falling in love with grease paint, costumes, backstage, drama," and she "married" herself to them for life.

Anita Bush was only sixteen when she secured her parents' reluctant permission to join the company of Bert Williams and George W. Walker, although she considered herself very untalented musically. When her concerned father asked Williams why he wanted his daughter to join his troupe, Williams gallantly assured him that she "would make a pretty picture on stage." Bush remained with the famous team until they discontinued their association and Williams went on to greater fame with the Ziegfeld Follies.

In 1915, driven by the constant dream of forming a group of actors to perform in serious drama, Bush gathered some of Harlem's favorite performers and began what at first was called the Anita Bush Players, a name the group retained until they moved to the Lafayette Theater from the Lincoln Theater in December of that year. Shortly thereafter, they began to be advertised in newspapers as the Lafayette Players, and the name stayed with the troupe throughout its seventeen-year existence.

The newly formed company consisted of such Harlem luminaries as Charles Gilpin, Dooley Wilson, Andrew Bishop, and Carlotta Freeman, who, prior to joining the group, had never performed professionally.

The Lafayette Players introduced legitimate theater to more than twenty-five cities across America. Performing more than 250 dramas never presented by a completely black group, either before or since, the Players became a virtual training ground for more than 300 black performers before they disbanded permanently in 1932. Bush herself starred with the Players for several years and then, in 1921, costarred with Lawrence Chenault in the first all-black western movie, *The Crimson Skull*. Later, in 1936, Bush was featured in the Works Progress Administration (WPA) Federal Theatre Project's *Swing It*.

During her long and varied career, Anita Bush was given credit for initiating the professional careers of more than fifty successful black performers. She died in February 1974 at the age of ninety-one knowing that her dream had been the seed that blossomed and changed the face of black theater forever.

SISTER FRANCESCA THOMPSON

C

Canty, Marietta (1906–1986)

When the camera scans the emotional landscape of family life in the fifties in *Rebel Without a Cause*, it reveals—among the older generation—hypocrisy, cowardice, and insensitivity, and then it focuses on a figure of dignity and compassion, sweetly played by Marietta Canty.

Marietta Canty was born in Hartford, Connecticut, in 1906, daughter of Henry C. Canty, a municipal employee, and Mary N. Canty. She attended the Hartford Northeast Grammar School and the Hartford Public Evening High. While in high school, she won prizes in elocution, sang in the choir of the AME Zion Church, took singing lessons from a local voice teacher, and, at eighteen, joined the Charles Gilpin Players. At the same time, she worked as a cleaner at local department stores and residences.

When Canty was twenty-four, she went to New York to audition for Hall Johnson, who accepted her into his famous choir. It was in this choir that she made her Broadway debut in the play *Run Little Chillun*. After touring with the show, she acted in the film version of *The Emperor Jones*. The amazingly energetic Canty managed, in the meantime, to study nursing and finish a probation term at Lincoln Hospital in Hartford.

In 1936, Canty had a principal role in the Clare Boothe play *Kiss the Boys Goodbye*. After several other appearances on the New York stage, Canty returned to Hollywood,

appearing in more than fifty films before she retired to care for her aging father in 1955. Her films included *The Searching Wind*, *Home Sweet Homicide*, *Father of the Bride*, *The Spoilers*, and *My Foolish Heart*.

In her last film, *Rebel Without a Cause*, Canty played the housekeeper who provides Sal Mineo with the only parental love and affection he has ever known. As she plays the role, this black woman does not care for the boy because she is a Mammy who sacrifices herself for white children. She cares for him because somebody has to and there is no one else to do it. Canty radiates decency and humanity.

After her retirement to Hartford, Connecticut, Marietta Canty became active in civic affairs. In 1961, she ran for the city council. She received many awards for service to her community, including the Citizenship and Civic Service Award of the Ararat Chapter of B'nai Brith. Canty died in 1986.

KATHLEEN THOMPSON

Carroll, Diahann (1935–)

For Diahann Carroll, as for many other black entertainers, success has sometimes been a two-edged sword, giving her notoriety in the mainstream but separating her from her roots. She once complained that she was a black woman with a white image. Although she has achieved some success, her career has been hampered by the limited opportunities available to black actresses both on stage and screen. However, as her

Actress and singer Diahann Carroll has achieved success in nightclubs and in film, television, and the Broadway stage but has had to struggle against the perception that she is a black woman with a white image. (SCHOMBURG CENTER)

tell-all memoir, *Diahann: An Autobiography* (1986), makes clear, her career aspirations were frustrated by marital struggles and rocky romances.

Carol Diahann Johnson was born on July 17, 1935, and raised in Harlem and the Bronx by her mother and her father, who was a subway conductor. Pretty and talented, at ten she won a Metropolitan Opera scholarship and at fourteen first prize on *Arthur Godfrey's Talent Scouts,* for which she began to use the name Diahann Carroll. As a teen, she attended New York's High School of Music and Art, and by the time she graduated she was working steadily as a model for *Ebony*, *Jet*, and *Sepia* magazines.

Carroll studied psychology briefly at New York University, but she left when she won the costarring role of Ottilie in Truman Capote and Harold Arlen's Broadway musical, *House of Flowers* (1954), directed by Peter Brook. Although the show closed in the face of unusually strong Broadway competition, Carroll's singing and acting won her a small role in the film *Carmen Jones* (1954). She then studied acting with Lee Strasberg and spent a number of years as a nightclub singer in New York and other major entertainment centers; as her record albums show, her own singing was influenced by Frank Sinatra's style.

In 1956, she married Monte Kay, a white casting agent, and in 1960 gave birth to a daughter, Suzanne. A long-term romance with Sidney Poitier, whom she met while playing the small role of Serena in the 1959 film *Porgy and Bess*, eventually destroyed the marriage.

In the early 1960s, Carroll continued to sing and play supporting film parts, but her most important role was the lead in Richard Rodgers' Broadway musical *No Strings* (1962). This story of a doomed interracial romance ran for more than a year and won Carroll a Tony Award. When Hollywood then promised the lead in the film version to a Eurasian actress, Carroll created a minor scandal by complaining to the press of the film industry's racism; the film was, in fact, never made. (In 1965, Rodgers was said to be at work on another Broadway musical for Carroll, but it never materialized.)

By the mid-1960s, Carroll was a frequent guest on television talk shows, and in 1968, in *Julia*, she became the first black star of a television situation comedy. This slick, popular, and generally unimaginative show, produced by Hal Kanter, ran for three seasons; Carroll played a single mother, the widow of an American who had died in the Vietnam War. She gained a tremendous viewership, but the change in her image from glamorous to maternal later diluted her nightclub success.

In 1972, Carroll was briefly engaged to the television interviewer David Frost and then unexpectedly married Freddie Glusman, a white Las Vegas shopowner. Their stormy marriage lasted only four months and ended with Carroll's charges against Glusman of physical abuse.

In 1974, Carroll starred in what is generally considered her best film, *Claudine*, directed by John Berry and costarring James Earl Jones. Her uncharacteristically gritty portrayal of a single welfare mother garnered her an Academy Award nomination as Best Actress.

In 1976, she married Robert DeLeon, an editor of *Jet* magazine and a dozen years her junior, and largely abandoned her career. DeLeon died in a car crash.

After DeLeon's death, Carroll devoted herself completely to rebuilding her career, beginning all over again as a nightclub singer. Finally, in the late 1970s and early 1980s, she earned major roles in the TV specials *Roots: The Next Generation* (1979) and *I Know Why the Caged Bird Sings* (1979) and in the Broadway drama *Agnes of God* (1982).

For several seasons beginning in 1984, Carroll played the unscrupulous Dominique Deveraux on TV's *Dynasty*. She considered this introduction to prime-time audiences of a black character as vicious as her white counterparts to be a high point of her career.

"I wanted," as she later put it, "to be the first black bitch on television."

In 1987, Carroll married Vic Damone, a white singer and subsequently made frequent appearances as the mother of Whitley Guilbert (played by Jasmine Guy) on the television situation comedy *A Different World*. Carroll and Damone were divorced in 1991. In 1995, she began a long-term run in the Canadian company of the musical *Sunset Boulevard* in the lead role of Norma Desmond.

PAUL NADLER

Carroll, Vinnette (1922–)

Vinnette Carroll drew national attention in 1972 when she became one of the first black women to direct a production on Broadway. Carroll was born March 11, 1922, in New York City but spent much of her childhood in the West Indies. Before turning to the theater, she was a clinical psychologist, having received a B.A. in 1944 from Long Island University and an M.A. in 1946 from New York University.

As founder and artistic director of New York City's Urban Arts Corps (UAC) in 1967, Carroll was instrumental in beginning the careers of many of today's leading performers. Her original works combine music, dance, and the spoken word and have played to audiences around the world. She directed the Broadway hits *Don't Bother Me, I Can't Cope* (1972) and *Your Arms Too Short to Box with God* (1976). Her production of *When Hell Freezes Over I'll Skate* (1979) was performed at Lincoln Center and on national public television. Through UAC, Carroll developed many works that reached major audiences. She has also acted and directed for stage, film, and television throughout the world. Among her many honors are three Tony Award nominations, an Emmy Award, an Obie Award, the **National Association for the Advancement of Colored People** Image Award, the Los Angeles Drama Critics Circle Award, the New York Outer Critics Circle Award, and induction into the Black Filmmakers Hall of Fame.

Her work continues as the producing artistic director of the Vinnette Carroll Repertory Company in Fort Lauderdale, Florida.

KATHY A. PERKINS

It would be difficult to name a theatrical honor that has not been awarded to actress/director Vinnette Carroll. Her productions, including Don't Bother Me, I Can't Cope *and* Your Arms Too Short to Box With God, *have won three Tonys, an Emmy, an Obie, and dozens of other awards.* (SCHOMBURG CENTER)

Carter, Nell (1948–)

Nell Carter, 4 feet 11 inches and 250-plus pounds with a singing voice that one critic said "can blare like a trumpet," parlayed her unique characteristics into stardom despite a difficult personal life. Carter was born in Birmingham, Alabama, on September 13, 1948 (some sources say 1949). Four of her eight brothers and sisters were older, four younger. Her parents were army sergeant Horace Hardy and homemaker Edna Mae Humphrey. Her father was killed when he stepped on a live power line; Carter, still a toddler, witnessed the incident.

She began to sing with a group called the Renaissance Ensemble in coffeehouses and clubs during her junior year of high school. In her senior year, she was raped at gunpoint and made pregnant by an acquaintance who had offered her a ride home from a performance. For many years, Carter kept this part of her history secret and said that her daughter was the offspring of an early marriage. Going public about it for the first time, she recalled, "We never called the police. Rape wasn't something you talked about then outside the family" When she found herself unable to handle raising the child alone, an older sister who already had a family of her own took the baby in.

Carter went to New York City when she was nineteen and began to sing in clubs and cabarets. Three years later, she appeared in her first musical comedy, *Soon*, costarring Richard Gere. Other plays followed, including *Jesus Christ Superstar*, and in 1978 she had her first major Broadway success, winning Theater World and Tony awards for her performance in *Ain't Misbehavin'*, a revue featuring the music of Fats Waller. Her big break in television came in 1981 when she landed the role of the feisty house-keeper in the NBC sitcom *Gimme a Break*, which ran for six years. When it went off the air, Carter resumed her nightclub career. Her film appearances include *Hair* (1979) and *Modern Problems* (1981). In 1993 she returned to television as the high school principal in the ABC sitcom *Hangin' with Mr. Cooper*.

Behind the scenes, Carter often battled personal demons: two troubled marriages that ended in divorce, overeating, alcohol abuse, and an addiction to cocaine. Searching for spiritual guidance, she converted to Judaism around 1983. She was finally able to give up cocaine after being in and out of drug treatment programs during the mid-1980s. After three miscarriages, she adopted two baby boys in 1992. Later that year, she underwent two bouts of major surgery to remove life-threatening aneurysms pressing on her brain. "That's when I began to learn what was important in life," Carter said. She gave up alcohol and began to work on controlling her weight.

One writer analyzing Carter's appeal summed her up as ". . . short, chunky, bubbly, playful, and campy. . . . She represented the lovelorn, agreeably bossy woman with a self-deprecating humor (calling attention to her size whenever possible) and a sentimental streak as well," and she ain't misbehavin' any more.

Cash, Rosalind (1938–1995)

Talented, trained in her craft, sexy, intelligent, independent, ambitious, with a résumé that includes Shakespeare, sitcoms, and some of most things in between, Rosalind Cash might have become a major star if Hollywood's head hadn't been screwed on crooked.

Cash was born in Atlantic City, New Jersey, on December 31, 1938, to John and Martha Curtis Cash. She attended the City College of New York and also studied acting with Vinnette Carol and Edmund Cambridge. In 1958, she made her stage debut in Langston Hughes' *Soul Gone Home* at the Harlem YMCA. Like most actors, she also worked at other jobs: hospital aide, waitress, salesgirl. Cash first appeared on Broadway in 1966 in *The Wayward Stork*, a comedy about artificial insemination. One critic said the play ". . . happily has few equivalents in recent Broadway history for lack of humor, charm, taste, or any trace of skill." None of the major New York reviews mentioned Cash, and under the circumstances she was probably glad to be ignored.

More rewarding work was to come. In 1967, Douglas Turner Ward, Robert Hooks, and Gerald S. Krone founded the **Negro Ensemble Company**. The only fully professional black theater company in the United States, its mission was to provide a forum for the development of black theater artists and to produce plays that illuminate all aspects of black life for a primarily black audience. Cash became one of the fifteen original members of the ensemble, which was housed in a small theater in New York's East Village and began its work with three months of training in acting, dance and movement, voice, and karate. Beginning with its first production, *The Song of the Lusitanian Bogey*, which opened on January 2, 1968, Cash appeared regularly with the group for three seasons, during which it won Drama Desk, Tony, and Obie Awards.

Cash had her first shot at the big time in 1971, when she won a role that virtually every black actress in Hollywood wanted: Mounted on a motorcycle, she roared on-screen to rescue Charlton Heston in *Omega Man* and became ". . . a glorious symbol, . . . the beautiful black woman who comes out of nowhere and saves man from his own sad plight, a dream woman to be fought for but never conquered."

The next year, in *Melinda*, her performance as a strong but troubled woman involved in a love triangle established her appeal among young black women as well. But in the early 1970s, Hollywood was more interested in making a superficial appeal to the black audience's box-office dollar than in presenting authentic aspects of black experience. All too often, writers and directors shied away from creating black characters, especially black women, who displayed the rough edges of individuality, and as a result black actors seldom had the opportunity to express the full range of their talents. This effect can be seen even in *Omega Man*; as the story progresses, Cash's character is diluted until she is almost a token presence.

On television, Cash appeared in Melvin van Peebles' *Sophisticated Gents*, **Maya Angelou**'s *Sister Sister*, *A Killing Affair*, and the American Playhouse adaptation of James Baldwin's *Go Tell It on the Mountain;* she also played Mary Mae Ward on the soap opera *General Hospital.*

Cash's other credits include the films *Uptown Saturday Night* (1974), *Cornbread, Earl and Me* (1975), *Wrong Is Right* (1982) [in which she played the first woman Vice President of the United States], and *Tales From the 'Hood* (1995), as well as numerous stage appearances. When *Who's Who in the Theater* asked her to name her favorite roles, she answered, "Those performed for the Negro Ensemble Company."

Cash died of cancer on October 31, 1995 in Los Angeles.

Childress, Alice (1920–1994)

Playwright, novelist, actress, essayist, columnist, lecturer, and theater consultant, Alice Childress was never flattered by the litany of firsts that were often used to refer to her works. She believed that when people have been barred from something for so long, it seems ironic to emphasize the "first." Childress, instead, looked to the day when she would be the fiftieth or hundredth African-American artist to accomplish something.

Long regarded as a champion for the masses of poor people in America, Childress wrote about the disparity between rich and poor, underscoring that racism and sexism are added burdens forced upon people of color. A reticent and private person, Childress boldly spoke out in her works against a United States government that either exploits or ignores poor people in the name of capitalism. One of Childress' strongest convictions was that black authors must explore and include black history in their writings. Her sagacity and commitment to preserving black culture and history are evident in her refusal to tell lies about black people, even at the expense of Broadway options.

Alice Childress was born on October 12, 1920, in Charleston, South Carolina. When she was five, she moved to Harlem to live with her grandmother, Eliza Campbell, who reared her after her parents divorced. Although Childress grew up very poor, she was enriched by her grandmother's love, patience, and appreciation for the arts. It was her grandmother who taught her the art of storytelling and who took her to museums, art galleries, and Wednesday-night testimonials at Salem Church in Harlem. Childress's inspiration for writing came from these testimonials because in them she heard the troubles of many poor people.

Childress attended Public School 81, the Julia Ward Howe Junior High School, and, for three years, Wadleigh High School, which she left when her grandmother and mother died in the late 1930s. Mostly self-taught, Childress remembers discovering the public library as a youngster and voraciously reading two books a day. She took on a series of odd jobs in the 1940s to support herself and her daughter from her first marriage, Jean. Childress worked as assistant machinist, photo retoucher, domestic worker, salesperson, and insurance agent—jobs that kept her in close contact with the working-class people that she characterizes in her works.

Childress began her writing career in the 1940s. In 1943, she began an eleven-year association with the American Negro Theater, where she studied acting, performed in Broadway productions, directed, and served on the board of directors. One of Childress' major accomplishments during her tenure with the American Negro Theater was initiating in the early 1950s advanced, guaranteed pay for union off-Broadway contracts in New York City. Childress benefited from this effort because her *Just a Little Simple* (1950) and *Gold through the Trees* (1952) became the first plays by a black woman to be professionally produced, that is, performed by unionized actors.

Childress wrote more than a dozen plays, including *Florence* (1949); *Wedding Band: A Love Hate Story in Black and White* (1966), which was televised on ABC in

Attacking stereotypes and institutional racism, Alice Childress' plays have shaken up audiences and the American theater for four decades. Her Trouble in Mind *was the first play by a black woman ever to receive an Obie.* (SCHOMBURG CENTER)

1974; *Wine in the Wilderness* (1969), which was produced on National Educational Television in 1969; *Mojo: A Black Love Story* (1970); and *Moms* (1987). Her plays attack institutional racism and stereotyped roles assigned to African Americans.

Childress became the first black woman ever to receive an Obie Award, for the off-Broadway production of *Trouble in Mind* (1955), a play about white directors who know little about black life yet insist on presenting stereotypes. Running for ninety-one performances at the Greenwich Mews Theater, Childress' two-act drama drew rave reviews and generated interest from commercial backers. *Trouble in Mind* was scheduled for a Broadway production in April 1957 but was withdrawn by Childress because of changes required by the director.

Childress also wrote novels, including *Like One of the Family: Conversations from a Domestic's Life* (1937), *A Hero Ain't Nothin' but a Sandwich* (1973) [which Childress adapted for a 1979 film that starred **Cicely Tyson** and Paul Winfield], *A Short Walk* (1979), *Rainbow Jordan* (1981), and *Those Other People* (1990).

Her novels, like her plays, portray poor people who struggle to survive in capitalist America. She incorporates in them black history in order to inform black children of the heroic lives that paved the way for them to succeed. *Like One of the Family* is a collection of vignettes in which the maid enlightens her employers about their shortcomings. Playwright Ed Bullins' review of *A Hero Ain't Nothin' but a Sandwich* in *The New York Times* concludes: "There are too few books that convince us that reading is one of the supreme gifts of being human. Alice Childress, in her short, brilliant study of a 13-year-old heroin user, achieves this feat in a masterly way." *A Short Walk,* another exceptional novel, chronicles Garveyism and the black experience through the 1960s. *A Hero Ain't Nothin' but a Sandwich, Rainbow Jordan,* and *Those Other People* are novels for adolescents and deal with sexuality, drugs, and growing up in a homophobic society.

Childress' innovativeness garnered her several major awards and honors, including writer-in-residence at the MacDowell Colony; featured author in a BBC panel discussion on "The Negro in the American Theater"; a Rockefeller grant administered through the New Dramatists and the John Golden Fund for Playwrights; and a Harvard appointment to the Radcliffe Institute for Independent Study (now Mary Ingraham Bunting Institute), from which she received a graduate medal. Noted American authors Lillian Hellman and Tillie Olsen were instrumental in recommending Childress to Radcliffe. During her stay at Radcliffe, she wrote *Wedding Band* (1966), a play that deals with interracial love and the objections raised by members of both races.

Alice Childress wrote for the stage for more than four decades, and she played a major part in the development of African-American theater. **Lorraine Hansberry**, who would later author the 1959 Broadway success *A Raisin in the Sun*, wrote the 1950 review of Childress' play *Florence* in Paul Robeson's *Freedom* magazine, evidence of the impact Childress' work would have on future generations of black dramatists. She was a master craftsperson whose deft handling of language aligns her with America's most brilliant authors.

Childress married professional musician and music teacher Nathan Woodward on July 17, 1957. Her daughter Jean died in 1990. Childress died of cancer in August of 1994 in Queens, New York.

ELIZABETH BROWN-GUILLORY

Clough, Inez (c.1870–1933)

James Weldon Johnson called April 17, 1917, "the date of the most important single event in the entire history of the Negro in the American theater." On that date, an evening of three one-act plays with black casts opened on Broadway. Inez Clough, playing one of the leading roles, was singled out for critical praise.

Clough was born in New England in the 1860s or 1870s and began her career as a concert singer in Worcester, Massachusetts. In the late 1890s, she toured with John Isham's Oriental American Company around the United States and in Europe. After returning to the United States, Clough began to appear in music halls before joining the Walker and Williams company.

With George Walker and Bert Williams, she appeared in *Dahomey* in 1902, *In Abyssinia* in 1906, and *In Bandanna Land* in 1907. She worked with another legendary team in black musicals when she joined cast of *Shoo Fly Regiment*, written by James Weldon Johnson and his brother J. Rosamond Johnson and produced by Bob Cole.

Clough was one of the original members of the **Lafayette Players**, founded by **Anita Bush**. Many of the acting ensemble were among the casts of the Ridgely Torrence one-acts. What made this production so remarkable was that it was a serious dramatic evening. To this time, black actors had appeared on Broadway almost exclusively in musicals. The occasional black role in a serious drama was usually a servant, a character of little or no consequence in the play. In these plays by white poet Ridgely Torrence, Inez Clough and her fellow actors played characters written with sensitivity and intelligence. Drama critic George Jean Nathan chose Clough and another cast member, Opal Cooper, among the best ten performers of that year on Broadway, an exceptional tribute.

During the 1920s, Clough appeared in the landmark musical *Shuffle Along* by No-

ble Sissle and Eubie Blake and its successor, *The Chocolate Dandies*.

Inez Clough died in December of 1933, in Chicago.

KATHLEEN THOMPSON

Cole, Olivia (1942–)

Commenting on Olivia Cole's performance as a mammy in the 1985 TV miniseries *North and South*, one critic remarked that even in "the dopiest of roles," she "refuses not to take acting seriously."

Cole was born in Memphis, Tennessee, on November 26, 1942, to William and Arvelia Cage Cole. During her childhood, the family moved to New York's Harlem neighborhood, and her parents eventually divorced. Cole recalled that her mother, a tennis teacher, "would take me to the museum because she couldn't afford a babysitter. But . . . I never had to pick cotton. I had a first-rate education." She attended Hunter College High School, then majored in drama at Bard College in upstate New York, and studied acting on a scholarship at the Royal Academy of Dramatic Art in London for two years. Back in the States, she appeared in *Romeo and Juliet*, *Coriolanus*, and *The Taming of the Shrew* at the American Shakespeare Theater in Stratford, Connecticut, in 1965 and obtained an M.A. in drama from the University of Minnesota.

During the early 1970s, Cole worked in many highly respected theaters, playing roles that ranged from the motherly Nerissa in Shakespeare's *The Merchant of Venice* to the stuffy-nosed Adelaide in the musical comedy *Guys and Dolls*. For more than four years, she had a major role on the soap opera *The Guiding Light*. When she moved to Los Angeles, she had every reason to expect that movies and prime-time television would embrace her. Instead, she was all but ignored. She was ready to give up and return to the East Coast when her agent called with an offer to read "for something called *Roots*." Her work in the landmark ABC miniseries earned her the 1977 Emmy as Best Supporting Actress in a Single Performance. The parts that followed were smaller, as in her first two films, *Heroes* and *Coming Home*, or less challenging, as in the quickly forgotten TV sitcom *Szysznyk*, but she approached them with the same skill and commitment she brought to her starring role of Maggie Rogers, who worked for all eight U.S. presidents from Taft to Eisenhower, in the 1979 NBC miniseries *Backstairs at the White House*. That performance brought her no official awards, but when the question who's the best black actress around? was debated, **Cicely Tyson**'s name wasn't the only "right" answer anymore.

Cole welcomed the opportunity to play one of the great roles for black women, the mother in *A Raisin in the Sun*, at New York's Roundabout Theater in 1986, although she continued to work mostly in films and television plays, including *Something About Amelia*, a highly acclaimed drama about incest (ABC, 1984), and *The Women of Brewster Place* (ABC, miniseries 1989, series 1990). In descriptions of characters she has played, certain words are used again and again: dignity, discipline, control, self-respect, integrity. As her NAACP Image Award confirms, they apply equally well to Cole herself.

D

Dandridge, Dorothy (1922–1965)

Dorothy Dandridge was one of the most acclaimed actors of her time; yet Hollywood producers' inability or unwillingness to see past race meant that she was often without acting roles unless the part called for the stereotypically exotic, sexual black temptress. Dandridge always rose above stereotypes, even when playing the temptress. Her story lies in both the brilliance of her talent and in Hollywood's willingness to squander such brilliance.

Dorothy Dandridge was born on November 9, 1922, in Cleveland, Ohio. Her father, Cyril Dandridge, was a cabinetmaker and minister. Her mother, Ruby Dandridge, was an aspiring actress. They separated shortly before Dandridge was born. When she was still a young child, she performed with her older sister, Vivian, in an act called the Wonder Kids. They toured all over the country, not in vaudeville, but in Baptist churches, singing, dancing, acting in skits written by their mother, and doing acrobatics. At the end of the act, the children would stand on stage and answer personal questions about their lives as performers. Dandridge blamed those question sessions for her aversion to interviews later in life, remembering them as painful and difficult.

She also remembered a time when her father followed and found them. "I remember one night when I was about three," she said in a 1962 *Ebony* interview, "and Vivian and I were sleeping, and Mother had to put both of us up in the attic so our father wouldn't find us. He was looking for us to take us away, and Mother didn't want this, so she hid us. I remember that horror because I wanted so desperately to see him. I just wanted to know what he was like."

In the early 1930s, Dandridge and her mother and sister moved to Los Angeles. Ruby found work on radio and television,

Dorothy Dandridge was one of the most acclaimed actors of her time. She is shown here in the 1954 film Remains to Be Seen. (PRIVATE COLLECTION)

83

eventually appearing in such films as *Tish*, *Cabin in the Sky*, and *My Wild Irish Rose*. She also became a regular on the radio and television show *Beulah* and, later, *Father of the Bride*. Her daughters joined with a third girl, Etta Jones, and changed their stage name to the Dandridge Sisters. When Dorothy Dandridge was sixteen, the trio went to New York and performed at the Cotton Club, often appearing on the same bill with Cab Calloway, W. C. Handy, and Bill "Bojangles" Robinson. While there, she met her father for the first time.

The Dandridge Sisters debuted in Hollywood in a short turn near the end of the Marx Brothers film *A Day at the Races*. Soon after the film was made, the trio split up. In 1941 and 1942, Dandridge appeared several times in the 1940s version of the music video, the musical film short. Her appearances included the classic Mills Brothers *Paper Doll*, in which she appeared as the paper doll that each Mills brother wanted to "call my own." She also played bit parts in *Lady from Louisiana*, *Sun Valley Serenade*, *Bahama Passage*, *Drums of the Congo*, and *Hit Parade of 1943*.

In 1942, Dandridge married Harold Nicholas, one of the famous dancing Nicholas Brothers, and had a child. For about six years after the child was born, she remained at home and supported her husband in his bid for a movie career. However, the child, Harolyn, was discovered to be severely brain damaged and was eventually institutionalized. The marriage ended in divorce.

At this point, Dandridge singlemindedly set out to become an actress. Her first step was to support herself by singing. She appeared with the Desi Arnaz Band at the Macombo in 1951 and, in 1952, at La Vie en Rose. That New York nightclub was just about to close when she opened there. She sold out for two weeks, stayed on for fourteen more, and saved the club from bankruptcy. *Theater Arts* magazine referred to her act as "vocalized sex appeal." When she returned a year later, she had toned down that aspect of her performance, hoping to be taken more seriously.

In the meantime, Dandridge had been spending every penny she earned singing on trying to develop an acting career. Her life was a round of auditions, lessons of all kinds, and singing performances. In 1953, she made her first important step toward an acting career when she was cast opposite Harry Belafonte in the film *Bright Road*. She played a southern schoolteacher. It was a good film, and Dandridge made her mark, but she almost missed out on her biggest screen opportunity because of her class and dignity. Otto Preminger was not going to let her read for the title role in his black musical *Carmen Jones* (1954) because he thought she was too "regal." However, by appearing at an interview with him dressed for the part in skirt and low-cut blouse with tousled hair, she snared the role.

Dandridge's performance in the film, an adaptation of Bizet's opera *Carmen*, was dazzling. *Life* put her on its cover, and the critics went wild. *Time* said she "holds the eye—like a match burning steadily in a tornado." Comparing her role with the one she played in *Bright Road*, *Newsweek* said, "The range between the two parts suggests that she is one of the outstanding dramatic actresses of the screen." She won an Academy Award nomination, the first for a black woman in the category of Best Actress, and she was suddenly an international star. She would not make another film for three years.

When Dandridge finally appeared in front of the camera again, it was in the first of a series of films in which she played opposite white actors. Hollywood did not really know what to do with her. A 1966 article in *Ebony* summed up the situation. Dandridge was a leading lady, it pointed out, and that was the problem. "Except for Harry Belafonte and the quietly but brilliantly rising Sidney Poitier, there were no prominent Negro romantic male leads about. Besides, a Negro male can be made a star without becoming a leading man. He may play a variety of roles not involving romance. But a leading lady such as *Dorothy had to set male hormones sizzling*" [emphasis added].

So Dandridge was relegated to temptress roles in films such as *The Decks Ran Red* (1958), *Tamango* (1959), and *Malaga* (1962). Her love scenes were played with white men who were not allowed to kiss her for fear of alienating southern theater owners and audiences. The situation was reminiscent of the career of Chinese actress Anna May Wong, who, in order to avoid an interracial happy ending, died in every single one of her films.

In 1959, Dandridge was cast as Bess in the film version of *Porgy and Bess*. The cast was a virtual duplication of that in *Carmen Jones*—Dandridge, **Pearl Bailey**, Brock Peters, Roy Glenn, and **Diahann Carroll**. The major substitution was Sidney Poitier for Harry Belafonte, who had flatly refused to do the film on the grounds that it was an insult to black people. (Poitier tried to refuse but was coerced.) The major addition was Sammy Davis, Jr. Again, Dandridge rose above her material. She won the Golden Globe Award for best actress in a musical.

Dandridge made two more films, but her film career was essentially over. When Rouben Mamoulian was selected to direct *Cleopatra*, he told Dandridge that he wanted her for the part. "You won't have the guts to go through with it," she said. "They are going to talk you out of it." Of course, they did. The role of the greatest black temptress in history went to violet-eyed Elizabeth Taylor. (Mamoulian himself was fired from the film soon after shooting began.)

During the late 1950s, Dandridge was linked romantically with Peter Lawford, Otto Preminger, and many others. Dandridge was the first Hollywood celebrity to sue the magazine *Confidential,* when it printed an article accusing her of an affair in Reno with a musician. Then, in 1959, she satisfied all of the speculation about her personal life when she married white nightclub owner Jack Denison and revealed that they had been seeing each other secretly for four years.

In 1962, Dandridge divorced Denison and, five months later, declared bankruptcy. In 1959, her income had been $250,000; in 1963, it was less than $40,000. She was no longer able to pay for the private institutionalization of her daughter, who was suddenly deposited, disoriented and violent, at her home. She was eventually transferred to a state institution.

Dandridge was on the rebound from her problems in late 1965. She had a huge success in a nightclub engagement in New Mexico and was contracted to open in New York at Basin Street East. She signed contracts for two films with Mexican producer Raul Fernandez for $100,000. She had been hired to do an American western for $25,000. She was finishing up her autobiography, for which she had an eager publisher. Then, on September 4, she was found dead in her apartment from an overdose of an antidepressant. The drug, Tofranil, is not one that causes drowsiness or forgetfulness, making an accident unlikely.

Dorothy Dandridge was a fine actress with a wide range who was forced into a destructive stereotype for reasons of race and gender. Her talents were wasted because she was a woman and because she was black. Her autobiography, *Everything and Nothing*, was published posthumously in 1970. In 1977 she was inducted into the Black Filmmakers Hall of Fame.

KATHLEEN THOMPSON

Dandridge, Ruby (1904–1991)

While confined to playing maids and servants by the race codes of her day, Ruby Dandridge still succeeded in carving out a place for herself in the entertainment industry. Her success helped make it possible for two of her daughters, Vivian and the famous **Dorothy Dandridge**, to advance to more rewarding roles.

Born in Memphis, Tennessee, in 1904, Ruby married Cyril Dandridge, a cabinetmaker and minister, when she was still in her teens. She separated from her husband in 1922, shortly after their second daughter was born. Dandridge and the two children then toured the country with an act written by Dandridge and sung, danced, and acted by the girls.

In the early 1930s, Dandridge and her daughters moved to Los Angeles. There, she found work for herself in show business. She played supporting roles in several radio series, including *The Judy Canova Show* and *The Gene Autry Show*. She was also part of

the radio cast of *Beulah* and moved with it to television. During the fifties, she had a popular nightclub act that played in many of the best clubs in Hollywood. In the 1961 season, she appeared as the maid in the television series *Father of the Bride.*

Dandridge also worked in movies during the era of the Hollywood studio system. Her film credits include *Midnight Shadow* (1939), *Tish* (1942), *Cabin in the Sky* (1943), *Gallant Lady* (1943), *Melody Parade* (1943), *Junior Miss* (1945), *Three Little Girls in Blue* (1946), *My Wild Irish Rose* (1947), *The Arnelo Affair* (1947), and *A Hole in the Head* (1959).

ANDRA MEDEA

Dash, Julie (1952–)

The success of Spike Lee's first film, *She's Gotta Have It*, in the mid-1980s signaled the beginning of trends in the movie business that have given black independent filmmakers more and more opportunities to create and market their work. Still, there are very few women among them. Of those few, Julie Dash, creator of the stunning *Daughters of the Dust*, stands out.

Dash was born in 1952 and grew up in the Queensbridge Projects in Long Island City, New York, a short subway ride from Manhattan. While in high school, she went to visit a friend at the Film Workshop at the Studio Museum in Harlem and "just kind of fell into shooting 16-mm film and editing it. We were doing documentary films for a while, but I never consciously decided at that time that I was going to be a filmmaker." She went to City College of New York to study psychology but changed her major to film and television production and graduated with a B.A. degree in 1974. Dash then moved to Los Angeles, where she attended the prestigious American Film Institute for two years, then did graduate work at UCLA.

Losing interest in making documentaries by this time, Dash would later willingly return to the form when she worked with the National Black Women's Health Project on a series of videotapes addressing various health concerns of black women. She had come to believe "that you can reach a wider audience by providing a story with the same facts and entertain them a little bit and educate them and all that." While a student in Los Angeles, she directed *Four Women*, an experimental dance film based on a Nina Simone song, which won the 1977 Golden Medal for Women in Film at the Miami International Film Festival, and *Diary of an African Nun*, based on a short story by **Alice Walker**. The film won a 1977 Directors Guild Award at the Los Angeles Film Exposition.

In 1989, *Illusions*, a thirty-four-minute black-and-white film produced, directed, and written by Dash in 1983, was named Best Film of the Decade by the Black Filmmaker Foundation. The two main characters in *Illusions* are black women working in Hollywood during World War II. One is a singer who is only useful to the studios as the dubbed-in singing voice of white actresses; the other, who is passing as white, is a studio executive. The women are drawn into friendship, at least in part because each one, in her own way, must remain invisible in order to succeed.

Dash spent several years writing and fund-raising for *Daughters of the Dust*, her first feature-length film. During the process, she relocated to Atlanta, Georgia. Set in 1902 on the isolated island of Ibo Landing

off the coast of South Carolina, *Daughters* depicts a critical time in the life of a family that is part of the unique Gullah culture. Interviewed while making the film, Dash said, "It's about the struggle to maintain their own family unity as half of the family wants to migrate North and the other half wants to stay behind and maintain cultural traditions and beliefs. So there's a lot of mysticism in it and magic in it."

Hard-won grants from the Public Broadcasting System and the Fulton County (Georgia) Arts Council among other sources made filming possible, and the result was well received at the 1991 Sundance Film Festival in Utah, but getting what one critic called the "extravagantly poetic" movie into theaters proved difficult. One thing that has remained unchanged since the earliest days of the film industry is that most of the people who hold the power to market and distribute films are white men, and it seemed impossible to convince them that there was an audience out there willing to pay to see Dash's film. Finally, with the involvement of the small but savvy black marketing company Kino International, the film was released in 1992. That same year, it aired in the *American Playhouse* series on PBS television. It has been referred to as "the critically acclaimed *Daughters of the Dust*" so many times that "critically acclaimed" might as well be part of the title!

Dash may never come up with a box-office blockbuster, but then she's not trying to. Although she is well aware of "the bottom line" and very knowledgeable about the business of filmmaking, for her, telling the story is the important thing. She believes that black independent filmmakers "have to take chances and just see what's gonna happen, because we're really creating the road and breaking the trail. . . . We're trying to redefine images and show people as we know them, and so present something very different. It's very easy to write formula and stereotypes, but it's very different to hold onto your cultural base and have that depicted clearly on the screen."

INDIA COOPER

Dearing, Judy (1940–1995)

Judy Dearing designed costumes for more than a dozen Broadway productions, including *for colored girls who have considered suicide/when the rainbow is enuf, Checkmates, The Babe, The Mighty Gents,* and *Once on This Island.* One of the few black female designers on Broadway, Dearing inspired many young women to pursue a career in costume design.

Judy Elizabeth Dearing was born February 28, 1940, in New York City to Charles and Elizabeth Dearing. One of six children, she attended City College of New York and the Sapho School of Design. Her earliest stage designs were for dance, for such choreographers as Alvin Ailey, Rod Rodgers, and Donald McKayle. She was inspired to design for theater by actors Bill Duke and Garrett Morris.

In 1974, Dearing designed her first Broadway production, *What the Wine-Sellers Buy.* The next year, she became a member of United Scenic Artists Association (USAA). Her other major credits include *A Soldier's Play* for the **Negro Ensemble Company** and *The Dance and the Railroad* for the New York Shakespeare Festival. Dearing designed throughout the country for regional theaters and taught on numerous university campuses.

Her many awards include seven Audience Development Committee (AUDELCO) Awards, a Tony Award nomination, **National Association for the Advancement of Colored People** Image Award, and an Obie. In 1970, Dearing married choreographer/dancer John Parks. They had one daughter. She died on September 30, 1995 of acute pneumonia in New York City.

KATHY A. PERKINS

Dee, Ruby (1924–)

The history of black actors in American film has often been one of exploitation and repression. In theater, it has been one of careful isolation from the mainstream. Among the handful of actors who have risen above that condition by sheer intelligence, dignity, and determination is Ruby Dee.

Born Ruby Ann Wallace on October 27, 1924, in Cleveland, Ohio, she was the third of four children of Marshall and Emma Benson Wallace. When Ruby was an infant, the family moved to New York City and settled in Harlem. Her mother, who was a schoolteacher, was determined that her children should escape the ghetto that the area was fast becoming. She saw that they studied literature and music, and in the evenings the family read aloud to one another from the poetry of Longfellow, Wordsworth, and Paul Laurence Dunbar.

By the time she was in her teens, Ruby Dee, the name she adopted when she went onstage, was also adept at art and was submitting poetry to the *New York Amsterdam News,* a black weekly newspaper. During this time, she became involved in political activity as well. She spoke at a mass meeting protesting the cancellation of a federally funded music program, the result of which

One of the greatest actors of all time, Ruby Dee has done it all, from Lorraine Hansberry's play A Raisin in the Sun *to Spike Lee's film* Do the Right Thing. *She is shown here in a western with Sidney Poitier.* (PRIVATE COLLECTION)

had been the suicide of a teacher whose job had ended.

After high school, Dee went to Hunter College where she majored in French and Spanish and began to study acting. She also joined the American Negro Theater (ANT), a Harlem group founded by playwright/director Abram Hill. From 1941 to 1943, Dee appeared in a variety of ANT productions. In December 1943, Dee made her Broadway debut as a native girl in a drama entitled *South Pacific*. It was a walk-on role, but just three years later she was back in a principal role in the play *Jeb*, the story of a black World War II veteran. Ossie Davis, whom she married two years later, played the lead.

In 1944 and again in 1947, Dee played the title role in touring productions of a black adaptation of *Anna Lucasta* that appeared first at ANT and then on Broadway. The play drew national attention to many of its actors. In 1946, Dee appeared in her first film, *Love in Syncopation*.

Through friends she had made while protesting the treatment of Julius and Ethel Rosenberg, Dee received a role in 1953, *The World of Sholem Aleichem*. She credits that production with changing her consciousness about theater and about the universality of oppression.

During the late 1940s and the 1950s, Dee appeared frequently in both plays and films, including *The Jackie Robinson Story*, in which she played the great baseball player's wife. She also worked in radio, performing the title role in the serial *This Is Nora Drake*, a nonblack part. In 1959, on Broadway, she created the role of Ruth Younger in *A Raisin in the Sun*, by **Lorraine Hansberry**, a play that has been called perhaps the most important event in the history of modern black theater. Two years later, Dee played Ruth in the film version of the play. Sidney Poitier played her brother, the lead male role. It was the fifth time the two had played opposite each other.

In earlier films, both Dee and Poitier had been forced to play sexless, self-effacing stoics. In *Raisin*, they broke that mold for themselves and others. Dee made another break from her "Negro June Allyson" image when she appeared in her husband's satirical play *Purlie Victorious* that same year. (It was later made into a film entitled *Gone Are the Days* and musicalized as *Purlie*.) In 1965, she became the first black actress to appear in major roles at the American Shakespeare Festival at Stratford, Connecticut, playing Kate in *The Taming of the Shrew* and Cordelia in *King Lear*.

A year later, Dee won the Drama Desk Award for her performance in the lead role in **Alice Childress'** prize-winning play *Wedding Band*. Widely acclaimed and financially successful, the work focuses on an interracial love affair; in 1974, a televised version again starred Dee. In the meantime, she appeared in Athol Fugard's *Boesman and Lena*, for which she won an Obie in 1971.

When scholarship brought about renewed interest in the work of **Zora Neale Hurston**, a folklorist and writer during the Harlem Renaissance, Dee penned a stage-play entitled *Zora Is My Name* in which she starred on PBS in 1990, receiving a two-star rating. Her most recent theater work shows her ardent support of the Crossroads Theater Company, founded by African Americans. Dee played "Miss Leah" in its production of *Flyin' West* at the Kennedy Center in 1994.

Dee's performances in such films as *The Balcony*, *The Incident*, *Uptight*, *Black Girl*, and *Buck and the Preacher* gained her a reputation for powerful, honest, and highly skilled performances. In 1974, however, frustrated by the attitudes and actions of those in power in Hollywood, Dee took a break from films to work with her husband on the radio series *The Ossie Davis and Ruby Dee Hour*. The series lasted until 1976, but Dee did not return to films until 1982, when she starred in *Cat People*.

In 1989, her portrayal opposite Ossie in Spike Lee's critically and historically important film *Do the Right Thing* was marked by a dignity and humanity that reflect the values she stands for in the black community and in the dramatic community at large; roles in *Jungle Fever* (also directed by Spike Lee) and in *Just Cause* (with Blair Underwood and Sean Connery) followed.

Since the 1960s, Dee has appeared regularly on television in prestigious dramas, in nighttime soap operas, in historical treatments of black heroines such as Harriet Tubman, and in police and detective dramas. In 1981, Dee and Davis had their own series on PBS, *With Ossie and Ruby*. In 1983, she played Mary Tyrone in an all-black televised production of Eugene O'Neill's *Long Day's Journey into Night*. In 1991, she won an Emmy Award as Outstanding Supporting Actress in a Miniseries or Special for her performance in *Decora-*

tion Day, an NBC Hallmark Hall of Fame production. She recently appeared in Stephen King's *The Stand* on ABC and was featured in *Homeward Bound*, an American Movie Classics TV special.

Dee has also long been politically active. Following the 1963 church bombing in Montgomery, Alabama, and the assassination of President John F. Kennedy, Dee and Davis mounted a campaign to encourage people to donate to the promotion of civil rights instead of buying Christmas presents. They have consistently supported and lent their names to such leaders as Martin Luther King, Jr., Bayard Rustin, and A. Philip Randolph. Dee regularly performs at benefits and serves on national committees; she has also established a scholarship for young women entering the field of drama.

As if all of this were not enough, the lady has written an award-winning book! *Two Ways to Count to Ten*, Dee's adaptation of an African folk tale, won the Literary Guild Award in 1989. Other writings include, for children, *Tower to Heaven*; a volume of poetry, *Glow Child and Other Poems*; and, *My One Good Nerve*, a collection of short stories and poetry.

She and Ossie Davis were the first African-American couple to narrate the *New Testament* on cassette tape.

MARGARET D. PAGAN

Dickerson, Glenda (1945–)

"As a black female director," said Glenda Dickerson at a symposium on Non-Traditional Casting held in 1986, " . . . for all my professional life, when I have gone into rooms and theaters, classrooms, and offices . . . I felt like the Indians were perceived in those old movies. You could see in peoples' faces and hear in their attitude, 'Oh my God, here come the rioting Africans again with their big Afros and their switchblade knives and their big radios . . .'"

One can understand why the sight of this striking and dramatic woman might call up images of a crowd approaching. Glenda Dickerson is not only a formidable and determined crusader, but a multitalented artist who has achieved success in an impressive number of artistic capacities: actress, director, playwright and adaptor, as well as an educator, folklorist, and choreographer.

Dickerson was born in 1945 in Houston, Texas, and her childhood was marked by the constant traveling that is the lot of the family of a career army officer. After taking her Bachelor of Fine Arts from **Howard University** in 1966, she received her M.F.A. from Adelphi University in 1968. Although she originally wanted to work as an actor, she grew frustrated with the herd mentality of New York theater and founded her own company. She named it TOBA (Tough on Black Actors), in honor of the similarly named black vaudeville circuit.

For the next several years she worked as a director to create a theater form that dynamically combined elements of black history and culture, poetry, dance, and drama. "My vision as a creative artist was firmly rooted in the traditions of African slaves, of the masking miming ritual spied on the plantations, in the knowledge that in African art the audience is chorus." She speaks of this as a journey of reclamation. "I wanted to lead the choral dance of the misplaced people—the flying Africans—and thus experience ecstasy, to inspire the dance of the serpent as she becomes the luminous flying bird."

This vision led her to adapt many of the world's great myths and legends to reflect the black experience, as in her *Haitian Medea*. This play refashioned the Greek tragedy into a drama of voodoo set in Dahomey in the nineteenth-century. Her production of the Japanese classic tale *Rashomon* reconceived it as an exploration of African trickster legends, set in thirteenth-century Ethiopia. Dickerson has also adapted a number of black literary works to the stage, most notably *Jump at the Sun*, a stirring version of **Zora Neale Hurston**'s *Their Eyes Were Watching God*. Her 1978 production of *Magic and Lions*, based on the writings of Ernestine Walker, won her an AUDELCO Award.

A pivotal experience was her 1983 collaboration with writer Alexis DeVeaux to create what they called a "literary collage" entitled *"NO!" a new, experimental work of neoliterary events, political messages, and innovative stories for the stage.* Created out of a number of DeVeaux's poems, stories and a short play, "NO" gave Dickerson access to what sociologist bell hooks has called the "liberatory voice." Dickerson describes this as "that of the uppity black woman. I came to voice by shining the clean light of day on the things unspoken, the taboos, the personal stuff."

Dickerson has found a number of forums to continue speaking out in her liberatory voice. As a theater educator, she has taught at Howard University, Rutgers, Fordham, and the State University of New York at Stony Brook. She is currently Chair of the Theater Department at **Spelman College**. Her directing career has taken her throughout the United States, from the Seattle Repertory Theater to the St. Louis Black Repertory, from New Jersey's Crossroads Theater to the John F. Kennedy Center for the Performing Arts in Washington, D.C.

In New York, she has worked both on and off-Broadway, most notably with the New Federal Theater, the Woman's Interart Theater, and as a resident director with the **Negro Ensemble Company**. In the most public forum of all, television, her work has earned her an Emmy nomination for a 1972 production of *Wine in the Wilderness* and a Peabody Award for her production of *For My People*.

Glenda Dickerson's work, in all her many roles, exalts the color and gleam of ideas and honors the secrets of history and the deep truths hidden in legend. One recent work of reclamation, *Re/Membering Aunt Jemimah: an act of magic*, probed one of the most prominent icons of black American womanhood. Taken as a whole, her body of work celebrates the liberatory dream of "Bad Girls talking back, being loud, being rowdy, ANNOUNCING!"

RICHARD E. T. WHITE

Douglas, Marion   (1920–)

"Io mangio dove voglio. Eh! Tu! . . . Va te ne!" ("I'll eat where I want. As for you, beat it!") European child star Marion Douglas snapped to bewildered Atlantans who had introduced her to Jim Crow practices. Marion Douglas had performed on the stages of Switzerland, France, and Italy in her father's *Louis Douglas Revue*; her father had choreographed on Broadway and in Paris for **Josephine Baker**; her grandparents, ragtime composer Will Marion Cook and the legendary singer **Abbie Mitchell**, had performed for royalty; and Uncle Mercer Cook was head of the French department at **Spelman College**. No monolingual backwater plebe was going to tell *her* where she could or could not dine.

Marion Douglas, also known as "Maranantha Quick," was born Abbie Louise Douglas in 1920 in North Marylebone, England. She grew up between the world wars touring Europe with her parents, based in Italy and Germany. Billed as an acrobatic dancer, she performed matinees with the revue while at the same time attending school in Catholic convents. With the rise of Mussolini and Hitler, her father decided that the family should return to the United States and that she should become educated as a black American woman at Spelman College. With greater fluency in French and Italian than in English and no knowledge of racism, Douglas arrived in Atlanta in 1937. Her interest in languages and theater became her means of coping with the "unreality" of life around her.

Her work with the Atlanta Repertory Players at Spelman and the Hampton Institute's Summer Theater program under the direction of Owen Dodson gave her a dramatic outlet for her frustration with America in 1938. She performed in *Les précieuses ridicules* in French, and in 1941 she played several roles, including the Countess in a noted production of *The Cherry Orchard* and major parts in *Tovarich*, *Cyrano de Bergerac*, and racial plays *Outward Bound* and *Elijah's Ravens*.

The most noted role of her career was as Ophelia in Dodson's 1945 production of *Hamlet* at the Hampton Institute. Gordon Heath, who played the lead, recalls in his autobiography that Dodson felt she had overresearched the part, exclaiming, "Oh, how I hate *thinking* actors!" In spite of her excessive industry, Heath wrote, "Marion was still the best Ophelia I ever saw."

Before *Hamlet*, she had already been working on the New York stage. In the 1945 season, she played the part of Sophie Baines in *A Young American*, produced by the Blackfriars Guild, an off-Broadway troupe that performed plays with Catholic and racial themes. In this play she worked with a young black actor and fellow Dodson pupil who was to become a prolific filmmaker, William Greaves. In 1982 and 1985, Douglas had cameo roles in his two award-winning films commissioned by the National Park Service: *Frederick Douglass: An American Life* and *Booker T. Washington: The Life and Legacy*. Maintaining contact with the theater throughout her life, she worked in *Uncle Vanya* in 1984 as well as *The Threepenny Opera* and *The Confidential Clerk* at the Cynthia Belgrave Studio Theater in Brooklyn.

When not on stage, Marion Douglas has been an educator, teaching French in the New York City public school system since the 1950s. Always committed to the theater, she designed a program for teaching languages to children through drama. In the late 1960s, she directed the Children's Theater at the Harlem School of the Arts, where she introduced and wrote black-centered material for the program. From 1971 until 1983, she set drama aside to investigate mysticism and tour as a psychic.

Late in life, Douglas stated her career objectives: "To express and create through humor; to enhance the vitality of life, and to communicate the mature outlook of age as a desirable achievement." She has continued to pursue these goals, working in Jesse Jackson's 1988 presidential campaign and serving on the New York State Committee on Multicultural Education. Although modest about her contribution to the theater, she offers the unique perspective of a black American who grew up in Europe and has touched a wide network of dramatists and educators.

DAVID A. GOLDFARB

DuBois, Shirley Graham (1896–1977)

When Shirley Graham wrote in a 1933 *Crisis* essay, "Black man's music has become America's music. It will not die," she summed up one of her life's ambitions: to bring to the foreground the many accomplishments of African Americans in every field. One of Graham's concerns was that African Americans would eventually abandon their spirituals, with their unique rhythms and haunting melodies. In an effort to preserve black music, she became the first African-American woman to write and produce an all-black opera, *Tom-Toms: An Epic of Music and the Negro* (1932). This was just one successful effort in a lifetime devoted to the preservation of black history and culture.

Professional writer, composer, conductor, playwright, and director, Shirley Lola Graham was born on November 11, 1896, on a farm near Evansville, Indiana, to Reverend David Andrew Graham and Etta Bell Graham. Graham and her four brothers were encouraged by their father, a Methodist missionary, to discover black culture and music and to work to uplift the race. Shortly after graduating from Lewis and Clark High School in Spokane, Washington, Graham married Shadrach T. McCanns in 1921. McCanns died three years later, leaving her with two children, Robert and David.

In 1935, she completed a Master's degree in music history from **Oberlin College**, after studying music at the Sorbonne in 1926 and at **Howard University** in Washington, D.C., and Morgan State University in Baltimore in 1929–32.

During her first year at Oberlin, Graham converted her play *Tom-Toms* into an opera, which was produced by the Cleveland Opera Company in 1932. Drawing national media attention because of the monumental cast of 500 and the novelty of a black female composer, librettist, and dramatist, the opera played to a house of 10,000 on the first night and 15,000 for the second and final performance. Tracing African music through the United States, *Tom-Toms* began a trend that popularized musicals and dance concerts based upon African and West Indian themes. Dancers such as **Katherine Dunham** and Asadata Dafora became prominent on the heels of Graham's successful production of an opera that generated mass appeal.

With the success of her opera, Graham chose to develop her craft as a dramatist. She accepted a position in 1936 as director of the black division of the Chicago Federal Theatre Project, a job that allowed her to combine her expertise in music with theater. Between 1938 and 1940, Graham studied at the Yale Drama School, where she wrote and produced five plays: *Dust to Earth, I Gotta Home, It's Mornin', Track Thirteen,* and *Elijah's Raven*. Most notable is *It's Mornin'*, which centers on a black slave woman who kills her teenaged daughter to protect her from a lecherous master. At the end of the decade, Graham worked on a doctorate in English and education at New York University.

Feeling a need to record black progress, Graham published thirteen book-length biographies between 1944 and 1976, including *Paul Robeson: Citizen of the World* (1946), *There Was Once a Slave: The Heroic Story of Frederick Douglass* (1947), *The Story of Phillis Wheatley* (1949), *Booker T. Washington: Educator of Hand, Head, and Heart* (1955), and *A Political History of W. E. B. DuBois* (1976).

Graham had corresponded with W. E. B. DuBois since 1936, seeking advice and job opportunities. They married in 1951 and together worked for justice and world peace. Her efforts to end discrimination against black soldiers and other civil rights activities in the 1940s had prompted her dismissal from her job as director of the **Young Women's Christian Association**–United Service Organizations. Her activism in Ghana led the U.S. government to hold Graham suspect. After her husband's death in Ghana in 1963, she was denied entry to the United States on the basis of alleged un-American activities. She lived in Cairo, Egypt, for several years before being invited by the Chinese government to take up residence. She died in Beijing.

Shirley Graham DuBois lived up to her commitment to uplift the black race. Evidence of success in her several simultaneous careers came in the form of prestigious awards, including a Julius Rosenwald Fellowship in 1938–40, a Guggenheim Fellowship in 1945–47, the Julian Messner Award in 1946, the Anisfield-Wolf Award in 1949, and the National Institute of Arts and Letters Award in 1950. She also was a founding editor of *Freedomways*, a journal of black literature and culture. Her aim was to preserve black history and culture, and she succeeded from the mammoth production of *Tom-Toms* to working for world peace with a home base in China.

ELIZABETH BROWN-GUILLORY

E

Ellis, Evelyn (1894–1958)

Evelyn Ellis was an accomplished actress whose career spanned some thirty-five years on stage, television, and films. From her beginnings with the famous Lafayette Theater to her work in major motion pictures, directed by such venerable directors as Orson Welles, Ellis performed a wide variety of roles with realism and finesse.

Evelyn Ellis was born on February 2, 1894, in Boston. Little is known about her childhood and education, but her stage career began in 1919 in a production of *Othello* by the celebrated Lafayette Theater in Harlem. Shortly thereafter she was given parts in several Broadway shows, including Nan Bagby Stephen's *Roseanne*. In 1927, she won critical praise in the role of Lucy Bell Dorsey in *Goat Alley*, a play about life in the slums of Washington, D.C. That same year she performed to even greater acclaim as Bess in the hit show *Porgy*, forerunner of George and Ira Gershwin's opera *Porgy and Bess*.

Ellis's career was greatly affected by the Great Depression, as work for performers dried up across the country, but in 1937 she made her comeback as director of Dorothy Hailparn's comedy *Horse Play*, a production financed by the federal government's Negro Theatre program through the renowned Works Projects Administration (WPA). In 1941, Ellis played the part of Hannah Thomas in Orson Welles' staging of Richard Wright's *Native Son*; the follow-ing year she again played the role in another, equally acclaimed production. A succession of successful performances followed, first in 1945 as a housekeeper in *Deep Are the Roots* and then in 1951 as Della in *The Royal Family*. In 1950, Ellis directed and acted in an all-black production of *Tobacco Road*, staged by the Negro Drama Group.

Her last Broadway show was William Stuckey's *Touchstone* in 1953, but by that time her television and movie career was growing. She had played the part of Bessie in Orson Welles' film *The Lady from Shanghai* in 1948, and in 1953 Ellis took on the role of Mrs. Barrow, the fighter's mother, in *The Joe Louis Story*. Also in 1953, Ellis made her final film appearance, playing a dignified maid in *Interrupted Melody,* starring Eleanor Parker and Glenn Ford.

Evelyn Ellis died in the Will Rogers Memorial Hospital in Saranac Lake, New York, on June 5, 1958.

FENELLA MACFARLANE

Evans, Louise (1921–1992)

During the 1940s, when opportunities for black Americans and particularly women were rare behind the scenes in theater, Louise Evans achieved distinction as a costume, scenic, and lighting designer. Evans also became the first black woman to be admitted into the prestigious United Scenic Artists Association (USAA) in 1952.

Born in St. Louis, Missouri, on March 29, 1921, Louise Evans was one of three children born to Alexander E. and Johncie Hunter Evans. She attended Northwestern University (1940–42) to study children's theater and directing. As a director, Evans believed it was important to know the design side of theater and so took several design courses. After two years at Northwestern, Evans transferred to the Art Institute of Chicago to study at the Goodman Theater, where she specialized in design. At Goodman, Evans worked on numerous productions as a designer of costumes, scenery, and lighting, as well as lighting technician and property manager. Evans also directed and designed with the Chicago Negro Art Theater and served as director of drama with the Chicago Park District.

In 1946, Evans moved to New York to pursue a professional career as a designer. She designed and worked as the technical director for the Broadway Stock Company in Milford, Pennsylvania. In New York City, she designed for off-Broadway productions, particularly at the Equity Library Theater. Evans also worked with the **American Negro Theater** during the late 1940s, where she met her actor husband, Austin Briggs-Hall. They were married in 1948 and had two sons. They were later divorced. Evans gave up her career in theater to become a nun with the Third Order of Carmelites. She died on December 27, 1992 in New York City.

KATHY A. PERKINS

F

Falana, Lola (1943–)

An outsider would describe Lola Falana's career in terms of charismatic singing, dancing, and acting talent that was critically checked twice by life-threatening diseases. Falana would say it has actually been a back-and-forth struggle between the beguiling fruits of worldly success, much of it amid the glitter of Las Vegas hotel stages, and a long unfocussed yet never absent commitment to God.

Born to Cleo Twine and Bennett Falana in Camden, New Jersey, on September 11, 1943, Lola Falana was reared Catholic in Philadelphia. She was to say later that, as she grew up, "I wanted to be like everything I saw in the movies, on television, and in videos—hot, sassy, sexy. That's the image and that's the mold that was sold. And I bought it because people rewarded me for it."

She found dancing venues on the East Coast and in 1964 appeared on Broadway with Sammy Davis, Jr., in a musical version of Clifford Odets' *Golden Boy*. Davis became a mentor—as did, for varying reasons, Dinah Washington, Bill Cosby, and Wayne Newton. She has credited each with a role in her climb to success, during which, in the late 1960s, she married singer Butch Tavares. They divorced five years later.

Her singing had meanwhile found its way to Frank Sinatra's Reprise Label and Berry Gordy, Jr.'s Motown Records. She became a regular on CBS's *The New Bill Cosby Show* in the 1972 season and was one again on NBC's even shorter-lived 1975 *Ben Vereen—Comin' at Ya*, both variety hours. Later she made film appearances and had two specials of her own on ABC.

But by far the most successful part of her career was her time in Las Vegas, where she eventually equaled "King of Las Vegas Entertainment" Newton when she earned $2 million for performing for five months in the town's Aladdin Hotel and was named "First Lady of Las Vegas Entertainment." She broke nearly every Las Vegas nightclub attendance and box-office record, became Las Vegas' highest-paid entertainer, was bestowed its Georgio award, and for years would call Las Vegas "my hometown." She received a Clio award "from the advertisers around the world because they liked the Tigress commercials" she had done.

Her 1983 bout with peritonitis, an abdominal lining inflammation, was not her first health crisis, nor was it her last. Returning to Las Vegas in 1987 from an engagement in Orlando, Florida, she was seized with strokelike symptoms—no voice, impaired vision and hearing, sagging facial muscles, and left-side numbness. Diagnosed with MS, a degenerative disease that attacks the central nervous system, she suffered five more such attacks. Her doctor attributed her amazing recovery from it two years later to her "dancer's stamina" and "strong constitution." She attributed it, mainly, to "talks with God."

Her 1990 comeback secured with work offers from Las Vegas, Los Angeles, Atlantic City, and Boston as well as from talk show and speaking invitations, she startled fans with the news she was leaving show business to dedicate her life to the church.

She announced her decision around March that year and explained it to rapt listeners in the 3,500-seat auditorium of Chicago's Christ Universal Temple. "I was out on that road dancing and singing my heart out—and shaking that thing. And then I found that every time I went back to my hotel room, I was crying . . . . I started to pray to God—please, God, the thing that I begged you for, to let me be in show business and let me be noticed and let me be a star in the world, I don't want it anymore. It doesn't fulfill me at all."

Since then, Falana has moved back to Philadelphia to be near her family. She gives lectures to churches, schools, and women's organizations and is becoming active in political activities.

GARY HOUSTON

Foster, Frances (1924–)

"I don't know how many roles I have created since I've been with the NEC [**Negro Ensemble Company**]," said Frances Foster in an interview with Holly Hill. "Every new play that I did, I was the first to do that role. What more could an actress ask? I wanted to be the best actress I could be, and I decided when I was very young that I didn't care about being a star. I think that was very good for me and kept me healthy. I just wanted to work and to be good."

These words are eminently worthy of Frances Foster, the exemplary actor, teacher, and director who spoke them. She is of a pioneering generation that knew that acting jobs for African Americans were meager and too often thankless, and that rewarding ones had to be created, not awaited.

Foster was born in Yonkers, New York, on June 11, 1924. She always wanted to be an actor, but her parents wanted her to attend **Howard University** and then go into law. Their reasoning was sound. There were no roles for black women that they wanted their daughter to play.

Young Frances inched around this obstacle. She had her godmother, dancer Frances Atkins, vouch for the Harlem YMCA where she had begun to act in plays; when one of these was reported as "dirty"—Oscar Wilde's *Salome*, in which Foster acted and danced the wanton title role—Foster told the YMCA board she couldn't see how a Bible story could offend.

Salome continued and caught the attention of Fred O'Neal of the **American Negro Theater**, founded in 1940 and based across the street from the YMCA. O'Neal suggested Foster follow high school with study at the American Theater Wing on 44th Street, which offered scholarships. Not telling her parents, she auditioned and was awarded tuition for three years, starting in 1949. She was the Wing's sole black student, except for James Earl Jones, who was in Foster's television acting class for one semester. While at the Wing she got her first professional job in a radio soap opera, *The Right to Happiness* in a part that had not been written for a black actor.

Foster received her B.A. in 1952 and while she auditioned was a sales clerk, a barmaid, and an actor in many no-pay showcase productions. She also joined in demonstrations for increased minority opportunities.

Her next professional job was on the CBS-TV Sunday morning religious program, *Lamp Unto My Feet*. Making more TV appearances, she had union memberships in both the Screen Actors Guild and the American Federation of Television and Radio Artists. The right to join Actors Equity, the stage actors' union, still eluded her.

But in the mid-1950s a Wing teacher cast her in a revival of Louis Peterson's play, fittingly titled *Take a Giant Step*, which ran Off-Broadway for a year. It led to her Broadway debut in 1955 as Dolly May in *The Wisteria Trees*.

That decade, she was not above taking understudy jobs and did so as Tituba in an off-Broadway production of *The Crucible*, eventually replacing the departed Vinnette Carroll. Such a task came again in 1959, when Foster understudied both **Diana Sands**' Beneatha and **Ruby Dee**'s Ruth in **Lorraine Hansberry**'s *A Raisin in the Sun*, which starred Sidney Poitier. She replaced Dee occasionally and, in time, permanently as the show toured the continent.

The Hansberry play was 1959's best opportunity for black actors. Foster and such colleagues as Douglas Turner Ward often met to decide, as she told Hill, what plays "we were going to do and how we were going to raise money. . . . We all knew each other and were constantly talking about the need for a theater of our own where we could develop black actors, playwrights, directors, stage managers, administrators, crews."

In 1967, under Ward's leadership, they made that theater happen. Foster acted in "Day of Absence" and "Happy Ending,"

both by Ward, the 1965 pair of one-acts whose production led to NEC's founding.

A river of NEC credits followed: *Summer of the Seventeenth Doll, Kongi's Harvest,* and *God Is a (Guess What?)* (1968); *String, Malcochan, Song of the Lusitanian Bogey,* and *Man Better Man* (1969); *Brotherhood* and *Akokawe* (1970); *Rosalee Pritchett* (in the title role) and *The Sty of the Blind Pig* (1971); *A Ballet Behind the Bridge* and *The River Niger* (1972); *The First Breeze of Summer* (1975), *Livin' Fat* (1976), *Nevis Mountain Dew,* and *The Daughters of the Mock* (1978); *Plays from Africa* (1979); *Big City Blues* (1980); *Zooman and the Sign* (1981); and *Henrietta* (1985, in the title role). She also directed NEC's 1974 production of Steve Carter's *Terraces*.

Foster did not act exclusively with NEC. She performed in Brecht's *Good Woman of Setzuan* at the Lincoln Center Repertory Theater (1970), a production of *Behold! Cometh the Vanderkellans* (1971), and in New York and regional theaters in *The Gin Game* and *The Amen Corner*, as well as plays by Arthur Miller, Athol Fugard and August Wilson.

In James deJongh's *Do Lord Remember Me* at American Place Theater, she played an 86-year-old ex-slave and for it won the Audelco Best Actress award and won an Obie in 1985 for Sustained Excellence of Performance. She was again on Broadway in the 1991 revival of *Mule Bone*, by Langston Hughes and **Zora Neale Hurston**.

Some 100 credits are cited for her work on film and television, including *All My Children* and the miniseries *King*.

Foster, mother of four children from her marriage to Martin Goldsen, in her later years has showed increasing interest in the generations to follow hers: She took up teaching with some reluctance but discovered that she liked it. She was a City College of New York artist-in-residence between 1973 and 1977 and later, into the 1990s, held acting classes at the Herbert Berghoff Studio.

GARY HOUSTON

Foster, Gloria (1936–)

Where do you find great roles for women? In Shakespeare, of course. And O'Neill. And Chekhov. And Sophocles, and Wilder, and Brecht. Gloria Foster has them all, and more, on her résumé.

Foster was born in Chicago on November 15, 1936, and raised by her grandparents Clyde and Eleanor Sudds on farms in Wisconsin and Illinois. Her godmother, Gloria Brown Dunklin, one of the first black women to work as a supervisor at Illinois Bell Telephone, was also an important part of her early life. Foster began to study speech education at Southern Illinois University and then transferred to the Goodman Theater School in Chicago after realizing that she wanted to be an actress, not a teacher. (But in 1978, she earned a master's in education from the University of Massachusetts, just in case.)

Although color-blind casting was rare in the commercial theater, in the art-for-art's-sake atmosphere of that conservatory school, a student's ability was the only criterion. In the Goodman's three-year program, Foster acquired strong technique, high standards, and a taste for the classics in roles that included the title character in *Medea* (*Theater World* Award in 1966) and Sabina in Thornton Wilder's *The Skin of Our Teeth*. She also worked at the University of Chicago's Court Theater, playing Jocasta in *Oedipus Rex*, Hecuba in *The Trojan Women*, and Volumnia in *Coriolanus*.

In 1961 and 1962, Foster was cast as Ruth in a production of *A Raisin in the Sun* that played Syracuse, New York, and later toured for ten weeks. She also worked as a secretary for the electrician's union and as an understudy in *Purlie Victorious* on Broadway, her only venture into musical comedy. In her off-Broadway debut, she had the chance to be seen the way she saw herself: not just as an actress, but specifically as a dramatic actress. Martin Duberman's *In White America* used real documents from different historical periods to examine the black American experience. It opened at the Sheridan Square Playhouse in Greenwich Village on November 2, 1963, and Foster's performance earned her—besides Obie and Drama Desk Awards—something most actresses long for their whole lives and never get: a rave review in the *New York Times*. "Most moving of all is Gloria Foster, a young actress with talent and intensity to burn," Howard Taubman wrote.

He went on to suggest that someone should write a play for Foster. In a way, as it turned out, someone already had: Her stage work over the next thirty years focused almost exclusively on the classics, from necessity as much as from choice. Unlike many actors, Foster refused to work just for the sake of working: She demanded challenging, rewarding, leading roles in important, life-affirming plays, and contemporary drama offered few of those for any actress, black or white. She worked frequently with Joe Papp's New York Shakespeare Festival, where she appeared in *Long Day's Journey into Night*, Chekhov's *Cherry Orchard*, Brecht's *Mother Courage* (adapted by

Ntozake Shange), and Shakespeare's *Corio-lanus*, among others, and was a member of its short-lived black and Hispanic Shakespeare Company. In 1995, she and costar **Mary Alice** enjoyed major Broadway success in *Having Our Say*, a contemporary play in which characters based on two real women look back over their long and interesting lives. Mary Alice played Bessie Delany, 101 years old; Foster played her sister Sadie, 103.

According to one writer, Foster "seemed born for films because . . . she did everything with her eyes," but she never developed the kind of enduring relationship with the camera that she had with the stage, although she worked in both film and television. She costarred with Bill Cosby in several projects, including the Emmy-winning TV movie *To All My Friends on Shore* (CBS, 1972), in which they played the parents of a child with sickle-cell anemia, and the forgettable film *Leonard, Part 6* (1987). Her first two movies, *The Cool World* (1963) and *Nothing But a Man* (1964), have been called "landmark films about black life." She played Mrs. Thurgood Marshall in *Separate but Equal* (ABC, 1991, costarring with Sidney Poitier) and appeared in *Law and Order* (NBC, 1992) and *The Atlanta Child Murders* (CBS miniseries, 1985), among others.

"No matter what role she plays," Susan Dworkin wrote about Foster, "she seems always to represent our most powerful secret selves." Great role or not-so-great role—that's what a great actress does.

Franklin, J[ennie] E[lizabeth] (1937–)

Audiences, critics, and the New York theater scene took notice when *Black Girl* arrived in 1972. With her affecting and observant play about a young black woman who dreams of becoming a dancer and who struggles with the inevitable moment of defining herself as separate from her family, J. E. Franklin experienced an almost unprecedented success for a black female playwright. The play touched a basic core of human experience because it had its roots in her own life and reflected the tensions she felt in her family as she struggled to come to terms with her own passionate desire to write.

Born in Houston, Texas, on August 10, 1937, Jennifer Elizabeth Franklin was one of thirteen children who made up the family of Robert and Mathie Franklin. The urge to write came at a young age, as she took in the world about her and put her feelings down on paper.

She was educated at the University of Texas, graduating with a B.A. in 1964, and later studied at the Union Theological Seminary in New York. During the 1960s, she worked in a number of occupations, moving from teaching primary school in Mississippi to serving as youth director for the Neighborhood House Association in Buffalo, New York. She then worked for the Office of Economic opportunity in New York and lectured in the Education Department at Herbert N. Lehman College in the Bronx, a branch of the City College of New York.

Franklin's early writing combined keen observation of human nature and family ties with a strong sense of social commitment. Her first play, written while she was working at the Freedom School in Mississippi, was entitled *First Step to Freedom* and was intended to encourage student awareness of the power of literacy. In 1967, after she moved to New York, she wrote *The In-Crowd*, about gang violence and the healing power of family ties, for Mobilization for Youth. The play was performed that year at the Montreal Expo. Ten years later, she would expand it into a full-length rock musical, under the auspices of the pioneering New Federal Theater in New York.

The play that followed, *Black Girl*, was as much a phenomenon as a theater piece. Produced by the New Federal Theater, its popularity with audiences quickly outgrew that small venue. The play transferred to the Theater de Lys, where it ran for 247 performances from June 16, 1971 to June 16, 1972. Franklin won the Drama Desk Award as the most promising new playwright of 1971–72, as well as the Media Women Award (1971) and the CAPS Award (1972). In the wake of the production's success in New York, she also wrote the screenplay for the 1972 film based on her play. Directed by Ossie Davis, it featured a powerhouse cast including **Leslie Uggams**, **Ruby Dee**, and Brock Peters.

For her next major project, she turned for source material to an earlier one-act play of hers that had been produced as a street-theater project in New York and the Bronx. This eventually became a full-blown musical collaboration with composer and colyricist **Micki Grant**. Entitled *The Prodigal Sister*, it recasts the Biblical tale of the prodigal son in a contemporary light, telling the story of a young black woman who becomes pregnant and bitterly leaves her rural home to come to the city. After experiencing enormous difficulties, she returns home to the care and forgiveness of her family. While unable to duplicate the success of *Black Girl*, the production at the Theater de Lys ran for forty performances, earning praise for its innovative use of a "Doo-Wop" chorus.

Although Franklin has continued to write plays, her main emphasis has shifted to using the arts to educate and heal. Her training as an artist-therapist led her to the directorship of the Theater of Artcentric Living at the Church of Crucifixion in New York City. She has written a number of articles about the positive influence of the arts on the educational process and has also attempted in her work to explore what she has called the "theological roots of racism."

Theater for Artcentric Living has produced a number of her plays, including *Throw Thunder at this House* about racial violence at the University of Texas and *The Hand-Me-Downs* about sibling rivalry and the stigma of illiteracy. While *Black Girl* remains the pinnacle of Franklin's commercial success, her work is still infused with the commitment to social justice and sensitivity to human interaction that has characterized it from the beginning.

RICHARD E. T. WHITE

G

Gaines-Shelton, Ruth (b. 1872–)

Ruth Gaines-Shelton was a grandmother at the time she won $40 for her play *The Church Fight*, published in *Crisis* in May 1926. Her play, a comedy, pokes fun at the internal squabbles that parishioners engage in when they are not sufficiently preoccupied with spiritual matters or social action. There is a critical edge in Gaines-Shelton's naming of two of her characters, Sister Sapphira and Brother Ananias: In the bible their namesakes deceptively withheld money and lied in an attempt to cheat their local church. Sources reveal that Gaines-Shelton wrote many other plays, but it is unclear whether the manuscripts, presumably unpublished, survive. Some of her other plays were *Aunt Hagar's Children*, *The Church Mouse*, *Gena*, *The Lost Child*, *Lord Earlington's Broken Vow*, *Mr. Church*, and *Parson Dewdrop's Bride*.

The daughter of AME Church minister the Reverend George W. Gaines and his wife Elizabeth Gaines, Ruth was born on April 8, 1872, in Glasgow, Missouri. Her mother died when Ruth was small, and Ruth assisted her father with church work as he directed the building of the Old Bethel AME Church on Dearborn Street in Chicago. She attended Wilberforce University in Ohio, graduating in 1895 and taught school in Montgomery, Missouri, until she married William Obern Shelton in 1898. Gaines-Shelton continued to write plays while raising her three children.

Her work, like that of other playwrights of her time, is significant because it documents the creative activities of black women within their own communities during an era when most other avenues of opportunity were closed to them.

LORRAINE ELENA ROSES

Gentry, Minnie (19??–)

A Minnie Gentry performance can be counted on to be unpredictable. On stage, in films, and on television for more than three decades, she has made strong, interesting choices that result in fascinating portrayals.

Minnie Gentry was born Minnie Lee Watson. Her early career took place in Cleveland at the Karamu Theater, one of the country's first and most important regional theaters. At the Karamu, casting was multiracial, and Gentry had the opportunity to play roles that black actors in more traditional theaters are never allowed to attempt.

Gentry's New York stage credits date from Jean Genet's *The Blacks*, which was produced in 1961 and ran for several years. This production was a training ground and jumping-off place for dozens of today's most famous black actors. As cast members replaced each other, went on to better-paying projects, and returned to the show, actors such as **Cicely Tyson**, James Earl Jones, Louis Gossett, **Helen Martin**, Godfrey Cambridge, and Cynthia Belgrave formed a talent pool that is still being drawn upon. Minnie Gentry was part of that pool.

While in New York, she participated in several other landmark productions in black theater including *Black Girl* in 1971. In that play, Gentry enacted with warmth and wisdom the role of the grandmother, Mu'Dear, who is the only member of Billie Jean's family who is willing to help her fulfill her dreams. Also in 1971, she performed in *Ain't Supposed to Die a Natural Death*, a controversial musical written by filmmaker Melvin Van Peebles.

Gentry also appeared in mainstream shows such as *The Sunshine Boys*, in 1972, and in productions of the **Negro Ensemble Company**, before moving her attention to film and television. She was in the 1974 television dramatic special *Salty* and worked with Van Peebles again in his television dramas *Just an Old Sweet Song* and *The Hollow Image*. In the latter, according to Donald Bogle in *Blacks in American Film and Television*, the soap-opera quality of the show was "relieved only when Minnie Gentry shows up."

Gentry costarred with **Diana Sands** in 1972 in *Georgia, Georgia*; its screenplay by **Maya Angelou** was the first written by a black woman for a feature film. Gentry played with eccentric passion the enigmatic Mrs. Anderson who strangles Georgia for betraying her blackness with a white lover. The same year, Gentry was seen in *Come Back Charleston Blue*, the sequel to *Cotton Comes to Harlem*, with Godfrey Cambridge and Raymond St. Jacques, followed by *Black Caesar* with Fred Williamson. Still in the seventies, Gentry appeared in *Claudine* with **Diahann Carroll** and James Earl Jones and in 1984 in the unusual John Sayles movie *The Brother from Another Planet*.

To quote Bogle again, "Gentry . . . brings to her work a clear character actress person (indeed, it's a star persona although no one's ever seemed to note that): she always strikes us as a fundamentally proper woman living by high personal standards—of dress, demeanor, use of language. Yet she often comes across as streetwise. She's a strange, crazed personality who stands apart from the productions she's in."

She's also an actor who has lent her skills and unconventional personality to many important ventures in the history of black theater and films.

KATHLEEN THOMPSON

Gibbs, Marla (1931–)

As a gutsy maid or a busybody housewife, Marla Gibbs helped set the pace in American popular culture in the past two decades. First as a star in the long-running TV comedy *The Jeffersons* and then starring in her own series, *227*, Gibbs has been a prominent comedienne in prime-time television since 1975. That is a record few comics can match.

Marla Gibbs was born Margaret Bradley on the south side of Chicago in 1931. Her parents separated when she was four, and she was raised by her father, Douglas Bradley, an auto mechanic. Her mother took the stage name Ophelia Kemp and left to follow her calling as a radio evangelist. Though Gibbs adored her father, she grew up missing her mother and feeling somehow displaced without her.

Margaret married her childhood sweetheart, Jordan Gibbs, and had three children. Restless as a housewife, the young Gibbs tried a series of jobs and finally became a reservations clerk for United Airlines. In

1969, her husband Jordan took a job transfer that took the family to Los Angeles. There Gibbs took acting classes "just to take my mind off my troubles." Soon she discovered her own calling in life. She shortened her name to Marla, divorced her husband in 1973, and set out to find herself as an actress.

Now in her early forties, with three children to support, Gibbs made good on her determination. In 1974, she auditioned for *The Jeffersons* and won a small part as a maid. Within a year, the small part turned into a steady role as Marla wowed the public with the sharp-tongued, tell-it-like-it-is Florence. Florence never took any nonsense from her boss, George Jefferson, and she also never did much work. As Gibbs described Florence's appeal, "The audience could release through me all the people who pressured them." Florence spoke up for all the people who couldn't talk back to the boss, and the audience loved it.

In 1981, Gibbs' success as Florence led to a spin-off series, *Checking In*. The series, however, was a casualty of a TV writers' strike, and she soon returned to *The Jeffersons*. She then stayed with the show until it closed after eleven years on the air.

Even after returning to *The Jeffersons*, Gibbs continued to take her career into her own hands. She founded Crossroads Arts Academy and Theater, where talent from the black community could develop their work. One of the plays she produced, *227*, became the basis of her next television success. Written by Chicago playwright Christine Houston, *227* was a comedy centering on the everyday life in an apartment building in Washington, D.C. Gibbs played a busybody housewife in the original play.

227 was brought to television in 1985, just months after *The Jeffersons* ended its run. Gibbs remained as star of *227* and also took on the role of creative consultant. As creative consultant, she helped mold the style and character of the show, influencing everything from scripts to casting.

In addition, Gibbs has launched a number of other enterprises to serve the black community. One project is a jazz supper club, Marla's Memory Lane, in south-central Los Angeles. Another organization is CHOICE (Concerned Helpers of Inner Community Endeavors), which sponsors entertainment events that support causes such as the Black Alliance for Student Education in Los Angeles.

Gibbs was the recipient of consecutive NAACP Image Awards from 1979 through 1983. She also was repeatedly nominated for Emmy Awards from 1981 to 1985 for Outstanding Performance by a Supporting Actress in a Comedy.

Starting at a time in life when many aspiring actors are giving up, Marla Gibbs created a career for herself and an enduring place in the American spotlight. What is more, she worked to expand opportunities for other black talent and for the community at large.

ANDRA MEDEA

Gilbert, Mercedes (d. 1952)

In the 1920s, when Mercedes Gilbert first appeared on Broadway, there were few parts for black actors. The few that existed were in musicals, such as *Bamboola*, in which Gilbert played a major role. It took extraordinary dedication to pursue a career in the theater.

In 1930, Marc Connelly's play *The Green Pastures*, though it did not reflect the reality of black life or the complexity of black folklore, did create work for many black actors. Mercedes Gilbert was one of them. She moved into prominence in 1935 when, upon Rose McClendon's death, she took over the leading female role in *Mulatto*, the Langston Hughes play dealing with the tragedy of a child born to a plantation owner and a family servant.

For more than two decades, Gilbert was a strong presence in black theater: In 1937, she appeared in *How Come, Lawd?* produced by the Negro Theater Guild; she was in *Carib Song* in 1945, directed by and starring **Katherine Dunham**.

In 1950, the Apollo Theater, usually the site of comedy and music performances, hosted three dramatic productions: all-black versions of *Rain* with **Nina Mae McKinney**, *Detective Story* with Sidney Poitier, and *Tobacco Road* with such black actors as **Evelyn Ellis**, Jimmy Wright, and Mercedes Gilbert.

Gilbert was in the cast of the classic Oscar Micheaux film *Body and Soul,* appeared on radio and television, and created several one-woman theater performances. A songwriter, she wrote the songs "Decatur Street Blues" and "Got the World in a Jug," among others.

Mercedes Gilbert died on March 1, 1952, in New York.

Goldberg, Whoopi (1949–)

Whoopi Goldberg will tell anyone who will listen that she is not a comedienne. Indeed, her talents as an actress are recognized to go far beyond the limits of what that term might seem to imply. Still, if Gold-

Whoopi Goldberg's glowing humor and humanity have won the name she created a permanent place in entertainment history. She is shown here in the 1986 film Jumpin' Jack Flash. (DONALD BOGLE)

berg's career is historically significant for black women, it is because she is funny.

Born in 1949 in a New York City housing project, Goldberg has worked hard to keep her real name a secret. She received a Catholic education and started acting at the age of eight at the Helena Rubinstein Children's Theater at the Hudson Guild. She spent her childhood and adolescence watching old movies and television comedy and then dropping out of high school, became an active part of the counter-culture during the 1960s. While participating in civil rights marches and demonstrations, she performed in the choruses of *Hair*, *Jesus Christ Superstar*, and *Pippin*. She was married for a short time and has a daughter from that marriage, Alexandrea Martin.

In 1974, a series of circumstances took Goldberg to San Diego, where she became a founding member of the San Diego Repertory Theater, joined an improvisational comedy troupe called Spontaneous Combustion, and created her name. Six years later, with an impressive theatrical and stand-up résumé behind her, she moved to Berkeley. There she continued to work on her comedy while supporting herself and her daughter in a variety of jobs from bricklayer to licensed cosmetician and sometimes had to depend on public assistance.

In 1983, Goldberg put together an hour-long, one-woman show. It was made up of four characters she had been developing for several years and was called *The Spook Show*. Its telling social satire was informed by a compassion that has since become characteristic of Goldberg. *The Spook Show* opened in Berkeley, went on the road in the United States and Europe, and ended up in New York as part of a workshop series at Dance Theater Workshop. A popular and critical success, the show was seen by Mike Nichols, who asked to produce it on Broadway.

Goldberg did not immediately take Nichols up on his offer. First, she returned to Berkeley to appear as the great **Moms Mabley** in *Moms*, a show written by Goldberg and Ellen Sebastian. Then, for the 1984–85 Broadway season, she expanded *The Spook Show* and opened in it as *Whoopi Goldberg* at the Lyceum Theater. Critical response was mixed. Some reviewers were enthralled by Goldberg's skills and

her spirit. Others were frankly uncomplimentary about the quality of her material. Audiences loved it.

Her position was cemented when she played the lead role in the film version of **Alice Walker**'s *The Color Purple* (1985), directed by Steven Spielberg, for which she received an Academy Award nomination. Although her next few films were critical and/or box-office failures (*Jumpin' Jack Flash*, 1986; *Burglar* and *Fatal Beauty*, both 1987; *Clara's Heart* and *The Telephone*, 1988; *Homer & Eddie*, 1989), she scored a personal triumph in *Ghost* (1990), winning the Oscar for her supporting performance and thereby becoming the first black actress to win an Oscar since Hattie McDaniel in 1939 for *Gone With the Wind*.

After her Oscar, that the question was being asked as to whether she could really build not just a good but a *major* career in Hollywood was a tribute to Goldberg. The answer, through 1990's *Long Walk Home* and 1991's *Soapdish*, was unclear. *Sarafina*, in 1992, was an inspiring performance, and Goldberg was clearly in demand. But the question still hung in the air until there was *Sister Act*.

The film didn't have the most original, or plausible, plot line—a lounge singer witnesses a murder and hides out in a convent disguised as a nun. In other hands, it would probably have been mildly entertaining and mildly successful summer fare. In Goldberg's it was a $139 million hit. She became a major, *bankable* star, one of the few women who could claim that status.

What Whoopi Goldberg did in this film was to find the magic formula that has eluded black comic actors so often in the past . . . and still does today. She played a role where being black was part of her comic persona, but being black was not what was funny.

When Goldberg confronts the rigid, wonderfully stuffy, upper-class Maggie Smith as Mother Superior, she uses the elements of her personality that contrast with Smith. When she listens to the other nuns talk with stunning naïvete about the world, she reacts with the elements of her personality that differ from them. One of those elements is being streetwise black.

Judy Holliday did the same with her working-class New Yorker in *The Solid Gold Cadillac*. Barbara Stanwyck did it with her jazz-baby stripper in *Ball of Fire*. Bette Midler would probably have done it in her own special way if she had played the role in *Sister Act*, as was originally intended.

With Goldberg, being black is part of what she has to offer a role, whether she's being funny in *Sister Act* or celestially wise in *Star Trek: The Next Generation*.

Goldberg was able to follow up *Sister Act* with another hit, *Made In America*, establishing herself as a romantic lead, a real coup for a woman who does not fit this society's established standards of beauty. In 1994, she hosted the Academy Awards show.

Goldberg, who has always been politically aware and active, was a founding member of the Comic Relief benefit shows on cable's Home Box Office, which raise money to assist the homeless. In early 1992, she became the first African-American actor to star in a film shot on location in South Africa. Before she accepted the role—that of a Soweto high-school teacher in a movie version of the South African musical *Sarafina!*, which was a Broadway hit—she sought and received the permission of the African National Congress and, after some conflict, of the Azanian People's Organization.

Although she has done some television work—a short-lived series based on the film *Bagdad Cafe* and a recurring role on *Star Trek: The Next Generation*—Goldberg is best known for her work in motion pictures. There have been other great black film actresses—**Ethel Waters**, **Dorothy Dandridge**, and **Ruby Dee**, to name only a few—but Goldberg's unique contribution and remarkable talent is her comic voice.

Black women found it once before in Moms Mabley, but it has been rare. The comic, as opposed to the clown, stands up and tells us what she thinks about life, death, politics, taxes, hairstyles, and the human condition. To be successful, the comic must be someone we are willing to hear. Until recently, the general public has not been willing to listen to black women. Mabley was an exception, and her success was a tribute to her genius. With Goldberg's talents to lead the way, perhaps the rules are changing. In 1996, Goldberg probably could have won the prize for hardest working film star in Hollywood, appearing in *Bogus*, *Eddie* and *The Associate*.

KATHLEEN THOMPSON

Grant, Micki (1941–)

Few people in the American theater have convincingly worn so many hats as Micki Grant has during her career. After first establishing herself as one of the New York theater scene's most versatile and spirited performers, she unleashed an outburst of creativity in the 1970s that revealed the breadth of her talents as playwright, composer, and lyricist.

Born Minnie Perkins in Chicago, Illinois, in 1941, Micki Grant attended the University of Illinois, Roosevelt University, and DePaul University, and then moved to Los Angeles to seek work as an actor. Before long, however, her music-theater talents had brought her to New York, where she appeared in *Brecht on Brecht* and Jean Genet's *The Blacks*, both in 1961. During the 1960s, she was a regular on and off Broadway, appearing in *Fly Blackbird,* in which she had also performed in Los Angeles; *The Cradle Will Rock;* **Adrienne Kennedy**'s *Funnyhouse of a Negro;* a theatrical program of songs by Leonard Bernstein; and, in 1969, **Lorraine Hansberry**'s final play, *To Be Young, Gifted, and Black.*

Grant also appeared in television, in continuing roles on the daytime dramas *Another World*, *The Edge of Night* and *The Guiding Light* and hosted the children's program *Around the Corner* on CBS.

In 1970, she began to work with Vinnette Carroll, the charismatic head of New York's Urban Arts Corps. Under Carroll's direction, Grant began to utilize the full range of her talents. She created the book, lyrics, and music for a musical look at the problems of contemporary city life and the black American experience. What emerged was what critics called a lively and colorful tapestry of songs and dances that wove together jazz, blues, gospel, pop, calypso, and spiritual influences to create a highly charged theater piece. Although its subject matter was serious, the overall effect of this musical, which Carroll and Grant provocatively titled *Don't Bother Me, I Can't Cope*, was vibrant and uplifting. After touring small theaters in New York and performing in Washington D.C., Micki Grant's *Don't Bother Me, I Can't Cope* opened on Broadway on April 19, 1972. It had a good run of 1,065 performances, making it a solid Broadway's hit, and was produced for a time by major theaters all over the country. Both as creator and performer, Grant won an impressive number of awards for the show, including two Drama Desk Awards, an Obie for outstanding work off Broadway, two Tony nominations for outstanding work on Broadway, a Grammy Award for the cast album, and an Image Award from the NAACP.

Grant's collaborations with Carroll continued to bear fruit in following years. Their work together included *Croesus and the Witch* in 1971, the antiwar musical *Step Lively, Boys* in 1972, and the ribald fantasy *The Ups and Downs of Theophilus Maitland* in 1975. Carroll adapted the last play from a West Indian folk tale. Grant also contributed music to Carroll's other great Broadway success, *Your Arms Too Short to Box With God*, in 1975; in 1976 provided music for Carroll's adaptation of poetry from the 1973 anthology *A Rock Against the Wind*, which they called *I'm Laughin' But I Ain't Tickled,* and made another team attempt to mount for Broadway an update of *Alice in Wonderland* and *Through the Looking Glass* called, simply, *Alice.* It featured book and direction by Carroll and music and lyrics by Grant; however, after a short tryout in Philadelphia, the troubled production closed prior to Broadway.

While her position as artist-in-residence with the Urban Arts Corps provided her with the primary forum for her musical creativity, Micki Grant has also worked with a variety of other collaborators, including *Black Girl* author J. E. Franklin, with whom Grant collaborated on *The Prodigal Sister* in 1974, *Godspell* creator Stephen

Schwartz on the 1977 musical *Working* and **Rosetta LeNoire**'s AMAS Musical Theater, providing music and lyrics for the 1988 production *Step Into My World*. Based on the book by Chicago writer Studs Terkel, Grant's *Working* premiered at Chicago's Goodman Theater and then had a brief run on Broadway.

Micki Grant has earned a place in the landscape of the American theater as a creative artist whose achievements as a wordsmith is on a par with her musical compositions. She is a multitalented creative force who has chosen to use her gifts to reflect the troubled spirit of her times, but she has done so by harnessing the power of music to engage our attention, to communicate her ideas, and, ultimately, to uplift our spirits.

RICHARD E. T. WHITE

Grier, Pamela (1949–)

Because she was an actress who embodied sexual power and the sexual revolution, critics and audiences have not always been sure what to make of Pam Grier. Is she a talented actress trapped in the cheap blaxploitation flicks of the 1970s or a dynamic symbol of pride and self-determination?

Pam Grier grew up as a self-described Air Force brat, the daughter of a military man stationed in Europe. She spent ages eleven and twelve at various European air force bases, where her view of life grew to be cosmopolitan, a position that influenced her throughout her life. Finally, Grier's family returned to the States and settled in Denver, Colorado; while still in her teens, Grier left home for Los Angeles and the film industry.

After an early stint as a switchboard operator for American International Films, she began to win small parts in action and exploitation films. The Black Power movement and the sexual revolution, which both occurred in the 1960s, combined to create a new film image. By the 1970s, a new stereotype appeared—the black woman as wild, tough, rough sexual powerhouse.

These were the movies in which Pam Grier made her mark, turning out fantasy/action films at a tremendous pace. She made *The Big Doll House*, *The Big Bird Cage*, *Black Mama, White Mama*, *Hit Man*, *Women in Cages*, *Coffy*, *Scream*, *Blacula*, *Scream*, *Twilight People*, *The Arena*, *Foxy Brown*, *Bucktown*, and *Drum* all in the five years between 1971 and 1976.

Stunning Pam Grier became an icon of the times: In her films, she stood against the forces of evil and could shoot, stab, or debilitate anyone who got in her way. She also took whatever men she wanted.

While there was no mistaking that movies like *Scream, Blacula, Scream* were not great art, Pam Grier brought an unmistakable style to them—she was nothing if not memorable. Many women found her an uncomfortable caricature of the modern black woman; others found her a meaningful symbol. She was featured on the cover of *Ms.* magazine as a liberated figure—certainly, her combination of cleavage and machine guns was a far cry from the old film image of black women as maids and cooks.

Grier tried to break out of blaxploitation films in the later part of the 1970s with *Sheba Baby*, and *Friday Foster*, both in 1975, and *Greased Lightning*, in 1977. However, like many typecast actresses, Grier had difficulty winning acceptance in more-complex roles. Refusing to give up, Grier began in the 1980s to find avenues for her talent. She put in a strong performance in *Fort Apache: The Bronx* in 1981 and followed that success with a Disney film, *Something Wicked This Way Comes* in 1983.

She rounded out her film work with television appearances, as a regular on *Miami Vice* and playing occasional roles in *Crime Story* and *The Cosby Show*. She went on to play the lead in Sam Shepard's *Fool for Love* at the Los Angeles Theater Center. In recognition of her scope-broadening roles, she was awarded a NAACP Image award as Best Actress in 1986. In 1988, she costarred in the film *Above the Law*.

It seems clear that the film producers of the 1970s did not do justice to the complete Pam Grier. Aside from her looks, reviewers describe her vitality, outrageousness, and unexpected sense of humor. While blaxploitation films were limited to a fad, Pam Grier's talent encompasses much more.

ANDRA MEDEA

Grimké, Angelina Weld (1880–1958)

In Angelina Weld Grimké's poem "Under the Days," the persona asks who will ever find her because she is being crushed, covered, and smothered under ceaseless black, gray, and white days. Perhaps this poem best expresses Grimké's personal life, which was filled with feelings of rejection, alienation, and suppression. Although recent critics label Grimké as neurotic and paranoid, a close look at her life reveals a delicate and highly sensitive woman who felt pain more acutely than most. Her sensitivity found its way into her literary works: Grimké's play *Rachel* (1916), the first staged play by an African-American woman, illustrates the author's keen awareness that black Americans are victimized.

Playwright, poet, and short-story writer, Angelina Weld Grimké was born in Boston on February 27, 1880, to Archibald Henry and Sarah Stanley Grimké. Her father was from a prominent biracial family, and her mother was white. Three years after Grimké was born, her mother left her father and took Angelina with her. Four years later, she returned the seven-year-old to her father and never saw her again.

Grimké spent much of her childhood as the privileged child of Archibald Grimké, a nationally known lawyer and the executive director of the **National Association for the Advancement of Colored People** (NAACP). Under the tutelage of her white great-aunt, Angelina Grimké Weld, a noted abolitionist

Rachel, *by Angelina Grimké, was the first play by a black writer to receive a fully staged professional production. Its heroine vows not to bring children into a world of racism and bigotry.* (MOORLAND-SPINGARN)

and suffragist, Grimké attended some of the finest schools in Massachusetts, including Carleton Academy in Ashburnham. A graduate of Boston Normal School of Gymnastics in 1902, Grimké moved to Washington, D.C., where she taught English at Armstrong Manual Training School. In 1916, she transferred to Dunbar High School, where she developed close relationships with a host of black women poets and playwrights who taught at the school.

Grimké wrote and staged *Rachel* in her first year at Dunbar. Produced by the NAACP on March 3 and 4, 1916, at the Myrtill Miner Normal School, the play centers on the numerous humiliations that African Americans suffer, ranging from lynchings to restricted job opportunities. Rachel, the play's heroine, vows never to bring black children into the world because of the suffering they would have to endure.

Rachel marked the beginning of staged or produced black theater. Prior to *Rachel*, plays had been written without staging in mind, as was the case with William Wells Brown's costume dramas, which he read to white abolitionists. Grimké had responded to W. E. B. DuBois' call for black theater by, for, and near black people.

Although Grimké's plays and fiction show evidence of race consciousness, the majority of her poems reflect a romantic influence, as does the poetry of many of her contemporaries, including **Jessie Fauset, Georgia Douglas Johnson**, Countee Cullen, and William Stanley Braithwaite. Her poems often contain images of isolation, no doubt the result of being abandoned by her mother.

Some of Grimké's unpublished poetry, mostly love poems, alludes to her lesbianism and resonates with signs of rejection, despair, and thoughts of death. Probably because she chose to suppress her emotions —with the possible exception of a love affair with poet, playwright, and co-worker at Dunbar High School, **Mary Burrill**—her creativity was stifled long before she died.

ELIZABETH BROWN-GUILLORY

H

Hall, Adelaide (1901–1993)

Music-theater star Adelaide Hall has had a long career as a singer. In the 1930s and 1940s, she appeared with bands such as the Duke Ellington Orchestra and the Mills Blues Rhythm Band and she was particularly known for her performance of "Creole Love Call" with Duke Ellington.

Before, during, and after her career as one of the most successful black women on the music-theater stage, Hall sang in nightclubs and on records. During the last decades of her life, she lived in London and, in her nineties, was still a sought-after performer. In 1992, she made a return appearance in New York. Adelaide Hall's biographical entry is in the *Music* volume of this encyclopedia.

Hall, Juanita (1901–1968)

Juanita Hall was born to Abram and Mary Richardson Hall on November 6, 1901, in Keyport, New Jersey, and educated in the public schools of Keyport, though her formal musical training was to come later. Many persons recognized the unusual talent of the young mezzo-soprano as she sang in the local Catholic church choir. She also played the organ, although she could not yet read music. These early musical experiences led to her acceptance as a voice student at the Juilliard School of Music in New York City.

From her 1928 portrayal of the torch-carrying mulatto Julie in Show Boat *to her 1949 performances as the loud, bawdy, vital Bloody Mary in* South Pacific *and the genteel Americanized Chinese aunt in* Flower Drum Song, *Juanita Hall showed herself to be a singer and actress of remarkable gifts.* (SCHOMBURG CENTER)

While still in her teens, she married Clement Hall, who died shortly thereafter in 1920.

As a vocal performer, Hall's first successful role was Julie in *Show Boat* in 1928. She captured the attention of the eminent Hall Johnson, with whom she began a rewarding association. She appeared in *Green Pastures* in 1930 with the Hall Johnson Choir and became Johnson's assistant conductor until 1936. Her interest and success as a choral conductor resulted in her becoming the conductor of various choirs in the New York metropolitan area: the Works Progress Administration Chorus, 1935–44; the Westchester Chorale and Dramatics Association, 1941–42; and her own choir, the Juanita Hall Choir, in 1942.

Simultaneous with her radio performances with such personalities as Rudy Vallee and Kate Smith, Hall sang in Broadway productions from 1943 to 1947: *The Pirate, Sing Out, Sweet Land, Saint Louis Woman, Deep Are the Roots,* and Kurt Weill's opera *Street Scene.*

Although classically trained, Hall turned her vocal talents to the nightclub scene, which for her became a fortunate venture. Not only was she a great success, but she was "discovered" by Richard Rodgers and Oscar Hammerstein II and cast in the role of Bloody Mary in their new musical, *South Pacific.* The first performance of the much-heralded new musical, which was an adaptation of James Michener's novel *Tales of the South Pacific,* was April 7, 1949, at the Majestic Theater on Broadway. The stars of the production were the established Broadway star Mary Martin and the celebrated Metropolitan Opera bass Ezio Pinza, but Hall was a stunning success and was awarded the prestigious Donaldson Award for her supporting performance. She was later to play the same role in the 1958 film version of *South Pacific.*

Bloody Mary became Hall's signature role, although other successes were to follow: *Flower Drum Song* and her one-woman show *A Woman and the Blues.* In addition, she continued her careers as a nightclub singer and a concert performer.

Juanita Hall's characters were always performed convincingly and with great authority. The eminent theater critic of the the *New York Times* Brooks Atkinson wrote of her performance as Bloody Mary: "She plays a brassy, greedy, ugly, Tonkinese woman with harsh, vigorous authentic accuracy, and she sings one of Mr. Rodgers's finest songs, 'Bali Hai,' with rousing artistry."

Cast as the flighty, mature Chinese lady Madam Liang in 1958's *Flower Drum Song,* again for Rodgers and Hammerstein, Hall was so convincing that she was assumed by many Chinese to be of Chinese origin. She repeated her role in the 1961 film version.

Complications from diabetes caused Hall's death on February 28, 1968, in Bay Shore, Long Island. Survived by a sister and a brother, Juanita Hall was buried in her home town of Keyport, New Jersey.

J. WELDON NORRIS

Hansberry, Lorraine Vivian
(1930–1965)

Celebrated black playwright Lorraine Hansberry was born in Chicago, Illinois, on May 19, 1930, and died in New York City on January 12, 1965, at the age of thirty-four after a scant six years in the professional theater. Her first produced play, *A Raisin in the Sun,* has become an American classic, enjoying numerous productions since its original presentation in 1959 and many professional revivals during its twenty-fifth anniversary year in 1983–1984. The roots of Hansberry's artistry and activism lie in the city of Chicago, her early upbringing, and her family.

Lorraine Vivian Hansberry was the youngest of four children; seven or more years separated her from Mamie, her sister and closest sibling, and two older brothers, Carl Jr., and Perry. Her father, Carl Augustus Hansberry, was a successful real-estate broker who had moved to Chicago from Mississippi after completing a technical course at Alcorn College. A prominent businessman, he made an unsuccessful bid for Congress in 1940 on the Republican ticket and contributed large sums to causes supported by the **National Association for the Advancement of Colored People** (NAACP) and the Urban League. Hansberry's mother, Nannie Perry, was a schoolteacher and later

Young, gifted, and black, Lorraine Hansberry changed the face of the American theater with her play A Raisin in the Sun. *(NATIONAL ARCHIVES)*

a ward committeewoman who had come north from Tennessee after completing teacher training at Tennessee Agricultural and Industrial University. The Hansberrys were at the center of Chicago's black social life and often entertained important political and cultural figures who were visiting the city. Through her uncle, Leo Hansberry, professor of African history at **Howard University**, Hansberry made early acquaintances with young people from the African continent.

The Hansberrys' middle-class status did not protect them from the racial segregation and discrimination characteristic of the period, and they were active in opposing it. Restrictive covenants in which white homeowners agreed not to sell their property to black buyers created a ghetto known as the "black metropolis" in the midst of Chicago's south side. Although large numbers of black Americans continued to migrate to the city, restrictive covenants kept the boundaries static, creating serious housing problems. Carl Hansberry knew well the severe overcrowding in the black metropolis. He had, in fact, made much of his money by purchasing large, older houses vacated by the retreating white population and dividing them into small apartments, each one with its own kitchenette. Thus he earned the title "kitchenette king." In *A Raisin in the Sun*, Lorraine Hansberry used the restrictive covenants and this type of apartment as its setting, with the struggle for better housing as the driving action of her plot.

Hansberry attended public schools, graduating from Betsy Ross Elementary School and then from Englewood High School in 1947. Breaking with the family tradition of attending Southern black colleges, Hansberry chose to attend the University of Wisconsin–Madison, moving from the ghetto schools of Chicago to a predominantly white university. She integrated her dormitory, becoming the first black student to live at Langdon Manor. The years at Madison focused her political views as she worked in the Henry Wallace presidential campaign and in the activities of the Young Progressive League, becoming president of the organization in 1949 during her last semester there. Her artistic sensibilities were heightened by a university production of Sean O'Casey's *Juno and the Paycock*. She was deeply moved by O'Casey's ability to universalize the suffering of the Irish without sacrificing specificity and later wrote: "The melody was one that I had known for a very long while. I was seventeeen and I did not think then of writing the melody as I knew it—in a different key; but I believe it entered my consciousness and stayed there" (*To Be Young, Gifted, and Black*, 1969). She would capture that suffering in the idiom of the Negro people in her first produced play, *A Raisin in the Sun*. In 1950, she left the university and moved to New York City for an education of another kind.

In Harlem, she began to work on *Freedom*, a progressive newspaper founded by Paul Robeson, and turned the world into her personal university. In 1952, Hansberry became associate editor of the newspaper, writing and editing a variety of news stories that expanded her understanding of domestic and world problems. Living and working in the midst of the rich and progressive social, political, and cultural elements of Harlem stimulated Hansberry to write short stories, poetry, and plays. On one occasion, she wrote the pageant that was performed to commemorate the *Freedom* newspaper's first anniversary.

In 1952, while covering a picket line protesting discrimination in sports at New York University, Hansberry met Robert Barro Nemiroff, a white student of Jewish heritage who was attending the university. They dated for several months, participating in political and cultural activities together. They married on June 20, 1953, at the Hansberry home in Chicago.

The young couple took various jobs during these early years. Nemiroff was a part-time typist, waiter, Multilith operator, reader, and copywriter. Hansberry left the *Freedom* staff in 1953 in order to concentrate on her writing and for the next three years worked on three plays while holding a series of jobs: tagger in the garment industry, typist, program director at Camp Unity (a progressive, interracial summer program), teacher at the Marxist-oriented Jefferson School for Social Science, and recreation leader for the handicapped.

A sudden change of fortune freed Hansberry from these odd jobs: Nemiroff and his friend Burt d'Lugoff wrote a folk ballad, "Cindy Oh Cindy," that quickly became a hit. The money from that hit song allowed Hansberry to quit her jobs and devote full time to her writing. She began to write *The Crystal Stair*. This play about a struggling black family in Chicago would eventually become *A Raisin in the Sun*.

Drawing on her knowledge of the working-class black tenants who had rented from her father and with whom she had attended school on Chicago's south side, Hansberry wrote a realistic play whose theme was inspired by Langston Hughes. In his poem "Harlem," he asks: "What happens to a dream deferred? . . . Does it dry up like a raisin in the sun? . . . Or does it explode?" Hansberry read a draft of the play to several colleagues. After one such occasion Phil Rose, a friend who had employed Nemiroff in his music publishing firm, optioned the play for Broadway production. Although he had never produced a Broadway play before, Rose and coproducer David S. Cogan set forth enthusiastically with their fellow novices on this new venture. They approached major Broadway producers, but the "smart money" considered a play about black life too risky a venture for Broadway. The only interested producer insisted on directorial and cast choices that were unacceptable to Hansberry, so the group raised the cash through other means and took the show on tour without the guarantee of a Broadway house. Audiences in the tour cities—New Haven, Connecticut, Philadelphia, and Chicago—were ecstatic about the show. A last-minute rush for tickets in Philadelphia finally made the case for acquiring a Broadway theater.

A Raisin in the Sun opened at the Ethel Barrymore Theater on March 11, 1959, and was an instant success with both critics and audiences. New York critic Walter Kerr praised Hansberry for reading "the precise temperature of a race at that time in its history when it cannot retreat and cannot quite find the way to move forward. The mood is forty-nine parts anger and forty-nine parts control, with a very narrow escape hatch for the steam these abrasive contraries build up. Three generations stand poised, and crowded, on a detonating-cap." Hansberry became an overnight celebrity. The play, whose cast included Sidney Poitier, **Claudia McNeil**, **Ruby Dee**, and **Diane Sands**, was awarded the New York Drama Critics Circle Award in 1959, making Lorraine Hansberry the first black playwright,

the youngest person, and the fifth woman to win that award.

In 1960, NBC producer Dore Schary commissioned Hansberry to write the opening segment for a television series commemorating the Civil War. Her subject was to be slavery. Hansberry thoroughly researched the topic. The result was *The Drinking Gourd*, a television play that focused on the effects that slavery had on the families of the slavemaster and the white poor, as well as the slave. The play was deemed too controversial by NBC television executives and, despite Schary's objections, was shelved along with the entire project.

Hansberry was successful, however, in bringing her prize-winning play, *A Raisin in the Sun*, to the screen a short time later. In 1959, a few months after the play opened, she sold the movie rights to Columbia Pictures and began work on drafts of the screenplay, incorporating several new scenes. These additions, which were rejected for the final version, sharpened the play's attack on the effects of segregation and revealed with a surer hand the growing militant mood of black America. After many revisions and rewrites, the film was produced with all but one of the original cast and released in 1961.

In the wake of the play's extended success, Hansberry became a public figure and a popular speaker at a number of conferences and meetings. Among her most notable speeches is one delivered to a black writers' conference sponsored by the American Society of African Culture in New York. Written during the production of *A Raisin in the Sun* and delivered on March 1, 1959—two weeks before the Broadway opening—"The Negro Writer and His Roots" is in effect Hansberry's credo. In this speech, since published in the *Black Scholar* (March/April 1981) as an essay, Hansberry declares that "all art is ultimately social" and calls upon black writers to be involved in "the intellectual affairs of all men, everywhere." As the civil rights movement intensified, Hansberry helped to plan fundraising events to support organizations such as the **Student Nonviolent Coordinating Committee** (SNCC). Disgusted with the redbaiting of the McCarthy era, she called for the abolition of the House Un-American Activities Committee and criticized President John F. Kennedy's handling of the Cuban missile crisis, arguing that his actions endangered world peace.

In 1961, amid many requests for public appearances, a number of which she accepted, Hansberry began work on several plays. Her next stage production, *The Sign in Sidney Brustein's Window*, appeared in 1964; before that, however, she finished a favorite project, *Masters of the Dew*, adapted from the Haitian novel by Jacques Romain. A film company had asked her to do the screenplay; however, contractual problems prevented the production from proceeding. The next year, seeking rural solitude, she purchased a house in Croton-on-Hudson, forty-five minutes from Broadway, in order to complete work on *The Sign in Sidney Brustein's Window*.

Early in April 1963, Hansberry fainted. Hospitalized at University Hospital in New York City for nearly two weeks, she underwent extensive tests. The results suggested cancer of the pancreas. Despite the progressive failure of her health during the next two years, she continued her writing projects and political activities. In May 1963, she joined writer James Baldwin, singers Harry Belafonte and **Lena Horne**, and other indi-

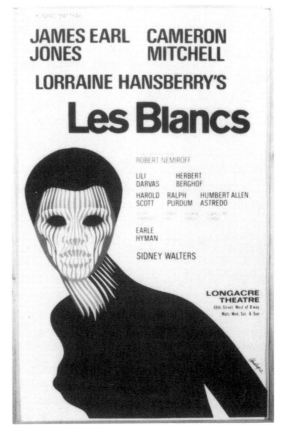

Les Blancs *premiered on Broadway in 1970, five years after Lorrainne Hansberry's death from cancer. The play is set in the midst of a violent revolution in an African country. In 1988, a revised version of the script was produced at Washington's Arena Stage.* (SCHOMBURG CENTER)

viduals, both black and white, in a meeting in Croton to raise funds for SNCC and a rally to support the Southern freedom movement. Although her health was in rapid decline, she greeted 1964 as a year of glorious work. On her writing schedule, in addition to *The Sign in Sidney Brustein's Window*, were *Les Blancs*, *Laughing Boy* (a musical adaptation of the novel), *The Mar-*

row of Tradition, Mary Wollstonecraft, and Achnaton, a play about the Egyptian pharaoh. Despite frequent hospitalization and bouts with pain and attendant medical conditions, she completed a photoessay for a book on the civil rights struggle titled *The Movement: Documentary of a Struggle for Equality* (1964).

Then, in March 1964, she quietly divorced Robert Nemiroff, formalizing the separation that had occurred several years earlier. Only close friends and family had known; their continued collaboration as theater artists and activists had masked the reality of the personal relationship. Those outside their close circle only learned about the divorce when Hansberry's will was read in 1965.

Throughout 1964, hospitalizations became more frequent as the cancer spread. In May, she left the hospital to deliver a speech to the winners of the United Negro College Fund's writing contest in which she coined the now-famous phrase, "young, gifted, and black." A month later, she left her sickbed to participate in the Town Hall debate "The Black Revolution and the White Backlash," at which she and her fellow black artists challenged the criticism by white liberals of the growing militancy of the civil rights movement. She also managed to complete *The Sign in Sidney Brustein's Window*, which opened to mixed reviews on October 15, 1964, at the Longacre Theater. Critics were somewhat surprised by this second play from a woman who had come to be identified with the black liberation movement. Writing about people she had known in Greenwich Village, Hansberry had created a play with a primarily white cast and a theme that called for intellectuals to become involved with social problems and world issues.

On January 12, 1965, Lorraine Hansberry's battle with cancer ended. She died at University Hospital in New York City at the age of thirty-four. Her passing was mourned throughout the nation and in many parts of the world. The list of senders of telegrams and cards sent to her family reads like a who's who of the civil rights movement and the American theater. *The Sign in Sidney Brustein's Window* closed on the night of her death.

Hansberry left a number of finished and unfinished projects, among them *Laughing Boy*, a musical adapted from Oliver LaFarge's novel; an adaptation of *The Marrow of Tradition* by Charles Chesnutt; a film version of *Masters of the Dew*; sections of a semiautobiographical novel, *The Dark and Beautiful Warriors*; and numerous essays, including a critical commentary written in 1957 on Simone de Beauvoir's *The Second Sex* (a book that Hansberry said had changed her life). In her will, she designated her former husband, Robert Nemiroff, as executor of her literary estate.

Hansberry's reputation has continued to grow since her death in 1965 as the now-late Nemiroff, who owned her papers, edited, published, and produced her work posthumously. In 1969, he adapted some of her unpublished writings for the stage under the title *To Be Young, Gifted, and Black*. The longest-running drama of the 1968–69 off-Broadway season, it toured colleges and communities in the United States during 1970–71; a ninety-minute film based on the stage play was first shown in January 1972.

In 1970, Nemiroff produced on Broadway a new work by Hansberry, *Les Blancs*, a full-length play set in the midst of a violent revolution in an African country. Nemiroff then edited *Les Blancs: The Collected Last Plays of Lorraine Hansberry*, published in 1972 and including *Les Blancs*, *The Drinking Gourd*, and *What Use Are Flowers?*, a short play on the consequences of nuclear holocaust. In 1974, *A Raisin in the Sun* returned to Broadway as *Raisin*, a musical, produced by Robert Nemiroff; it won an Antoinette Perry (Tony) Award.

In 1987, *A Raisin in the Sun*, with original material restored, was presented at the Roundabout Theater in New York, the Kennedy Center in Washington, D.C., and other theaters nationwide. In 1989, this version was presented on national television. In March 1988, *Les Blancs*, also with much of the original script restored, was presented at Arena Stage in Washington, D.C., the first professional production in eighteen years.

Hansberry made a very significant contribution to American theater, despite the brevity of her theatrical life and the fact that only two of her plays were produced during her lifetime. *A Raisin in the Sun* was more than simply a "first" to be commemorated in history books and then forgotten: The play was the turning point for black artists in the professional theater. Authenticity and candor combined with timeliness to make it one of the most popular plays ever produced on the American stage. The original production ran for 538 performances on Broadway, attracting large audiences of white and black fans alike. Also, in this play and in her second produced play, Hansberry offered a strong opposing voice to the drama of despair. She created characters who affirmed life in the face of brutality and defeat. Walter Younger in *A Raisin in the Sun*, supported by a culture of hope and aspiration, survives and grows; even Sidney Brustein,

lacking cultural support, resists the temptation to despair by a sheer act of will by reaffirming his link to the human family.

With the growth of women's theater and feminist criticism, Hansberry has been rediscovered by a new generation of women in theater. Indeed, a revisionist reading of her major plays reveals that she was a feminist long before the women's movement surfaced. The female characters in her plays are pivotal to the major themes. They may share the protagonist role, as in *A Raisin in the Sun*, where Mama is coprotagonist with Walter; or a woman character may take the definitive action, as in *The Drinking Gourd*, in which Rissa, the house slave, defies the slave system (and black stereotypes) by turning her back on her dying master and arming her son for his escape to the North. In *The Sign in Sidney Brustein's Window*, Sidney is brought to a new level of self-awareness through the actions of a chorus of women —the Parodus sisters. Likewise, the African woman dancer is ever present in Tshemabe Matoeseh's mind in *Les Blancs*, silently and steadily moving him to a revolutionary commitment to his people. Hansberry's portrayal of Beneatha as a young black woman with aspirations to be a doctor and her introduction of abortion as an issue for poor women in *A Raisin in the Sun* signaled early on Hansberry's feminist attitudes. These and other portrayals of women challenged prevailing stage stereotypes of both black and white women and introduced feminist issues to the stage in compelling terms. Recently uncovered documents revealing Hansberry's sensitivity to homophobic attitudes have further stimulated feminist interest in her work. When more of her papers are released for publication, the full scope of Lorraine Hansberry's work will be appreciated and assessed.

A recent reprint of *A Raisin in the Sun* and *The Sign in Sidney Brustein's Window*, edited by Robert Nemiroff (1987), contains material restored to both scripts, a foreword by Nemiroff, an appreciation by Frank Rich, and critical essays by Amiri Baraka and John Braine. Hansberry's published works appear in various English language editions (as well as in French, German, Japanese, and other languages). The uncompleted *Toussaint* appears in *9 Plays by Black Women*, edited by Margaret B. Wilkerson (1968).

[This entry was originally published in *Notable Women in the American Theater: A Biographical Dictionary*, ed. A. M. Robinson, V. Roberts, and M. S. Barranger (1989).]

MARGARET B. WILKERSON

Harvey, Georgette (1883–1952)

An adventurer and a maverick, Georgette Harvey created a life and a career with equal zest. She was born in St. Louis, Missouri, in 1883. Accounts differ as to how she got her start as an actor. Some say she went to New York when she was eighteen. Others say that, as a young girl, she was noticed by black actor, singer, and songwriter Ernest Hogan while still living in St. Louis. At any rate, her career began when Hogan got her a part in *Rufus Rastus*, a musical in which he starred. While in the show, she put together a quartet with three other women in the company, called the Creole Belles.

Harvey's quartet signed on for a six-month tour of Europe, but they didn't come home at the end but continued to work abroad. When the group broke up in St. Petersburg, Russia, Harvey stayed, living in

Russia for sixteen years, leaving only when the Bolshevik Revolution broke out in 1917. She made it to the Far East, where she taught English in China and Japan for a few years before coming back to the United States.

In 1923, Harvey was on Broadway in the show *Runnin' Wild*. She worked fairly consistently from then on, appearing in *Porgy* in 1927, *Five Star Final* in 1930, *The Party's Over* in 1933, *Porgy and Bess* in 1935 and again in 1942, *Brown Sugar* in 1937, *Mamba's Daughters* in 1939, *The Power of Darkness* in 1948, and the Maxwell Anderson-Kurt Weill musical *Lost in the Stars* in 1949. This last, an adaptation of Alan Paton's *Cry, the Beloved Country*, was a "musical tragedy" about apartheid and racial hatred in South Africa. It was Harvey's last appearance on Broadway. She died in 1952 in New York.

KATHLEEN THOMPSON

Haynes, Hilda (1914–1986)

She was almost certainly the first black woman to play a Jewish mother. That odd fact is characteristic of the theater world Hilda Haynes inhabited and helped to mold from the 1940s until her death in March of 1986.

The black theater movement in the United States began in the late 1930s–early 1940s. Hilda Haynes was one of the dedicated actors who formed that movement and propelled it forward. A member of the **American Negro Theater**, she appeared in some of its most important productions, including *On Striver's Row* in 1946. She was also a frequent performer at the Greenwich Mews Theater, a progressive, multiracial group that cast its shows regardless of color. It was here, in the play *Monday's*

Heroes, that Haynes played a Jewish mother in a primarily white cast.

Haynes was also in the cast of one of the few plays ever produced at the Apollo Theater. In 1950, the great center of black music presented all-black versions of *Tobacco Road*, *Rain*, and *Detective Story;* in the last, Haynes was part of the talented cast that supported young actor Sidney Poitier.

In 1955, the brilliant, funny *Trouble in Mind*, by **Alice Childress** was presented at the Greenwich Mews Theater with Hilda Haynes sharing the stage with **Clarice Taylor,** who also codirected. Haynes also appeared in Childress' *Wedding Band* when it was produced in 1972 by Joseph Papp and the New York Shakespeare Festival.

In the meantime, Haynes had appeared on Broadway in *King of Hearts*, *The Wisteria Trees*, *Take a Giant Step*, and *The Irregular Verb To Love*. She participated in black theater history again when she joined the Broadway cast of *Purlie Victorious*, by Ossie Davis, was in both the New York and London productions of *Golden Boy*, and supported James Earl Jones in *The Great White Hope*. She also appeared in the 1975 movie *Let's Do It Again*, with Sidney Poitier and Bill Cosby.

As important as her career onstage was her work with Actors Equity, the actors union. She was serving her fourth consecutive five-year term on the Equity Council when she died. During her time with Equity, she was a founding member of the Paul Robeson Citation Committee, served on the housing, national theater, and executive committees, and was an active and forceful voice for black actors on the council.

Hilda Haynes was a pioneer of black theater who, to the end of her life, worked to enlarge the role of black artists in the American theater.

KATHLEEN THOMPSON

Holiday, Jennifer (1960–)

"If the curtain didn't fall," said the *New York Times* critic of her performance in *Dreamgirls*, "the audience would probably cheer Jennifer Holiday until dawn." It was a remarkable triumph for a tenty-one-year-old girl.

Jennifer Holiday was born on October 19, 1960, in Houston, Texas, to Omie Lee and Jennie Thomas Holiday. Her Baptist-minister father and her mother were divorced while Jennifer was a baby; she remained with her mother, who early encouraged her to sing in a church choir. As a teenager, Holiday was student council president of her junior high and thought about being a lawyer, but she also sang gospel on a local television station. Music won out: At eighteen, she audition for the national company of *Your Arms Too Short to Box With God* and won a major role.

Holiday's performance in the show was highly praised and led to a role in a workshop production of a new musical called *Dreamgirls*. She and director Michael Bennett didn't get along and, for a time, it looked as though their differences would keep Holiday out of the Broadway production. However, her talent was an overwhelming lure. Bennett, who had found fault with Holiday's acting, took her to plays and sent her to old movies and, by the time *Dreamgirls* opened on Broadway, her acting was quite sufficient to back up her astonishing voice. She won a Tony and a Drama Desk Award for her performance.

Holiday was the rage. The *Dreamgirls* cast album won a Grammy in 1981. Holiday's show-stopping song "And I'm Telling You I'm Not Going" won another, in the category of Best Rhythm and Blues Performance–Female, in 1983. The young performer won an Image Award that same year. She even hosted *Saturday Night Live*.

In 1985, Holiday appeared on Broadway in *Sing, Mahalia, Sing*. She also performed in a television special, *In Performance at the White House*, in 1988 and has recorded several albums, winning another Grammy in 1986 in the category of Best Inspirational Performance–Female for *Come Sunday*.

It seems clear that, though she made her mark young, Holiday has staying power; she should be entertaining for a long time.

Holland, Endesha Ida Mae (1944–)

In 1965, a young woman in a "$3 dress and $2 suitcase" boarded a train that would take her from rural Mississippi to Minneapolis and a university education. Ida Mae Holland, the child of a former prostitute who became a respected midwife, took the first step of a journey that would lead her to write a very popular American play of the 1990s, *From the Mississippi Delta*.

Holland was born in Greenwood, Mississippi, in 1944. Her mother operated a rooming house that, according to Holland, everyone knew was used for other purposes. Raised in poverty and molested by an employer at an early age, Holland herself became a prostitute in her teens, but two things altered the young woman's life.

The first was her mother's other vocation of midwife. Holland's mother was known by all as "the Second Doctor Lady" because of her expertise. "She would go to see about

pregnant women at any hour, anytime; she saved old newspapers and baby clothes to carry with her on home deliveries, and she could turn a breech baby around in a woman's stomach." Ida Mae's mother was killed when the Ku Klux Klan burned their house in 1965.

The second great and transforming influence in her life was the civil rights movement. In her autobiographical play *From the Mississippi Delta*, Holland says, "I had never read a book written by an African American. I didn't know that black people could write books. I didn't know that blacks had done any great things. I was always conscious of my inferiority and I always remembered my place—until the civil rights movement came to the town where I was born and grew up." They came in the summer of 1963, and soon Ida Mae was deeply involved, marching in demonstrations and going to jail thirteen times.

The civil rights workers in Greenwood, seeing her intelligence and abilities, encouraged her to complete her education. Holland became a valuable speaker, traveling around the country to speak out for civil rights, and eventually she boarded that train to Minnesota. She received her B.A. in 1979, while also working with street people and former prostitutes, eventually forming the group Women Helping Offenders. Its purpose was to aid convicts returning to society after doing time in prison. As her range of activities expanded, so did her name, as she added Endesha, which is Swahili for "driver."

While at the University of Minnesota, Holland studied playwriting with Dr. Charles Nolte and began to turn the incidents of her life into theater. She possessed a remarkable ear for dialects and the idiosyncracies of character and, with the rich material of her past to draw on, she began to fashion a series of powerful plays. Her first, entitled *The Second Doctor Lady* (1980), honored her mother by recounting some of the midwife's experiences. Another, *The Reconstruction of Dossie Lee Hemphill* (1980), was inspired by memories of the women of Greenwood gossiping about town scandals. A third, *The Autobiography of a Parader Without a Permit* (1985), which served as her Ph.D. dissertation, dealt with her experiences in the civil rights movement and with other Southern crusaders who inspired her. Holland would later weave elements of those plays together into *From The Mississippi Delta.*

In 1982, she created *Miss Ida B. Wells*, a play about the famous black journalist/activist of the early twentieth century. She performed the play at universities and theaters around the country until 1986. She had begun a nine-year tenure in 1985 as Professor of Women's Studies at the State University of New York at Buffalo.

Born out of the events of her life and midwived through her early plays, *From the Mississippi Delta* began to grow into its final shape in 1987, when it received a production in New York under the auspices of the New Federal Theater. Shortly thereafter, the **Negro Ensemble Company** took it on tour. Nominated for a 1988 Pulitzer Prize, it was revived in 1990 at Chicago's Northlight Theater and went on to be produced at more than thirty theaters nationwide.

The frankness, power, and redemptive joy with which Endesha Ida Mae Holland has made her autobiography into communicative art of the highest order has brought her any number of honors, including the Key to the City of Greenwood, Michigan, and the 1993 Martin Luther King, Jr. Commission Life Achievement Award. True to her adopted name, she continues to drive ahead. She is working on a new play, entitled *Homeland.*

She resides now in California, where she is professor in the School of Theater and the Program for the Study of Women and Men in Society at the University of California at Los Angeles.

RICHARD E. T. WHITE

K

Kein, Sybil (1939–)

"I wonder if they know something we don't know?" is a line spoken by several characters from the older generation in Sybil Kein's play *Get Together* (1970); the implication is that the young are better equipped to deal with interracial or interethnic relationships than their parents. Kein maintains that once the mask is removed, people of all races and ethnic groups discover that while each ethnic group has certain culture-specific attributes, human beings are more alike than different. Her literary works celebrate diversity while underscoring the common ground or shared experiences among humanity.

Named Consuela Moore at birth, Sybil Kein was born on September 29, 1939, in New Orleans to Frank and Augustine Boudreaux Moore. One of thirteen children, Kein grew up in the seventh ward of New Orleans, an area historically inhabited by *gens du couleur* (free people of color, Creoles, or black Creoles). Kein, a Creole of Native American, French, and African ancestry, grew up speaking a French *patois* primarily and English secondarily.

Educated at Corpus Christi Elementary School and Xavier Preparatory High School, Kein went on to Xavier University in New Orleans to earn a bachelor's degree in instrumental music in 1958 and to the University of New Orleans to earn a master's degree in theater arts and communica-tion in 1972. Between 1958 and 1972, Kein had three children, Elizabeth, David, and Susan, and struggled through a divorce. At the age of thirty-three, Kein left New Orleans and three years later received a doctorate in American ethnic literature from the University of Michigan at Ann Arbor. She has taught English and theater at the University of Michigan–Flint since 1972.

A performing artist, poet, playwright, scholar, and recording artist, Sybil Kein has dedicated her life to researching the history and culture of Louisiana Creoles of color as well as writing poems and plays about them. Kein has published several volumes of poetry written in Creole and English, including *Visions from the Rainbow* (1979), *Gumbo People: Poésie Creole de la Nouvelle-Orleans* (1981), and *Delta Dancer* (1984). Many of her poems can be heard on two recordings: *Poetry and Music by Sybil Kein* (1979), by the National Federation of Community Broadcasters Program Service, and *Serenade Creole* (1987) by Mastertracks.

Kein's educational grounding is apparent in her twenty-eight plays, which incorporate poetry, music, and dance. Her most frequently produced plays include *Saints and Flowers* (1965), *Projection One* (1966), *The Black Box* (1967), *The Christmas Holly* (1967), *Deep River Rises* (1970), *The Reverend* (1970), *Get Together* (1970), *When I Grow Up!* (1974), *Rogues Along the River Flint* (1977), and *River Rogues* (1979). Kein's plays explore such subjects as the ramifications of slavery, miscegenation, teenage pregnancy, and, especially, class and color biases.

Garnering for her a Best Playwright Award from the University of New Orleans in 1970, Kein's play *Get Together* is representative of her wit. Her central message in this play is that members of different races are not very different from each other in that they all want good health, decent jobs, and security for their children. Kein pokes fun at both African Americans and white Americans who have preconceived, racist notions about each other; she further satirizes this by bringing up the possibility that these people may be related to each other because of mixed ancestry.

Kein has also won the Avery Hopwood Award for poetry (1975), the Creative Achievement Award (1978), the Amoco Foundation Grant (1979), the Michigan Council of the Arts Artist Award (1981), and the Michigan Association of Governing Boards Award (1982).

Sybil Kein is an important figure in the development of African American theater and poetry, particularly because of the local color in her work. She travels throughout the country performing and singing, often in English, French, Spanish, Kreyol, and Creole, her poetry about the family-oriented, education-minded, fun-loving, religious, and proud Creoles of color whose history, culture, and traditions are deeply entrenched in New Orleans and in Creole settlements across the country. A regionalist of the first rank, Sybil Kein's works are as important to understanding Louisiana culture as are the works of Flannery O'Connor and Ernest Gaines.

ELIZABETH BROWN-GUILLORY

Kennedy, Adrienne (1931–)

"My plays, " says Adrienne Kennedy, "are meant to be states of mind." Few writers have been so successful at breaking the bonds of realism on the stage and challenging notions of personal, racial and historical identity. Her plays use masks, carnival images, magic, and poetic incantations to take us into a world where deeply personal dreams and nightmares become ceremonies of transformation and awakening consciousness.

Kennedy was born Adrienne Lita Hawkins in Pittsburgh, Pennsylvania, on September 30, 1931. After a few years in Georgia, her family settled in Cleveland, where Adrienne attended school. In her memoir, *People Who Led to My Plays*, she talks about the influence of the movie characters during her early years, citing as an unusual but telling example, the Wolf Man: As she began to write plays, she says, "He still held a power over me. Metamorphosis and change of identity would become a theme that would dominate my writing."

She attended Ohio State University, earning her B.A. in education in 1953. Two weeks after her graduation, she married Joseph Kennedy. Six months after their marriage, Joe was sent to Korea, leaving a newly pregnant Adrienne at home in Cleveland. There she discovered a magazine called *Theater Arts* that contained an interview with Tennessee Williams, at that time perhaps America's most influential playwright. Moved by his essay, she read his *A Streetcar Named Desire* and shortly wrote her own first play. When Joe returned from Korea, the couple moved to New York, where she began graduate studies in creative writing at

Columbia and later the American Theater Wing.

In her early writing, Kennedy was influenced by Spanish poet Federico Garcia Lorca and by Williams, whom she called "the writer whose career and plays I coveted. It took ten years to stop imitating him, to stop using his form, and to stop stealing his themes, which were not mine." When she studied playwriting at the American Theater Wing, she was, like Laura in Williams' *The Glass Menagerie*, deeply shy and had to be encouraged to come to class.

Perhaps the greatest influence on her, however, was the playwright Edward Albee, who had electrified the New York theater scene in the early sixties with a group of plays that included *The Zoo Story* and *Who's Afraid of Virginia Woolf?* It was at Albee's playwriting workshop at the Circle in the Square Theater, which Kennedy attended from 1962 to 1964, that she experienced her first great success as a writer: *Funnyhouse of a Negro*, which she had begun to write on a journey to Africa, is a kaleidoscopic examination of racial identity and is a triumphantly original play in form and language.

The trip to Africa, taken in the fall of 1960, provided many of the images that would populate the funhouse dream world of her play. A stop in England exposed her to an image of Queen Victoria, ". . . the single most dramatic statue I'd ever seen. Here was a woman who had dominated an age." Other images from the African trip that would appear in the play included the dynamic Congolese leader Patrice Lumumba and the mask she bought in the streets of Accra of "a woman with a bird flying through her forehead." These inspired her to create the surreal characters who would soon populate her plays and establish her unique voice as a writer.

Funnyhouse of a Negro was first produced in Albee's workshop. It was then presented in 1964 in an off-Broadway production starring **Billie Allen** and won for the author a prestigious Obie Award. In the play, the central character Sarah's struggles to come to terms with her mixed racial heritage are represented in vivid imagery as she splits into a number of characters, including Jesus, the Duchess of Hapsburg, Queen Victoria, and Lumumba.

Kennedy's creativity unleashed itself with a series of other dramas steeped in ritual, spectacle, and myth, including *A Rat's Mass* and *The Owl Answers* in 1963, and *A Lesson in a Dead Language* in 1964. In 1967, she collaborated with British actor Victor Spinetti to create a stage piece based on the writings of an artist whose sensibility was as offbeat as her own—Beatle John Lennon. *The Lennon Play: In His Own Write* was performed at the National Theatre of Great Britain.

Adrienne Kennedy continued to write challenging and poetic plays; many of her more recent works have been written for educational institutions, such as *Black Children's Day* for Brown University, and *Orestes and Electra* for the Juilliard School of Music, both in 1980. In addition to her writing, Kennedy taught playwriting at Yale, Brown, and Princeton Universities. Divorced from her husband in 1966, she is the mother of two sons, Joe and Adam.

In 1994, Kennedy was the recipient of the Lila Wallace–Reader's Digest Fund's Writer's Award, which she used to establish an arts and culture program for minority children in Cleveland's inner-city schools.

RICHARD E. T. WHITE

L

The Lafayette Players

The Lafayette Players are enormously important for, and because of, black women in the theater. The group began in 1915 as the Anita Bush Players, founded by actor-director **Anita Bush**. The twenty-eight-year-old veteran of musical theater approached a movie-theater owner—after noticing that his Saturday matinee was almost empty—and suggested that she produce a play in his auditorium, the Lincoln Theater. He agreed, giving her two weeks to put it together.

The Lafayette Players, founded by actress Anita Bush, was one of the first black theater groups to perform serious, nonmusical theater. For seventeen years, the Players brought quality legitimate theater to black audiences. Shown here is a scene from Girl at the Fort, *featuring Anita Bush, Edward Thompson, Andrew Bishop, Dooley Wilson, and two unidentified actors.* (SISTER FRANCESCA THOMPSON)

On November 15, 1915, Anita Bush and her company, which included Carlotta Freeman and Charles Gilpin, opened *The Girl at the Fort*. It was written by Billie Burke (the Good Witch Glinda in *The Wizard of Oz*), who also directed the show for her young friend. Bush did everything else, from publicity to playing the lead role. The press reception was favorable, and the black community's response was beyond all expectations. The management of the Lincoln Theater, hoping to capitalize on a good thing, demanded that the Anita Bush Players become the Lincoln Players. Bush refused, gave two weeks' notice, and moved on to the Lafayette Theater. Once there, she agreed to a name change, and the company became the Lafayette Players. One suspects Bush just didn't like to be pushed around.

Bush stayed with the company until 1920, as it presented all-black casts performing the most popular plays of the day as well as classics. The cast members were paid well, and Bush helped set up companies in Chicago, Baltimore, Washington, D.C., and Philadelphia. There was also a touring company. Many of the women who got their start at this important black theater went on to have distinguished careers.

Edna Thomas went from the Lafayette Players to form her own company, the All-Star Colored Civic Repertory Company. She worked with Orson Welles and John Houseman, appeared on Broadway in *Lulu Belle*, became an active organizer for the rights of actors, and created the role of the Mexican Flower Woman in Tennessee Williams's *A Streetcar Named Desire* on Broadway. She repeated the role in the film version.

Abbie Mitchell was already famous as a singer when she began to perform with the Lafayette Players. Her experience there led to a remarkable second career as a dramatic actor on Broadway in such plays as *Abraham's Bosom*, *House of Shadows*, *Porgy and Bess*, and *The Little Foxes*.

Evelyn Ellis' career took off after she appeared at the Lafayette, and she was soon on Broadway in *Roseanne*, *Goat Alley*, and *Porgy*, the dramatic play on which the folk opera *Porgy and Bess* would be based. Ellis created the role of Bess. She went on to a career in films and television.

Evelyn Preer went from the Lafayette to Broadway, appearing in such plays as *Rang Tang* and *Porgy*. She was also a pioneer in films, appearing in many of the all-black movies produced by independent filmmaker Oscar Micheaux.

Laura Bowman came to the Lafayette after years with some of the larger black musical companies. She went on to have one of the most distinguished careers of any black actor of the time, eventually founding the National Art School, one of the first formal training grounds for black actors.

Bush herself stayed with the Lafayette for six years before going on to appear in the all-black film *The Crimson Skull*, a western mystery that was filmed in a black town in Oklahoma. She filmed another western in 1923. In the thirties she was active in the Federal Theatre Project and was also, for many years, executive secretary of the Negro Actors' Guild.

KATHLEEN THOMPSON

LeNoire, Rosetta (1911–)

"Bubbling Brown Sugar in a Crystal Ball" is the nickname that Rosetta LeNoire's godfather, Bill "Bojangles" Robinson, gave her when she was growing up in Harlem. Decades later, she reclaimed her nickname for

Bubbling Brown Sugar (1975), the award-winning musical revue that celebrates the African-American music and performers of her youth with "Uncle Bo." Rosetta LeNoire became well known in the 1980s and early 1990s through television sitcoms, appearing as Nell's mother on *Gimme a Break*, as Rolly's wife on *Amen*, and as the grandmother on *Family Matters*. At the age of eighty, she had become a nationally recognized television star with fifty years of theater successes to her credit, bouts with discrimination, numerous awards, and hu-manitarian work in the arts. She has made significant contributions to every major phase of the black experience in American theater history and served as her own manager.

Rosetta Olive Burton LeNoire was born in "Hell's Kitchen," Fifty-ninth Street in New York City, on August 8, 1911, to Marie Jacque and Harold Charles Burton, shortly after they migrated from Dominica, British West Indies, to the United States. Her early years dancing with Uncle Bo and singing lead in her church choir gave her the

Early in Rosetta LeNoire's career, Bill "Bojangles" Robinson called her "Bubbling Brown Sugar in a Crystal Ball." Fifty years later, this star of stage, screen, and television conceived the idea for the award-winning musical revue Bubbling Brown Sugar. *Here, she appears in the Broadway musical* Double Entry. (SCHOMBURG CENTER)

confidence to audition for the Federal Theatre Project in 1935, her entry into professional theater in New York City.

She became a member of the acclaimed Harlem unit of the Federal Theatre Project in 1936, performing the role of the First Witch in Orson Welles and John Houseman's production of *Haitian Macbeth*. Other Federal Theatre Project productions in which LeNoire performed (1935–39) were *Bassa Moona*, *Bluebirds*, *Haiti*, *Sing for Your Supper*, and *Underground Railroad*.

After Congress closed the Federal Theater Project in 1939, LeNoire made her Broadway debut in a principal role with Uncle Bo: *The Hot Mikado* was produced by Mike Todd. She completed the tour of *The Hot Mikado* after the bombing of Pearl Harbor and went on to perform in several productions of the United Service Organizations (USO) during World War II.

With her role as Rheba in *You Can't Take It With You*, she began to play female servant roles in some of the most prominent productions in New York, becoming highly respected as an actress who contributed to changing the stage image of the black female servant by performing with dignity and self-pride. This reputation has continued to the present.

Included among the plays in which she performed are *Decision* and *Three's a Family* with the New York Subway Circuit; *Four Twelves Are 48* (1948); *The Easiest Way* (1949); *Kiss Me, Kate* (1950); *Show Boat*, *Anything Goes*, and *Happy Birthday* (1951) stock; *The Ceremony of Innocence* (1954) and *The Name of the Game* (1967) off-Broadway; and the following Broadway productions: *Finian's Rainbow* (1955), *The White Devil* (1955), *Destry Rides Again*

(1959), *Sophie* (1963), *I Had a Ball* (1964), *The Great Indoors* (1966), *Show Boat* (1966), *The Sunshine Boys* (1972), *God's Favorite* (1974), *The Royal Family* (1976), and *The Little Foxes* (1983).

She participated in numerous off-Broadway shows by black writers and in plays written specifically for a black cast. After *The Hot Mikado*, she was featured in a principal role in Abram Hill's adaptation of Philip Yordan's *Anna Lucasta*, which was transferred from the **American Negro Theater** to Broadway, opening on August 30, 1944, and becoming the most successful black-cast production in the 1940s. Intertwined with her servant roles, she obtained principal roles in the following plays for mixed or an all-black cast off-Broadway: *O Distant Land* (1952), *Supper for the Dead* (1954), *Mister Johnson* (1955), *Take a Giant Step* (1956), *The Bible Salesman* (1960, 1961), *The Oldest Trick in the World* (1961), *Clandestine on the Morning Line* (1961), *Cabin in the Sky* (1964), and *Lady Day* (1972). On Broadway, she had roles in *Lost in the Stars* (1958), *South Pacific* (1961), *Tambourines to Glory* (1963), *Blues for Mr. Charlie* (1964), *A Cry of Players* (1968), *Hallelujah Baby* (1968), and *Lost in the Stars* (1972).

LeNoire was instrumental in establishing two of the most prominent organizations that contributed to the development of and more opportunities for black performers, the Negro Actor's Guild (NAG) and the Coordinating Council for Negro Performers (CCNP). She was one of the charter members of NAG, a welfare organization for performers in need, and she was one of the founders of CCNP, a political-action organization that in 1955 led a boycott against television to sensitize the sponsors to provide a fair share of jobs for black performers. In more recent years, she has been an active member of the Actor's Fund, the interracial welfare organization for performers.

Her proudest contribution to her profession was the establishment of Amas Repertory Theater in 1969 to encourage cultural pluralism and love in the world. The name of the theater, *Amas*, means "you love" in Latin, and its music theater productions reiterate that theme. LeNoire's primary reason for continuing to work as an actress, with all of the physical complications of her age, is to help subsidize the theater company, which is her greatest love. As she continues to work at Amas, refusing to accept a salary, her most immediate concern is to find a permanent building to house her institution.

LeNoire's contributions have not gone unrecognized. She has received almost as many major awards as the number of years she has been in theater: Since 1981, she has received thirty distinguished career awards including the Johnny Walker Award (1981); the Harold Jackman Award (1981); the St. Genesius Award from the Catholic Actor's Guild (1981); the Outstanding Pioneer Award (1982), Board of Directors' Award (1982), and Outstanding Musical Production of the Year (1979–84, 1991) from AUDELCO (Audience Development Committee); the Hoey Award from the Catholic Interracial Council (1985); Sojourner Truth Award from the Council of Negro Professional Women (1986); Mayor's Award for Arts and Culture (1986); Woman of the Year from the Caribbean Cultural Association (1986); Actor's Equity Award created especially for her called the Rosetta LeNoire Award (1989); the Living Legend Award

from the National Black Theater Festival (1991); and the Lucille Lortel Career Achievement Award (1991). The variety of presenters of these prestigious awards demonstrates that LeNoire has made an indelible mark on her profession and on her home, New York City.

LINDA NORFLETT

Livingston, Myrtle (1902–1973)

Myrtle Athleen Smith Livingston was one of the first black American playwrights to place the controversial question of interracial marriage openly on the stage. "For Unborn Children," published in *Crisis* in July 1926, provocatively explores the situation of a black lawyer who has fallen in love with a white woman and who plans to marry her over the opposition of his sister and grandmother. When he learns that his own mother was white and may have abandoned him because of his color, he begins to realize the cost of crossing the color line. As the play concludes, a lynch mob clamors outside his door and the audience realizes that it may be too late for him to escape being lynched.

Born in Holly Grove, Arkansas, on May 8, 1902, to Samuel Isaac and Lula C. Hall Smith, Myrtle Athleen Smith lived in Denver as a child, studied pharmacy at **Howard University** from 1920 to 1922, and transferred to Colorado Teachers College in Greeley. There she organized a dance group and began her lifelong involvement with theater arts. In 1925, she married William McKinley Livingston and in 1928 joined the faculty of Lincoln University, Jefferson City, Missouri, as sole member of the physical education and dance department and director of women's athletics. During her forty-four years of teaching, she also wrote and directed plays, and spent several sabbaticals studying in New York at Columbia University and New York University.

Livingston died in July 1973 in Honolulu. In accordance with Hawaiian custom, her ashes were scattered in the Pacific Ocean.

LORRAINE ELENA ROSES

M

Mabley, Jackie "Moms" (1897–1975)

Jackie "Moms" Mabley had a grandmother who lived to be 104 years old. "Moms" herself was a salty, wise, hilarious granny onstage for so long that, though she actually died at seventy-eight, it seemed that she had outdone that ancient slave grandmother.

Born Loretta Mary Aiken in Brevard, North Carolina, in 1897, Mabley was one of seven children. Her grandmother advised her to leave home if she wanted to make something of herself, and when she was thirteen years old, she did. She joined a minstrel show, claiming to be sixteen, and started to perform on the Theater Owners Booking Association circuit. Shortly after leaving home, she met and became engaged to a young Canadian man named Mabley. They were never married, but as she explained later, he took a lot from her, so she could at least take his name. She adopted "Jackie" as a first name simply because she liked it.

In Houston, Texas, a husband-and-wife dance team called Butterbeans and Susie saw her perform and persuaded her to join their act. As part of their routine, she performed her first significant role in *The Rich Aunt from Utah*.

When Mabley began her career, there was an extensive network of black-owned and -managed halls. They had arisen during the early years of the Jim Crow era, and though they owed their existence to discrimination and racism, they provided a home for black entertainers and audiences. Here entertainers could perfect their craft, and audiences could hear their own music, see their own dances, and relax in congenial laughter. In a sense, these clubs were sanctuaries that shut out an oppressive larger society. Whites might be admitted, but they clearly were there on the suffrance of the black majority. Dorothy Gilliam describes the Howard

The salty, wise, wisecracking Jackie Mabley was called "Moms" for so many years that it was easy to believe that she was ancient when she started out in show business. Hers was a remarkably durable career that stretched from minstrel shows to the Harlem Renaissance to movies to record albums to television. (SCHOMBURG CENTER)

Theater as the "one place in Washington where blacks and whites, school teachers and domestics, doctors and laborers mingled as equals."

This was Mabley's venue. She worked with Dusty (Open-the-Door-Richard) Fletcher in Washington, D.C., walked onstage with a stepladder and the American flag and "hipped her children" at the Earle Theater in Philadelphia, and was a standby at the Apollo in New York. In a 1941 letter to Arna Bontemps, Langston Hughes mentions his fondness for Mabley's performances at the Apollo to the extent of "splitting his money" with her. Mabley appeared at the Apollo more often than any other performer in its history.

In the 1920s, during the Harlem Renaissance, Mabley began to perform at nightclubs such as the Cotton Club, Connie's Inn, and the Savoy Ballroom, sharing billing with Duke Ellington, Louis Armstrong, Benny Goodman, Count Basie, and Cab Calloway. Later, she created comedy routines from her encounters and supposed love affairs with these immortals of entertainment. During the 1910s and 1920s, she also worked in the black theater in revues such as *Bowman's Cotton Blossoms*, *Look Who's Here*, and *Miss Bandanna*. In these revues, Mabley sometimes appeared in blackface.

During the Depression, black clubs and theaters had great difficulty staying open. Mabley found work at church socials, rent parties, movie houses, and show theaters. She recalled doing fifteen "jailhouse bits" in one day at the Monogram in Chicago, where she worked with Fletcher and Spider Bruce John Mason. She also appeared in the revues *The Joy Boat*, *Sidewalks of Harlem*, and *Red Pastures*.

Connoisseurs of the remarkable and the odd must cherish the thought of the Broadway play *Fast and Furious: A Colored Revue in 37 Scenes* in 1931, in which Mabley collaborated with Harlem Renaissance literary light **Zora Neale Hurston**, writing scenes and performing. In one skit, they appeared together as cheerleaders.

In 1933, Mabley appeared in her first film, playing a small role as a bawdy-house matron in O'Neill's *The Emperor Jones*, starring Paul Robeson. In 1939, she played Quince in a jazz adaptation of *A Midsummer Night's Dream*; inspired by the rude mechanicals' version of "Pyramus and Thisbe," she added that kind of satire of the classics to her comedy routine. Mabley returned to film in 1947 in *Killer Diller* and in 1948, had the lead role in *Boarding House Blues*, in which she played the character of Moms, who ran a boarding house for out-of-work entertainers.

Mabley acquired the name "Moms" from the fellow entertainers whom she helped and cared for, but she soon discovered that the persona was one that she could use to good effect on stage because it brought both protection and freedom: Female entertainers were often seen as either immoral or threatening, but Moms was safe. Mabley was, of course, not the first to draw on the power and associations of the maternal: there were **Ma Rainey** (Gertrude Pridgett), Big Mama Blues (Lillie Mae Glover), Sweet Mama Stringbean (**Ethel Waters**), and the Last of the Red Hot Mamas (Sophie Tucker), to name a few. Mabley, however, took the role to its limits, creating a character with the authority of a community elder in expounding folk wisdom, advising presidents, leveling bigots, and instructing the people about what and how to teach their young.

That persona proved durable, taking Mabley into television in the 1960s: She appeared on *The Smothers Brothers Comedy Hour* and on variety and talk shows hosted by Merv Griffin, Mike Douglas, Ed Sullivan, Garry Moore, and Flip Wilson. At Carnegie Hall, Mabley performed on a program with Nancy Wilson and Cannonball Adderley, and her act was popular at the Playboy clubs, the Copacabana, and the Kennedy Center. John F. Kennedy invited her to perform at the White House. Mabley was also a highly successful recording artist, making more than twenty-five comedy records; her first, *Moms Mabley: The Funniest Woman in the World*, sold more than a million copies.

The mother of three daughters and an adopted son, she made her home in Washington, D.C.; Cleveland, Ohio; and White Plains, New York.

In 1974, Mabley appeared in the motion picture *Amazing Grace*. Shortly after it was completed, she died on May 23, 1975.

ELSIE ARRINGTON WILLIAMS

Taking the role of the affable, advice-giving "mom" to its limits, Jackie Mabley created a character with the authority of a community elder in expounding folk wisdom, advising presidents, leveling bigots, and instructing the people about what and how to teach their young. Her character and her career took her to television in the 1960s, appearing on The Smothers Brothers Comedy Hour, *variety shows, and talk shows hosted by Merv Griffin, Mike Douglas, Ed Sullivan, Garry Moore, and Flip Wilson.* (MOORLAND SPINGARN)

Martin, Helen (1915?–)

Helen Martin understands patience and survival. "I worked at Western Union, in box factories and private family homes, operated elevators in hotels and served dinner parties," she once explained. "I always worked at something because I had to live. I have never been one of those people who was an actress only, eating peanut butter sandwiches the whole week. My telephone has never been cut off, and I've always paid my rent. I knew I had to make sacrifices."

Helen Dorothy Martin was born in St. Louis and grew up in Nashville in the 1920s. She was the only child of William and Amanda Frankie Fox Martin. "When I was growing up," she recalls, "wanting to be in show business was like working for the Devil." Hers was a family of musicians who expected her to be a concert pianist. In that line and to that end, she attended Fisk and Tennessee State universities and then, for a couple years, directed a twelve-piece orchestra. Domestic jobs on the side earned her just enough—$90—to allow a move to Chicago to pursue the work of "the Devil."

The time was the Great Depression, however, and only after more years of manual labor, including one in a chemical factory, did she join Chicago's WPA [Works Progress Administration] Federal Theatre Project company in the late 1930s. Following a short run in the play *The Great White Fog*, she married in 1939 and took her husband's advice to seek her stage livelihood in New York. He died three years later, and she never remarried.

In New York she joined the Harlem-based **Rose McClendon** Players, which was founded in 1937 and lasted until 1942. In 1940, still living on odd jobs, she and such others as Sidney Poitier, Harry Belafonte, and director Abram Hill formed the American Negro Theater in a Harlem library basement. Its only export to Broadway was Philip Yordan's *Anna Lucasta*, a comedy about a Polish family which the company adapted. The troupe dissolved before the 1940s ended.

But Martin's career had been launched. Her Broadway debut came in the 1941–42 season when Orson Welles, fresh from *Citizen Kane*, cast her as Bigger Thomas's sister in the Richard Wright–Paul Green stage version of Wright's 1940 novel *Native Son*. She auditioned for the play with some nervousness because she was lacking in Broadway credits: "There was a line all the way around the building," she said in an *Ebony* interview. "I was so scared, I was letting people by me." When she finally got the courage to audition, she was cast. The show was a hit.

She was on Broadway again—in an important role, albeit that of a maid—in Elia Kazan's 1945 production of *Deep Are the Roots* and went to London with it. Later, she became a member of another Harlem producing group, called The Committee for the Negro in the Arts (TCNA), at the Club Baron on Lenox Avenue.

Martin herself and others note that her long career was not one of steady work nor was her name a household word. Yet, her stage résumé with its many Broadway credits is enviable for almost any actor. A few of the shows she appeared in are *On Strivers Row* (1946), *The Little Foxes* and *The Petrified Forest* (1951), *Take a Giant Step* (1953), *Major Barbara* (1954), *You Can't Take It With You* (1954–55), *The Ballad of Jazz Street* (1959), *The Long Dream* (1960), *A Streetcar Named Desire* (touring in the 1950s), and Jean Genet's *The Blacks* (1961). This last show ran for four years with the unusual policy of allowing Martin and other actors to leave to do better-paying shows and then return.

She also appeared in 1961 in Ossie Davis's *Purlie Victorious*, in which she played Missy Judson, and in its musical version *Purlie*, in which she was Idella. Other important black plays whose casts she enhanced include *The Amen Corner* in 1964 and *Raisin* the musical version of *A Raisin in the Sun* which was produced in 1973.

Martin has also done many films, including *Where's Poppa?* (1970), *Cotton Comes to Harlem* (1970), *The Anderson Tapes* (1971), *Death Wish* (1974), and *A Hero Ain't Nothin' But a Sandwich* (1978). In 1987, she played the grandmother in Robert Townsend's independent film, *Hollywood Shuffle*, giving it a weight and credibility that few beginning films can boast.

Appearing in the ABC miniseries *Roots* in 1977, Martin garnered TV work on *Maude* and *Good Times* through the 1970s and 1980s. Regular roles on two sitcoms provided wider recognition: Denise Nicholas' mother Luzelle in *Baby, I'm Back* in 1978 and the nosy neighbor Pearl Shay nearly a decade later in NBC's *227*.

In 1992, after more than fifty years as an actor, Helen Martin was inducted into the Black Filmmakers Hall of Fame.

GARY HOUSTON

McClendon, Rose (1884–1936)

While watching Rose McClendon descend the winding staircase in the opera *Deep River*, producer Arthur Hopkins whispered to Ethel Barrymore, "She can teach some of your most hoity-toity actresses distinction." Barrymore later remarked, "She can teach them *all* distinction."

Rose McClendon was born Rosalie Virginia Scott in Greenville, South Carolina, in 1884, the daughter of Sandy and Lena Jenkins Scott. Around 1890 the family moved to New York, where Rosalie attended public schools, and in 1904, she married Henry Pruden McClendon, a chiropractor who supplemented his income as a Pullman porter. During the early years of marriage, McClendon directed and acted in church plays and cantatas at Saint Mark's AME Church, but it was not until she received a scholarship to the American Academy of Dramatic Arts in 1916 that she devoted her life to theater.

Hailed by the *Afro-American* as the "Negro first lady of the dramatic stage" (July 18, 1936), her acting credits included *Justice* (1919); *Roseanne* (1926) with Charles Gilpin (and later with Paul Robeson); *Deep*

Called the "Negro first lady of the dramatic stage," Rose McClendon worked with artists such as Paul Robeson, Ethel Barrymore, and Langston Hughes. (MOORLAND-SPINGARN)

River (1926) with Jules Bledsoe; *In Abraham's Bosom* (1926), Paul Green's Pulitzer Prize–winning drama for which she received the *Morning Telegraph* Acting Award along with Ethel Barrymore and Lynn Fontanne the following year; *Porgy* (1927); *House of Connelly* (1931); *Black Soul* and *Never No More* (1932); *Brainsweat* and *Roll Sweet Chariot* (1934); *Panic*; and her last appearance, as Cora in *Mulatto* (1935), a role Langston Hughes created for her.

In the late 1920s, McClendon was a director for the Negro (Harlem) Experimental Theater and in the 1930s worked in a supervisory capacity with the Federal Theatre Project. It was she who suggested that separate Negro units be established "to insure the production of plays dramatizing black themes and exhibiting black talents."

McClendon always envisioned the establishment of a permanent "Negro theater" that produced plays dealing "with Negro problems, with phases of Negro life, faithfully presented and accurately delineated" —a theater that would not merely develop "an isolated Paul Robeson, or an occasional Bledsoe or Gilpin, but a long line of first-rate actors." Toward this end, she and Dick Campbell founded the Negro People's Theater in Harlem in 1935. Unfortunately, on July 12, 1936, Rose McClendon died of pneumonia. To keep her dreams alive, Dick Campbell and his wife, **Muriel Rahn**, organized the Rose McClendon Players. Later, in 1946, philanthropist Carl Van Vechten established the Rose McClendon Memorial Collection of Photographs of Distinguished Negroes at Yale and Harvard Universities.

ANNETTA JEFFERSON

McDaniel, Hattie (1895–1952)

Character actress Hattie McDaniel presents a troubling figure on the landscape of American race relations. On the one hand, she had a fruitful career in the competitive industry of Hollywood cinema in the 1930s and 1940s, an era when the star system that enshrined white stars created few opportunities for black talent. On the other hand, she became famous for portraying mammy-like figures and thus perpetuated one of the most hated stereotypes of black women. Her admirers could point to her commitment to her race in providing an example of success for black youth and, when she could, by making small improvements for black actors in the industry. It is almost impossible

to reconcile these two opinions because McDaniel was so firmly defined by a paradoxical nature.

Fittingly, her early life was rooted in contradiction. Hattie McDaniel, the youngest of thirteen children, was born on June 10, 1895, to Henry and Susan (Holbert) McDaniel. In spite of her later fame as a deep-southerner, McDaniel was not raised in the South (she later had to teach herself southern dialect for film roles). Her birthplace was Wichita, Kansas, and her family soon moved to Colorado, where she grew up. The McDaniels first lived in Fort Collins and in 1901, when Hattie was six, moved to

After winning the Academy Award for her portrayal of Mammy in Gone With the Wind, *Hattie McDaniel found herself playing similar roles in* Gone With the Wind *imitations, such as* Maryland *(1940) with Ben Carter.* (DONALD BOGLE)

Denver where they remained throughout her life.

Although certainly not completely free from racism, Denver at the turn of the century was a relatively liberal town. Schools were not segregated; in fact, McDaniel attended predominantly white public schools. McDaniel eventually dropped out of Denver's East High School in 1910 to perform in minstrel shows, a form of vaudeville performed by black entertainers playing stereotypical roles. One of the groups with which McDaniel performed was the Henry McDaniel Minstrel Show, which costarred two of her brothers, Sam and Otis. The troupe was headed by her father, who had frequently supported himself and his family through minstrel shows since his emancipation from slavery at age twenty-five.

After her father went into semiretirement in 1916, Hattie McDaniel went solo. At first, she toured the Southwest and the Pacific Northwest with fellow black entertainer Professor George Morrison and his orchestra, the Melody Hounds; then, in late 1924, while continuing to tour, she began to sing on Denver radio station KOA with the Melody Hounds. These successes led to extensive travel on the black entertainment circuit in the late 1920s.

She was booked as a blues singer primarily through the Theater Owners Booking Association (TOBA), an organization that launched the careers of many blues greats: **Bessie Smith, Ethel Waters, Ma Rainey, Ida Cox, Mamie Smith,** and **Alberta Hunter** all got their start on the TOBA circuit, which was infamous for cheating entertainers out of their hard-earned money and for giving them grueling schedules. As a result, TOBA came to be nicknamed "Tough on Black Asses." Nevertheless, the organization did provide the performers with food and shelter and a certain amount of job security. McDaniel even got the chance to sing some of her own compositions, such as "I Wish I Had Somebody," "Just One Sorrowing Heart," "Any Man Would Be Better Than You," and "BooHoo Blues."

McDaniel's personal life during this early period in her career was as heartbreaking as her music. In 1922, she married George Langford, but soon after the wedding he died, reportedly of a gunshot wound. McDaniel remained a widow for sixteen years. In addition, her father, Henry, also died that year at the age of eighty-two.

After the stock market crash of 1929, the TOBA circuit went bust, and McDaniel found herself without a job. She worked for a while in the washroom of the Club Madrid in Milwaukee, Wisconsin, until she got her big break singing there on a night when the club was short on entertainment. She proved popular and soon became one of the club's regular performers.

In 1931, McDaniel was persuaded by her brothers, Sam and Otis, to join them in Los Angeles, where they had relocated. She found a few jobs singing in choruses and appearing in uncredited bit parts in Hollywood movies, including *The Golden West* (1932). Every Friday, she performed on Los Angeles black radio station KNX's *Optimistic Do-Nut Hour* as Hi-Hat Hattie, a bossy maid. Ironically, because McDaniel was paid only $5 a week at KNX and $5 per movie appearance, she had to support herself as a maid.

In late 1932, McDaniel was finally cast in a role big enough to be credited. Her early films included Josef von Sternberg's *Blonde Venus* (1932), in which McDaniel appeared briefly as a protectress of bombshell fugitive

Marlene Dietrich. McDaniel also appeared in *I'm No Angel* (1933), which paired Mae West and Cary Grant. As with *The Golden West*, these roles were primarily servile-but-sassy types with exaggerated southern accents. There were simply no other roles available for large black women in Hollywood; as a result, McDaniel began to find herself in competition with a small group of women who collectively portrayed all of Hollywood's mammies and maids. The group included Ethel Waters and **Louise Beavers** (who forced herself to overeat so that she would appear more mammylike).

McDaniel's reputation grew throughout the mid-1930s, and she was contracted to play bigger parts: In *Judge Priest* (1934), Aunt Dilsey, Judge Priest's (Will Rogers) spiritual-singing servant; Mom Beck in the 1935 Shirley Temple vehicle, *The Little Colonel*, which glorified antebellum plantation life; Malena Burns in *Alice Adams* (1935), with Katharine Hepburn in the title role; Queenie in *Show Boat* (1936); Lizzie in *Can This Be Dixie?* (1936); and Hilda in *The Mad Miss Manton* (1938), starring Barbara Stanwyck. She also appeared in many *Our Gang* shorts. Thus, by the end of the decade, McDaniel had established herself as one of the most successful mammy/maids of all time. By 1939, she had more than fifty credits in feature films and shorts. In 1936 alone, she appeared in fourteen movies.

It is clear that McDaniel relished her fame. She was able to move into an upscale Los Angeles neighborhood, and she gave generous donations to several charities. She began to count many of her glamorous white costars as friends and enjoyed giving advice to fledgling black actors, choosing not to dwell on the unavailability of nonra-cist, nonstereotypical roles for them in Hollywood. Indeed, she outwardly dismissed any criticism of her success as a mammy figure, saying, "I'd rather play a maid than be one." The only setback in McDaniel's life during this period was a mysterious, virtually unrecorded marriage to Howard Hickman, which ended in 1938.

On December 6, 1938, McDaniel tested for a choice role: Mammy in *Gone With the Wind*, the well-publicized movie adaptation of Margaret Mitchell's best-selling novel. After much deliberation, producer David O. Selznick offered McDaniel a contract on January 27, 1939, disappointing dozens of other actresses who also had auditioned.

McDaniel found herself being paid $500 a week to participate in a film shoot that took months and achieved mythical status even as it was unfolding. The sets and costumes were elaborate, even by Hollywood standards. The film's stars, Vivien Leigh and Clark Gable, were enshrined in movie magazines. While the minutiae of the filming were eagerly followed by millions of Americans, however, few thought to question why McDaniel was called "Mammy" both on screen and on the set. So great was the appeal of *Gone With the Wind* to a white public that the voices of those who worried about the film's possible racist message were lost in the uproar. When at last the film was complete, Selznick made a decision that clearly delineated the low status of black actors in Hollywood. He forbade McDaniel and all of *Gone With the Wind*'s other black actors to attend the Atlanta premiere in December 1939. He was afraid their presence would anger Southerners. McDaniel, as usual, accepted this injustice without complaint.

Hattie McDaniel clearly relished the fame and financial success her film career brought her. She dismissed any criticism of her success as a mammy figure, saying "I'd rather play a maid than be one." (SCHOMBURG CENTER)

Except for a few critics who were outraged by the portrayal of black characters in the film, white Americans loved *Gone With the Wind*. Especially appealing was McDaniel's beturbaned Mammy scolding Scarlett O'Hara (Vivien Leigh) in voice-coached Georgia sass. When McDaniel won the Best Supporting Actress Oscar for the role, Mammy's status as an indelible figure in America's cultural psyche was assured. As for McDaniel, she saw the award, the first ever given to a black actor, as a victory not only for herself but also for the black community. "[The Oscar] makes me feel very

humble, and I shall hold it as a beacon for anything that I may be able to do in the future," McDaniel said as she accepted the award. "I sincerely hope that I shall always be a credit to my race and to the motion picture industry."

McDaniel's words proved prophetic. *Gone With the Wind* was the beacon—or perhaps the burden—for her future. Soon after the Oscar awards ceremony, McDaniel toured the country on a series of David O. Selznick-conceived, ill-attended tours targeted at black communities to promote *Gone With the Wind*. She promoted herself as Mammy incarnate, publishing recipes for "Mammy's fried chicken à la Maryland" and posing for photographs in which she happily gazed at her prized collection of mammy figurines. In addition, McDaniel's career for most of the 1940s consisted mainly of Mammyesque roles in *Gone With the Wind* imitations, such as *Maryland* (1940) and *The Great Lie* (1941). She also played cheerful mammy Aunt Tempey in *Song of the South* (1946), the undeniably racist Disney version of antebellum days. The Old South roles were otherwise alternated with modern versions of Mammy: sassy maid roles in watered-down retreads of screwball comedies such as *Affectionately Yours* (1941), *George Washington Slept Here* (1942), *Three Is a Family* (1944), and *Family Honeymoon* (1948).

One important exception to the string of mammy and maid parts was Minerva Clay, McDaniel's role in the 1941 movie *In This Our Life*, starring Bette Davis and Olivia de Havilland. The movie was the first to represent black characters who were not one-dimensional, smiling servants/slaves but complex characters who were unjustly forced to cope with racism. McDaniel's character, Minerva Clay, whose son is falsely accused of killing someone, sums up the movie's sentiment when she sighs, "Well, you know those policemen. They won't listen to what a colored boy says."

For McDaniel, the 1940s were otherwise defined by her troublesome relationship with the **National Association for the Advancement of Colored People**. Led by executive secretary Walter White, the NAACP attacked the core group of black actors who perpetuated servile stereotypes; Waters and Beavers were chastised for their portrayal of mammies, while Stepin Fetchit and Clarence Muse were blasted for Uncle Tom roles. Because of her Oscar, McDaniel was the most visible black actor and received the harshest criticism. In response to the NAACP's condemnation, McDaniel and her fellow actors formed their own group, the Fair Play Committee (FPC), which emphasized slow change in the movie industry. The FPC pointed out the actors' own small attempts at change, such as asking that the word *nigger* be removed from their scripts or refusing to speak in dialect. For White, these small efforts were not enough.

In addition to her woes with the NAACP, McDaniel's 1941–45 union with Lloyd Crawford, though by far the longest of her four marriages, proved troublesome. Crawford found himself in financial difficulty and resented McDaniel's star status. In 1944, McDaniel announced (at the age of forty-nine) that she was pregnant, and she even received baby gifts from her Hollywood friends. When McDaniel was later diagnosed as having a so-called false pregnancy, she was crushed and slipped into depression. Not long after, she and Crawford divorced.

When White's campaign died out, McDaniel moved on to playing the role of

Beulah, the maid on the extremely popular radio show of the same name starting in 1947. McDaniel's health had begun to decline, however, a development her biographer, Carlton Jackson, partially attributes to the harassment by the NAACP. Her four-month marriage (1949–50) to Larry Williams probably contributed as well. She suffered from weight loss and had a series of slight strokes and heart attacks. After each physical setback, she would recuperate and then go back to work. For example, in the summer of 1951 McDaniel prepared to replace archrival Ethel Waters on the ABC-TV version of *Beulah*, which had been airing since 1950. She shot six episodes before becoming ill; the six shows were never aired. During the first few months of 1952, McDaniel improved and even recorded a season's worth of *Beulah* on the radio, but in May it was revealed that she had breast cancer, and from then on she was too ill to perform. Hattie McDaniel died on October 26, 1952, at the Motion Picture Country Home and Hospital in Woodland Hills, California. She was fifty-seven years old.

SARAH P. MORRIS

McIntosh, Hattie (c. 1860–1919)

From minstrelsy to vaudeville to the Broadway stage, Hattie McIntosh was one of the first black women to make a profession of the theater.

Hattie McIntosh was born in Detroit around 1860. She first performed in 1884 in McIntosh and Sawyer's Colored Callender Minstrels. Her husband, Tom McIntosh, was part-owner of the company and one of the country's leading black showmen. At a time when there were few black women onstage, many were wives of performers and producers; it was considered somewhat more respectable for a woman to go onstage with her husband than alone. There was very real protection in marriage, as well, from the hardships and dangers of touring.

In the early 1890s, the McIntoshes created a vaudeville act called "Mr. and Mrs. McIntosh in the King of Bavaria." In the next few years, they performed with the three important companies that broke out of the minstrel format and included women in their casts as well as men. In 1894, their act played with Sam T. Jack's Creole Shows, and they joined the legendary Black Patti's Troubadours in 1896. After that, they toured with John Isham's Octoroons Company. Hattie McIntosh soon had a leading role in Isham's King Rastus Company.

After the turn of the century, Hattie McIntosh joined the Walker and Williams company, going to England in 1902 in *Dahomey*. Tom McIntosh died in 1904, and in 1905, Hattie was in Chicago, a member of Bob Mott's Pekin Theater Stock Company.

Bob Mott was a saloon owner who turned his saloon into a music hall in 1904. He built a new building in 1905 calling it the Pekin Theater. He then formed a stock company to perform at the Pekin; eventually the company also toured the East and Midwest. It is not clear how long McIntosh stayed at the Pekin, but in 1909 she was back with Bert Williams in *Mr. Lode of Koal*. That was her last performance with the musical comedy great. In about 1911, she formed a vaudeville team with another woman, Cordelia McClain.

McClain and McIntosh took their act to the Billy King Stock Company in 1912, which toured the South and then opened at the Grand Theater in Chicago in 1915 or 1916. McIntosh married Billy King the same year that she and McClain joined the company.

Hattie McIntosh died in Chicago in December of 1919.

KATHLEEN THOMPSON

McKee, Lonette (1956–)

No doubt about it: one of the best women's roles in American musical theater is Julie in *Show Boat*. The to-die-for "Bill" and the show-stopping "Can't Help Loving That Man" are her songs, for one thing, but beyond that, the character is beautifully written and has great emotional depth. *Show Boat* is set on a Mississippi riverboat in the 1880s, and Julie is a mixed-race singer who passes for white and loses everything when her secret is revealed. Since the show premiered in 1927, only one black woman has played her on Broadway: Lonette McKee—and she's done it twice.

McKee was born in Detroit in 1956 and grew up in a working-class neighborhood. Her father, an autoworker, was black; her mother, white. Although she felt like an outsider around other children, her home environment was loving and supportive. She was playing the piano and singing in public by the time she was eight. At fifteen, she dropped out of high school to pursue her career. Her mother pawned her wedding ring to pay McKee's fare to Los Angeles.

McKee made her TV debut as one of the Soul Sisters, singer-dancers on *The Wacky World of Jonathan Winters* in 1972. For that job, she agreed to darken her complexion with makeup. "I was too young to know not to do it," she said later. Her performance as Sister, the streetwise leader of a female singing group in the 1976 film *Sparkle*, brought her excellent reviews, as well as predictions that she would soon be a major star. These didn't come true, in part because of her "exotic" looks. She lost some roles to white actresses, and "for a couple of films they said, 'You're not black enough.' It feels horrible because I consider myself a black woman."

Still, there was work. Onstage, she played Julie on Broadway for the first time in 1983 in the Houston Grand Opera production and portrayed Jackie Robinson's wife in *The First* and Billie Holiday in a one-woman show, *Lady Day at Emerson's Bar and Grill*. She appeared on television in *Spenser: For Hire*, *Miami Vice*, *The Equalizer*, and the miniseries *Queen*. Her film credits include *'Round Midnight*, *The Cotton Club*, *Gardens of Stone*, and Spike Lee's *Jungle Fever* and *Malcolm X*. Her first album, *Natural Love*, for which she cowrote the songs, was released on Lee's label in 1992.

Then, during a dry spell when McKee sometimes had to scramble for the rent, producer-director Hal Prince cast her in *Show Boat*, a huge success and a personal triumph for McKee from the day it opened in 1994. Film offers and other opportunities quickly started to come in, but, McKee reminded an interviewer, "If you're black in this business, you know there's no one magic role. It's to be one challenge after the next." McKee loves animals and has a special passion for birds. She believes she can "feel what they feel and actually pick up their thoughts!" They are so important to her, in fact, that *Queen of the Birds* is the working title of the autobiographical novel she is writing.

INDIA COOPER

McKinney, Nina Mae (1913–1967)

The first African-American actress to make her name in the American cinema, Nina Mae McKinney also presents an archetype of the exploitation and oppression of African-American women in Hollywood. Born Nannie Mayme McKinney in Lancaster, South Carolina, McKinney was reared by her grandmother on the estate of Colonel LeRoy Sanders, where her family had worked for many generations. Her parents lived in New York City. When she was twelve, they sent for her, and she went to live in the city where, just four years later, she began her entertainment career.

Dancing in the chorus line of Lew Leslie's *Blackbirds*, she was spotted and cast in the role of Chick in the film *Hallelujah* (1929), directed by King Vidor. Some say that, in this role, McKinney originated the stereotype of the "black temptress" that has haunted African-American actresses from that day to the present. Critics described her characterization of Chick as "half woman, half child"—McKinney was only seventeen years old when she played the role. She was a beautiful young woman and, on the strength of her performance, she was given a five-year contract at Metro-Goldwyn-Mayer (MGM).

That five years was a time of frustration for the young actress: She was a leading lady in an industry that had no leading lady roles for an African-American woman. MGM did not know what to do with her. As a result, she was cast in only two films, *Safe in Hell* (1931) and *Reckless* (1935). Her parts in both films were small. In the latter, she also dubbed Jean Harlow's songs. When her contract ended, so did her career in Hollywood.

An actress and singer who was once called the "black Garbo," Nina Mae McKinney, right, was a victim of Hollywood exploitation and oppression. Her film debut, some claim, originated the stereotype of the "black temptress." Her last film was Pinky *(1949), which starred Jeanne Crain (left).* (SCHOMBURG CENTER)

In 1929, McKinney went to Europe. She toured with pianist Garland Wilson and sang in major nightclubs in Paris and London. Billed as the "Black Garbo," she was greeted with enthusiasm by European audiences. She twice starred with Paul Robeson: in the play *Congo Road* and in the English film *Sanders of the River* (1935). The former took her back to New York City for its Broadway premiere. Yet, her native country was still unprepared to offer McKinney a career. She appeared in several independent films, including *Pie Pie Blackbird* with Eubie Blake, and then returned to Europe in 1932.

Eight years later she returned to the United States. She married jazz musician Jimmy Monroe and toured the United States with her own band. She also appeared in a number of black-cast films. Her last film was *Pinky*, released in 1949.

McKinney died in New York City on May 3, 1967, at the age of fifty-four. In 1978, she was inducted into the Black Filmmakers Hall of Fame.

KATHLEEN THOMPSON

McNeil, Claudia (1917–1993)

Claudia McNeil was born in Baltimore, Maryland, on August 13, 1917, to Marvin Spencer McNeil and Annie Mae Anderson McNeil. Shortly after her birth, the family moved to New York City, where Claudia lived for most of her life. Annie McNeil was six feet four inches tall and an Apache Indian. She owned a grocery store and ran the household singlehandedly after telling her husband to leave. Claudia credits her mother as her inspiration for her acting successes, but as a young girl, her relationship with her mother was not always harmonious. At the age of twelve Claudia went to work for the Heckscher Foundation as a mother's helper. Through this position, she met the Toppers, a Jewish couple of Romanian descent, who later adopted her. She became fluent in Yiddish, a skill she would use years later to score a comedic coup as a

Claudia McNeil (second from the right) became a star in 1959 with her portrayal of Lena Younger in Lorraine Hansberry's groundbreaking play, A Raisin in the Sun. *The cast also included Sidney Poitier, Ruby Dee, and Diana Sands, who reprised their roles in the film version (1961).* (DONALD BOGLE)

stereotypical (well, almost) Jewish mother named Sarah Goldfine in Carl Reiner's farce *Something Different* (1967).

At the age of twenty, with $500 from the Toppers, McNeil set out to become a professional singer. Her first job, at the Black Cat in Greenwich Village, paid $13.50 a week. Soon she moved on to bigger and better engagements, such as vocalist for the **Katherine Dunham** Dance Troupe on its tour of South America. She sang in vaudeville and nightclubs for years before acting on the advice of **Ethel Waters**; so, in her thirties, she landed her first Broadway role as a replacement in *The Crucible* in 1953.

Langston Hughes asked her to audition for his play *Simply Heavenly* (1957), based on his "Simple Takes a Wife" and other "Simple" stories. She won critical acclaim as Mami in *Simply Heavenly*, and two years later solidified her critical and popular appeal with her success in **Lorraine Hansberry**'s *A Raisin in the Sun* (1959). As Lena Younger, McNeil played a widow who mediates among the feuding factions in her family and leads them to take the first step toward integrating a lily-white Chicago suburb. She repeated the role in the 1961 film version as well.

Claudia McNeil became a star with her portrayal on stage and screen of the powerful, God-fearing matriarch. She so strongly identified with this role that she said, "There was a time when I acted the role. . . . Now I live it." She went on to play the part of Mama in Peter S. Feibleman's *Tiger, Tiger, Burning Bright* (1962), based on his novel *A Place Without Twilight*. Again, she received widespread praise, as well as a Tony nomination, for her acting.

In 1965, McNeil toured abroad as Sister Margaret in James Baldwin's *The Amen Corner*, performing in Paris, Israel, Edinburgh, and London, where she received the London Critics Poll award as Best Actress. After *Something Different* (1967), she played Ftatateeta in *Her First Roman* (1968), an expensive musical flop based on George Bernard Shaw's *Caesar and Cleopatra*, and starring **Leslie Uggams** (McNeil's roommate for a time) and Richard Kiley. She then played Mrs. Devereaux, a tenant in a Brooklyn tenement, in John Golden's *Wrong Way Light Bulb* (1969) and starred in two of the three one-act plays in Ted Shine's *Contributions* (1970).

Claudia McNeil acted in several films, beginning with *The Last Angry Man* (1959), starring Paul Muni, on television in the 1950s, and again in the 1970s when she acted on television more than in any other medium. She performed in such television productions as *The Member of the Wedding* (DuPont Show of the Month, 1958), *Do Not Go Gentle Into That Good Night* (CBS Playhouse, 1967), and *To Be Young, Gifted, and Black* (NET Playhouse, 1972). She was nominated for an Emmy Award for an episode of *The Nurses* in 1963.

She retired in 1983 and in 1985 moved into the Actors' Fund Nursing Home in Englewood, New Jersey, where she died of complications related to diabetes in 1993.

JOEL BERKOWITZ

McQueen, Butterfly (1911–1995)

Butterfly McQueen achieved fame primarily as a film actress in the 1940s. Noted for portraying seemingly dimwitted domestics prone to outbursts of hysteria, she elevated that convention to something approaching an art form with her first motion picture role as the slave, Prissy, in *Gone With the Wind*

The slave Prissy in the film Gone With the Wind *speaks the controversially immortal line,*
"Lawdy, Miz Scarlett, I don't know nuthin' 'bout birthin' babies!" Decades later, the actress
who played her, Butterfly McQueen, said about that type of role, "I didn't mind being funny,
but I didn't like being stupid." Her integrity by and large cost her a career in Hollywood.
(DONALD BOGLE)

(1939). In later years, she devoted herself to volunteer work with youth in Harlem.

She was born Thelma McQueen on January 8, 1911, in Tampa, Florida, the only child of a stevedore and a cleaning woman. She attended grammar school in Augusta, Georgia, and graduated from a Long Island, New York, high school where she was able to cultivate her interests in music and dance. She studied ballet with Mabel Hunt and modern dance with Venezuela Jones in the latter's Negro Youth Project. In a production of *A Midsummer Night's Dream* at City College of New York, she danced in the "Butterfly Ballet" and thus acquired her stage name. After a brief stint with the Federal Theatre Project, she made her Broadway debut in George Abbott's *Brown Sugar* in 1937; although the revue closed after only three days, McQueen received good critical notices. She went on to play in several other productions, including *Swingin' the Dream*, a Benny Goodman–Louis Armstrong collaboration. The musical brought her to the attention of David O. Selznick, producer of *Gone With the Wind*.

McQueen won excellent reviews for her labors in the classic Civil War epic, although, in retrospect, many African Americans regretted some of the excesses of the performance. Malcolm X, for example, recalled feeling both anger and shame the first time he saw Prissy on screen. In fairness to McQueen, however, it is important to note that she herself regarded Prissy as backward and that, on the set, she resisted offensive characterizations and situations. For instance, she refused to eat watermelon in one scene, and only after registering her displeasure did she submit to the scene in which Scarlett O'Hara (played by Vivien Leigh) slaps her in the face upon hearing her tearful confession, "Lawdy, Miz Scarlett, I don't know nuthin' 'bout birthin' babies!" Then, too, *Time* magazine cited the "sly humor" McQueen brought to the role: Although obliged to scream, "De Yankees is comin'!" as Sherman approaches Atlanta, Prissy also quietly sings to herself, "Jes' a few mo' days ter tote de wee-ry load." (According to historian Thomas Cripps, her casual reading material between takes included critics George Jean Nathan and Alexander Woollcott.)

McQueen's subsequent screen appearances constituted, for the most part, variations on the Prissy theme; she reprised squeaky-voiced foolish maids, for example, in *Affectionately Yours* (1941), *Mildred Pierce* (1945), and *Duel in the Sun* (1947). As Peter Nobel observed in *The Negro in Films* (1970), McQueen was fated "to act stereotypes or starve." In a sense, she decided to starve. To protest the lines she was asked to speak as a colored servant on Jack Benny's radio program, she walked out of the studio, and when she declined similar motion picture assignments, casting agents boycotted her for more than a year. The actress retired from films in 1947. "I didn't mind playing a maid the first time because I

In 1975, at the age of sixty-four, Butterfly McQueen earned a college degree. She immersed herself in various social welfare projects, and when this photo was taken in the early 1980s, she was working with black and Hispanic students in Harlem, primarily at Public School 153. "They're my children and I love them all." (SCHOMBURG CENTER)

thought that was how you got into the business," she told an interviewer decades later. "But after I did the same thing over and over, I resented it. I didn't mind being funny, but I didn't like being stupid." For a brief period in the early 1950s she played Oriole, the dizzy neighbor on the television series *Beulah,* but then she left Hollywood altogether. From the standpoint of her acting career, the next twenty-five years were not encouraging; she held menial jobs more often than not.

During this time, McQueen returned to Augusta, took a course in nursing at the Georgia Medical School, and managed Les Belles, a community service club for black children. Relocating in a one-room apartment in New York, she enrolled as an undergraduate at City College of New York (CCNY) and, in 1975, at the age of sixty-four, earned a bachelor of arts with a major in Spanish. She then immersed herself in various social welfare projects, such as the Mount Morris Marcus Garvey Recreational Center. From the early 1980s, she worked with black and Hispanic students in Harlem, primarily at Public School 153. "They're my children," McQueen, who never married, stated, "and I love them all."

Although she was lauded, in 1989, at the fiftieth anniversary celebration of the release of *Gone With the Wind,* movie offers remained infrequent; she played small roles in *Amazing Grace* in 1974 and *The Mosquito Coast,* starring Harrison Ford, in 1986. Occasionally, she performed in churches, singing, dancing, signing autographs, and talking about the making of *Gone With the Wind.* (She had an abiding fondness for Clark Gable.) In 1978, she wrote, produced, and starred in a bilingual one-act play, *Tribute to Mary Bethune,* in Washington, D.C.

For every bit of acting she ever did, Butterfly McQueen received uniformly fine reviews; had she come along a generation or so later, she might have enjoyed great artistic and commercial success, but fate and the historical calendar mitigated against her. For her stand against racist stereotyping, she was in effect punished by the Hollywood establishment and never recovered. This unfortunate turn in a promising career was the result of McQueen's decision to live by her principles. The children of Public School 153 no doubt loved her all the more because of it.

She died on December 23, 1995, in Augusta, Georgia, of burns suffered when a kerosene heater in her one-bedroom cottage just outside Augusta caught fire.

THOMAS J. KNOCK

Miller, May (1899–1995)

May Miller was one of the most outstanding black female playwrights of the Harlem Renaissance. She was also the most widely published black woman playwright of her era. Of her fifteen plays, nine were published; many of them were staged at numerous colleges and little-theater groups throughout the country.

May Miller was born January 26, 1899, in Washington, D.C. One of five children born to Kelly and Annie May Miller, she grew up on **Howard University**'s campus, where her father was a prominent professor and dean. Kelly Miller's position as a nationally recognized sociologist and educator put him in close social and political contact with many eminent black Americans. He was also a published poet, and his creative and oratorical skills influenced the young May. She attended the M Street School (later Dunbar High School), where she studied under playwrights **Mary P. Burrill** and **Angelina Grimké**. Under Burrill's tutelage, Miller was encouraged to write her first play, *Pandora's Box*, published in 1914. She graduated from Dunbar High School in 1916 and entered Howard University that same year, where she continued to develop her dramatic writing skills through the Howard Drama Club. Academically at the head of her class, she earned a B.A. in 1920; in recognition of her abilities, Howard University awarded Miller a playwright's award for best play for *Within the Shadows*, making her the first Howard student to win such an award.

The 1920s and 1930s were Miller's most prolific and productive years. After graduating from Howard University, she taught drama, speech, and dance at the Frederick Douglass High School in Baltimore. While in Baltimore, she wrote most of her plays. Miller was among those enriched by poet/playwright **Georgia Douglas Johnson**'s "S Street Salon," which was a gathering place at Johnson's Washington, D.C., home for writers to share their works. Miller commuted on weekends to S Street, where she cultivated an array of friendships among such writers as Langston Hughes, Carter G. Woodson, Willis Richardson, and **Zora Neale Hurston**. During the summer months, Miller studied playwriting at Columbia University under the prominent theater scholar Frederick Koch.

In 1925, her play *The Bog Guide* placed third in the Urban League's *Opportunity* contest. *Opportunity* also awarded her an honorable mention the next year for *The Cuss'd Thing*. During the 1930s, Miller wrote history plays to educate her students at Douglass High School. In 1935, she collaborated with and contributed four plays

An outstanding playwright of the Harlem Renaissance, May Miller focused in her works on social and political issues. Unlike most of her contemporaries, who wrote for all-black casts, Miller often included white characters as a way to deal with racial issues of the day. (MOORLAND-SPINGARN)

to playwright Willis Richardson on *Negro History in Thirteen Plays*, an anthology that dramatized the lives of black heroes and heroines that earned national recognition.

Like many of the black women writers of the 1920s and 1930s, Miller's plays focused on social and political issues. Her work stands out from that of other black women because she dared to venture from the home, and in several plays she incorporated white characters in major roles while most of her contemporaries utilized an all-black cast. She did this as an effective method of dealing with the racial issues of the time.

In 1943, Miller wrote her last play *Freedom's Children on the March*, and retired from the Baltimore school system and began to focus on writing poetry. She lived in Washington, D.C., with her husband, John

Sullivan, a high school principal whom she had married in 1940.

Miller's career as a poet is just as outstanding and expansive as her life as a playwright. In Washington, D.C., in 1943, she joined a poetry workshop conducted by Inez Boulton. Miller's poetry speaks of humanist issues; like her plays, her poetry poses the moral questions that confront a society without humanist values. Her poems have been published in many periodicals, anthologies, and journals; she has conducted readings throughout the Washington, D.C., area.

In 1986, May Miller won the Mister Brown Award (William Brown was manager of the African Company in New York from 1816 to 1823) for Excellence in Drama and Poetry, an award sponsored by the National Conference of African-American Theater. There has been a resurgence in the production and publication of her plays in the 1990s. Miller died in her Washington, D.C., home on February 8, 1995.

KATHY A. PERKINS

Mills, Florence (1896–1927)

Florence Mills, the leading black American musical-comedy singer and dancer of the Jazz Age and the Harlem Renaissance, was born January 25, 1896, in Washington, D.C., to John Winfree and Nellie (Simons) Winfree. She died from paralytic ileus and peritonitis in New York City on November 1, 1927.

Born in slavery in Amherst County, Virginia, the Winfrees migrated to Washington from Lynchburg because of economic depression in the tobacco industry where both were employed. They settled first in a middle-class neighborhood on K Street, where

Florence as born, but were soon forced to move to Goat Alley, one of the capital's most poverty-stricken, unhealthy, and crime-ridden black slums. John Winfree worked sporadically as a day laborer, and Nellie Winfree took in laundry to keep their family together. Both were illiterate, and even in a city with unusual opportunities for people of color, their prospects and futures were limited.

"Baby Florence," however, demonstrated early her extraordinary gifts for singing and dancing and as young as age three appeared at local theater amateur hours, where she won prizes. She was even invited to entertain the British ambassador, Lord Poncefort, and his guests. The child received public recognition that no doubt contributed to her developing sense of self-worth, and she became an important source of her family's income, which imbued her with a profound sense of responsibility for those around her.

The high point of Mills' childhood occurred in 1903 when she appeared as an extra attraction in the road-company production of Bert Williams and George Walker's *Sons of Ham*, where she sang, "Miss Hannah from Savannah." She was taught the song by **Aida Overton Walker**, the great cakewalk dancer and ragtime singer who had sung it in the original show. Walker was a beautiful, sophisticated, and highly talented star who took time with a ghetto child, thereby becoming Mills' mentor and role model. Walker demonstrated that blacks with ability and determination could find a successful vocation in entertainment.

As a result of her abilities, Mills was hired at about age eight by the traveling white vaudeville team of Bonita and Hearn, entertainers who used her as a singing and dancing "pickaninny" in their routine. Mills may well have felt both gratitude for the opportunity to work on the stage and support her family as well as resentment at the crude exploitation.

At age fourteen, Mills and her sisters Maude and Olivia organized their own traveling song-and-dance act as the Mills Sisters. They played East Coast black vaudeville houses and received good notices in the black press for their lively performances. Sometimes dressed in male attire, Florence Mills specialized in traditional ballads and the popular tunes of the day. In 1912, she contracted a brief marriage with James Randolph.

Just before World War I, Mills found herself in Chicago, weary of long hours, low pay, and the difficult traveling conditions all blacks faced. She decided to move from vaudeville to cabaret and through **Ada "Bricktop" Smith** obtained a job at the notorious Panama Cafe on State Street. In the heart of the South Side's honky-tonk and red-light district, the Panama was a black-and-tan club well known for sexual liaisons across the color line.

With Bricktop, Cora Green, and varying others, Mills formed the Panama Trio, a singing group with the legendary Tony Jackon on piano. This was an exciting time in Chicago: the city was the center of black migration from the rural South, and the white gangsters who controlled the cabarets in the black community fostered the new jazz music and an open social environment. "Respectable" people, both black and white, however, perceived the Panama as a center of vice, and it was finally closed down.

Mills returned to vaudeville and joined the Tennessee Ten, a traveling black show then on the Keith circuit. A member of the troupe was Ulysses "Slow Kid" Thompson, an acrobatic, tap, and "rubber legs" dancer of considerable skill. Born in Arkansas in 1888, Thompson had spent his life in various circuses, carnivals, medicine, and minstrel shows. He and Mills became romantically involved, were married, and established a devoted relationship that lasted until her death.

The connection with Thompson and the success of the Tennessee Ten brought Mills closer to the center of show business than she had been in cabaret and vaudeville. She was singing at Barron's Club in Harlem when she received an offer that moved her into public notice and the front rank of black entertainers. It was the opportunity to replace Gertrude Sanders as the lead in *Shuffle Along*.

Shuffle Along opened off-Broadway in New York in the spring of 1921. Music and lyrics were composed by Noble Sissle and Eubie Blake, and the book was written by Flournoy E. Miller and Aubrey Lyles. It was an instantaneous and total hit. Actually, there was little new about *Shuffle Along*; similar shows had existed in the black entertainment world for years; what was new was the discovery by white America of the zesty abandon of jazzy music and fast, high-stepping black dancing. Langston Hughes believed that *Shuffle Along* even initiated the Harlem Renaissance and inaugurated the decade when "the Negro was in vogue."

Besides reintroducing blacks into mainstream musical theater and setting the rhythmic beat for the roaring twenties, *Shuffle Along* presented Mills to a national audience. Now twenty-six years old, she was a dainty woman, five-feet-four, never weighing much more than 100 pounds, and bronze colored with beautiful skin texture. She moved deftly and in her strange high voice sang "I'm Simply Full of Jazz" and "I'm Craving for That Kind of Love."

The critics could never quite describe Mills' voice with its curious breaks, soft accents, sudden molten notes, and haunting undertones. Birdlike and flutelike were among the reviewers' frequently used adjectives. It was Mills' dancing, however, and the dancing in all the black shows spawned by *Shuffle Along* during the 1920s that completely stunned audiences. The jazz rhythms, accelerated pace, skilled precision, intricate steps, and uninhibited movement brought dance rooted in African-American folk culture to white audiences eager to break loose from restrained and respectable convention.

Mills' performances were memorable, too, for her charismatic effectiveness in presentation. Demure and modest personally and in her private life, onstage she was assured, vivacious, and as capable of intimate mutual interaction with her audiences as a black preacher. With her fey and fragile

So popular was the musical-comedy star Florence Mills during the Jazz Age that 150,000 people jammed the streets of Harlem for her funeral in 1927. (RICHARD NEWMAN)

appearance, she could be intense as well as melancholy, could communicate imprudence as well as pathos, and be risqué without being vulgar. Mills' popularity, however, did not mean that race and racism were no longer realities; Irving Berlin said if he could find a white woman who could put over a song like Mills, he would be inspired to write a hit a week.

Anticipating a fad for black entertainment and entertainers, white promoter Lew Leslie, hired Mills and Kid Thompson to appear nightly after *Shuffle Along* at the Plantation Club, a remodeled night spot over the Winter Garden Theater. The Plantation's decor included an imitation log cabin, a chandelier in the form of a watermelon slice, and black mammy cooking waffles. Featuring Mills, the revenue itself was a constellation of black talent: Will Vodery's orchestra, Johnny Dunn's cornet, Edith Wilson's double-entendre songs, and visiting performers such as Paul Robeson.

The Plantation was "the first high-class colored cabaret on Broadway." It drew fashionable white clientele and helped create an accepting atmosphere for things black, though old stereotypical images died hard. Florence Mills left *Shuffle Along* to work full time for Leslie, a mutually beneficial relationship that lasted throughout her career. Also, the Plantation established the format for Mills' and Leslie's future shows: unconnected singing and dancing and musical acts in the vaudeville style with a touch of minstrelsy, and with all black performers.

Leslie soon realized his nightclub production could be turned into a Broadway show. The *Plantation Review* opened at the Forty-eighth Street Theater on July 22, 1922. Sheldon Brooks presided as master of ceremonies and did a comedy routine; otherwise the bill was the same as the club's. Audiences and reviewers were impressed with the cast's genuineness and enthusiasm and the show's buoyant spontaneity, especially the breathtaking dancing. It was all "strutting and stepping and syncopating," said the New York *Tribune*.

The *Plantation Review* was important for Mills for it was here that she was first seen by the New York critics. They liked her energy and vitality, her sinuous dancing, and her lack of self-consciousness. She sang Irving Berlin's "Some Sunny Day" and led the Six Dixie Vamps in a "Hawaiian Night in Dixie Land" dance number. There was some criticism of her song "I've Got What It Takes But It Breaks My Heart to Give It Away," not quite the sweet, crooning number that was her specialty. But there was real appreciation for the authenticity of black song and dance, and the realization that black portrayals by blackface performers such as Al Jolson and Eddie Cantor were only imitations of the real thing.

With *Shuffle Along* and the *Plantation Review* behind her, Mills emerged as a preeminent black female performer with the potential of breaking into the racially restricted preserves of establishment show business. America was not ready for such a bold move, but the British impresario Sir Charles B. Cochran was looking for ready-made attractions for the London stage. He made arrangements to take the Plantation company to the Pavilion in the spring of 1923. There were immediate problems. British entertainers strenuously objected, citing the competition for jobs but reinforcing that fear with color prejudice. "Nigger Problem Brought to London" ran the headline of one of Hannen Swaffer's articles in the *Daily Graphic*.

The show Cochran devised was a hybrid called *Dover Street to Dixie*. A mild comedy with an all-English cast, "Dover Street" constituted the first half and was totally unrelated to "Dixie," the second half, which was Mills and the Plantation cast in a variation of their standard routines. Prejudice against the visiting black Americans had escalated, and demonstrations were expected in the theater on opening night. Tension intensified because "Dover Street" was a disaster and the audience was restless and bored.

"Dixie" began with a fast number by Vodery's orchestra, featuring a troupe of frantic dancers and Edith Wilson belting out a song. Then Mills quietly made her entrance and in a small plaintive voice sang "The Sleeping Hills of Tennessee." She electrified the audience. Any threat of opposition vanished, and for the rest of that night and the remainder of the show's run, she received a fervent ovation *before* every song she sang. This was a tribute, Cochran said, he had never known London to give to any other performer.

Perhaps the most significant consequence of *Dover Street to Dixie* was the serious attention it was paid by British intellectuals. The essence of their response was that Mills' performance and that of her fellow black Americans was art—even high art—and not mere entertainment. One reviewer made the astonishing statement that Mills was "by far the most artistic person London has ever had the good fortune to see." Constant Lambert, musical director of Sadler's Wells Ballet, was deeply inspired by Mills and "Dixie" and began to adapt jazz rhythms and techniques to his work, narrowing the separation between popular and "serious" music and infusing the latter with new vitality.

Upon her return to New York, Mills received an unusual invitation—to appear as an added attraction in the *Greenwich Village Follies* annual production, opening that autumn at the Winter Garden. With Bert Williams' death the previous year, there were now no blacks in mainstream shows. This was the first time a black woman was offered a part in a major white production. The *Follies* cast responded by threatening to walk out. Even after management smoothed their feelings, the white cast continued to resent Mills' participation.

Mills' talent and popularity brought an even more extraordinary opportunity. Florenz Ziegfeld offered her a contract to join the *Ziegfeld Follies*, the country's leading musical revue and the apex of show-business success, but Mills turned Ziegfeld down. She decided to stay with Lew Leslie and create a rival show—but with an all-black cast. Bert Williams had broken the color barrier as an individual, she said, but she could best serve the race not by merely following him herself but by providing a venue for an entire company.

Mills wanted to break through Broadway's racial restrictions *and* to create an opportunity for black American entertainers to demonstrate the uniqueness of their culture. Her decision, and what she meant by it, was not lost on the black community. The *Amsterdam News* said:

> Loyalty of Florence Mills to the race as against temptation to become a renowned star of an Anglo-Saxon musical extravaganza has saved for the stage and the race what promises to be one of the most distinctive forms of American entertainment ever created—an All-Colored revue.

The first step toward Mills' goal was *From Dixie to Broadway*, which opened at the Broadhurst Theater in October 1924. A black musical comedy in the heart of Broadway had been the dream of black entertainers since the turn of the century, and it was now realized. The price for this acceptance was a certain modification of the show's black elements by the whites who controlled the production, but the cast's superactive energy and expressive power broke through, and the show was a critical and popular hit.

The cooperative effort between black and whites set a pattern for "crossovers" from the black entertainment milieu to the larger, more lucrative, and more influential white world. This resulted in a minimum of traditional "darky" stage imagery. Some critics missed this absence, but the reviewers could only applaud the vital black American style and exuberant tempo, which was now more free from racist stereotypes.

In *From Dixie to Broadway*, Mills sang "Dixie Dreams," "Mandy, Make Up Your Mind," and the song that became her theme and trademark, "I'm a Little Blackbird Looking for a Bluebird"; behind the song's sentimentality, Mills saw a subliminal message: "the struggle of a race" seeking satisfaction. Most critics thought the show's high point was its satirical jazz treatment of Balieffe's "March of the Wooden Soldiers," in which Mills led the male dancers.

Mills clearly dominated *From Dixie to Broadway,* and the reviewers lauded her as "a slender streak of genius" and "an artist in jazz." Writing in the *New York Telegram and Evening Mail*, Gilbert W. Gabriel gives a fuller picture of the Florence Mills who captured Broadway, as well as revealing his inability to comprehend the distinctive black American elements in her art:

This sensational little personality, slim, jaunty, strung on fine and tremulous wires, continues to tease the public's sense of the beautiful and odd. There is an impudent fragility about her, a grace of grotesqueness, a humor of wrists, ankles, pitching hips and perky shoulders that are not to be resisted. Her voice continues to be sometimes sweet and sometimes further from the pitch than Dixie is from Broadway. She is an exotic done in brass.

After the show's road tour, Mills broke another racial barrier. On June 27, 1924, she was the first black woman to headline at "the Taj Mahal of vaudeville," the Palace Theater. On Broadway at Forty-seventh Street, the Palace was the country's premier variety theater, and it was every entertainer's dream to play there. Other blacks had been in Palace programs, but as a headliner, Mills received money, billing, the best dressing room, and courtesy from management—real and symbolic achievements for a black American woman.

Mills achieved her great goal of creating a major all-black revue, but she was destined never to return to Broadway. The new show was *Blackbirds*, and it opened at the Alhambra Theater in Harlem after having been constructed at Plantation Club performances. After successful runs in Harlem and Paris, *Blackbirds of 1926* moved to London's Pavilion Theater, opening September 26 and lasting for an impressive 276 performances, after which it toured the British provinces.

Blackbirds was an extraordinary hit. Mills sang "Silver Rose" and repeated "I'm a Little Blackbird." She was so popular that she became to London what **Josephine Baker** was to Paris. The prince of Wales saw *Blackbirds* more than 20 times and Mills played to him when he was in the theater. She and the cast were taken up by England's ultrasophisticated "Bright Young People" and joined their outrageous parties in London, Oxford, and Cambridge.

Mills is mentioned in all the diaries of the period and even turns up as a character in Evelyn Waugh's *Brideshead Revisited*. It is likely that she had an affair with the King's youngest son, the handsome, wild, and charming Prince George, who later became Duke of Kent. It was not only royalty and decadent aristocrats who were impressed, however; artists and intellectuals caught the infectious freedom and style of the black performers and the energizing tempo of their music and dance. "For the first time," exclaimed critic Arnold Haskell, "I was *seeing* true jazz."

Perhaps because she felt more secure in a less racially prejudiced country or perhaps because the British public and press treated her more seriously than the American public and press did, Mills expressed her race consciousness more strongly in England than at home. At an exclusive dinner party where she was lauded by Sir Charles Cochran as a great artist, she ignored his personal tributes in her response and instead made a moving plea for black freedom. "I am coal black and proud of it," *Variety* quoted her as announcing at a fashionable soiree where there was some question about black and white seating arrangements.

Mills saw her work as a crusade on behalf of racial justice and understanding, literally believing that every white person pleased by her performance was a friend won for the race. Her passion led her to drive herself without respite, and it broke her health. She left *Blackbirds* and after an unsuccessful attempt at a rest cure in Germany sailed for

New York. Her condition did not improve, however, and she entered the Hospital for Joint Diseases, where she died following an operation. She was thirty-one years old.

Mills was one of the most popular people in Harlem during the 1920s. Blacks understood that she had never forgotten her roots, that she never put on airs, and that she affirmed over and over again the heritage —and the struggle—they shared together. In appreciation for everything she meant to them, the people of Harlem gave her the grandest funeral within their considerable power; it was an outpouring of affection and recognition, music and flowers, tears and drama.

On a cold November day in 1927 a congregation of 5,000, a choir of 600, and an orchestra of 200 jammed Mother African Methodist Episcopal Church on 137th Street. More than 150,000 people crowded the Harlem streets to glimpse the famous mourners and to participate in a bit of history—but mostly to pay their own silent tributes and say good-bye to a sister they knew was their own. It is reported that a flock of blackbirds flew over the funeral cortege as it slowly made its way up Seventh Avenue toward Woodlawn Cemetery in the Bronx.

The public tributes were lavish. In an unprecedented editorial, the *New York Times* praised "the slim dancer who blazed the way" for others to follow. George Jean Nathan called her "America's foremost feminine player." Theophilus Lewis said Mills "always regarded herself as our envoy to the world at large, and she was probably the best one we ever had." One London newspaper commented that if Mills had been a white woman, she would have been acknowledged as one of the greatest artists of her time.

Except among the cognoscenti and in black folk legend, Mills did not achieve permanent fame. Plans for a memorial fizzled in disputes over money. There were no films or recordings to perpetuate her memory. The Great Depression of 1929 abruptly rang down the curtain on the vim and verve of the Jazz Age. Lew Leslie tried to continue the *Blackbirds* series, which was her dream for celebrating authentic black American performing art, but the effort faded without Mills' vibrant and vivacious presence.

Mills made her mark in several ways. *Shuffle Along* introduced jazz song-and-dance to Broadway musical theater. In *From Dixie to Broadway,* she starred in a black revenue built around female singing and dancing rather than traditional male blackface comedy. In *Blackbirds,* she created a major show composed of vital black American music and movement. She helped minimize the "darky" element in show business, while bringing special black qualities to her crossover numbers. Through it all, Florence Mills was first and foremost a "race woman" proud of her heritage, uncompromising in her identity, and always using her artistry to build bridges to the white world in the hope of securing greater justice for her people.

RICHARD NEWMAN

Mitchell, Abbie (1884–1960)

In 1929, while performing in Chicago with Helen Hayes in *Coquette,* Abbie Mitchell said, "All my work as an actress has been done with my singing in my mind." Despite the numerous roles she played on and off Broadway, Mitchell was first and foremost a singer.

Born on New York's Lower East Side in 1884 to a musically inclined African-American mother and a German-Jewish father, Abbie Mitchell was early discovered to be a prodigy. After completing her public school training in Baltimore, she returned to New York in 1897 to study voice with Harry L. Burleigh and to audition for *Clorindy, the Origin of the Cakewalk.* Recognizing her unusual talent, lyricist Paul Laurence Dunbar and composer Will Marion Cook cast her in their musical. A year later, Mitchell married Cook and in 1899 was given the principal role in the next Dunbar-Cook collaboration, *Jes Lak White Folks.*

In 1903, she was cast in *In Dahomey,* a Bert Williams–George Walker production written by Jesse Shipp. After playing in New York, the company moved to London's Shaftesbury Theater. While in London, Edward VII invited the company to perform at a birthday celebration for the Prince of Wales. When the king noted that Abbie Mitchell was not there, he sent his private coach for her so that he could hear her sing "Brownskin Baby Mine," the song she had made famous.

Back in New York, Mitchell became immersed in the theatrical life centered at the Marshall Hotel on West Fifty-third Street. She joined the Memphis Students, a playing, singing, and dancing group that opened at Proctor's Twenty-third Street Theater and played at Hammerstein's Victoria Theater and the Roof Garden in New York, the Olympia in Paris, the Palace Theater in London, and the Schumann Circus in Berlin.

Between 1904 and 1912, in addition to giving recitals, Mitchell appeared in *The Southerner* (1904) and *Bandanna Land* (another Williams and Walker show, 1908) and sang the lead in *The Red Moon,* which later

King Edward VII of England once sent his private carriage for Abbie Mitchell so that he could hear her sing "Brownskin Baby Mine," the song this theatrical performer made famous. (SCHOMBURG CENTER)

was performed for Czar Nicholas II of Russia. Beginning in 1912, a throat ailment prevented Mitchell from singing for a few years, during which time she became involved with the **Lafayette Players**, a Harlem theater company, as a lead actress until she left for Paris to study voice with Jean de Reszke and de Reszke's famous teacher, Szbrilla. She performed in concert throughout Europe, singing French classics, German lieder, and Negro folk songs.

When Mitchell returned to America, she appeared in *In Abraham's Bosom* at the Provincetown Theater (1926), *The House of*

Shadows (1927), and *Coquette* in Chicago (1929). Two years later, she accepted the position of head of the voice department at Tuskegee Institute. However, her work at Tuskegee did not prevent her from singing in concert. She appeared at Town Hall in New York City on November 22, 1931, and at the Mecca Temple and Aeolian Opera Company in *Cavalleria Rusticana* in 1934. That same year, she also appeared as Binnie in *Stevedore* and in 1939 as Addie in Lillian Hellman's *The Little Foxes*.

On March 16, 1960, Abbie Mitchell died in Harlem Hospital. She was survived by her son, Mercer Cook, and three grandchildren. Her husband had died in 1944, her daughter in 1950.

ANNETTA JEFFERSON

Monk, Isabell (1952–)

"I have exactly what I always wanted," says Isabell Monk of her life as a member of the Guthrie Theater's acting ensemble. "There's no difference between my life and my craft."

Isabell Monk, one of the most respected actors in American regional theater, was born in 1952 in Indianhead, Maryland, and grew up on a farm that lacked all the modern conveniences, including running water. It was a very hard life. "I'm fortunate to be alive," says Monk. "A lot of people I grew up with aren't." Indeed, Monk's mother died at the age of thirty-six, when Isabell was eighteen.

Monk herself escaped from Indianhead when she received a scholarship to Towson State University. There, she fell in love with acting and revealed a talent under the direction of Paul Berman. She resolved to go on to Yale's drama school, but the first time she applied she wasn't accepted. Instead, she got a job in a program sponsored by the state of Maryland. She toured schools around the state with a troupe of actors. The next year, the troupe was disbanded, so she collaborated with a fellow actor on a one-woman show called *We Ain't What We Was*. Playing a 300-year-old woman, Monk told stories about being black in America. The show was brought to the attention of PBS, which bought a part of it for an hour-long broadcast, for which Monk won a public television award.

Monk tried stand-up comedy next in New York and Los Angeles, but decided she it really wasn't for her. She returned to Maryland, worked as a teacher for two years to pay off student loans, and applied to Yale again. This time, going to the university to audition, she arrived at the New Haven railroad station in a blizzard and couldn't get a taxi; so she walked through the snow, arriving to find that the auditions had been canceled because of the weather. Some faculty members were called out of their cozy homes to watch her audition, and Monk went home.

This time, she was admitted, but the letter of acceptance was lost in the mail. She called to inquire at the school just one day before her place in the class would have been given to someone else.

At twenty-eight, she was the oldest person in her class, and things did not always run smoothly. However, she had a chance to live, work, and develop her skills for three years with other talented actors. Of her Yale training she says, "It's like getting an American Express card as far as acting is concerned. You have to pay the bills, but you get to play with the big boys." As a kind of graduation gift, the four women in her Yale class were all cast in a film that one of their acting teachers was directing—*The World According to Garp*, with Robin Williams and Glenn Close.

For several years, Monk auditioned and performed for regional theaters around the country. She was approached by director Lee Breuer about a small, half-hour version of *Oedipus at Colonus*, using gospel music. The show expanded, Morgan Freeman joined the cast, they toured everywhere, and Monk ended up on Broadway in a hit called *The Gospel at Colonus*. With Breuer, she also did a version of *King Lear* in which the genders were reversed. Ruth Maleczech

A member of the Guthrie Theater's acting ensemble, Isabell Monk is shown here in The Triumph of Love *as Leontine, with Reg Rogers (center) as Agis and Stephen Yoakam as Hermocrates.* (MICHAEL DANIEL)

One of the most gifted actors in American regional theater, Isabell Monk is shown here as Clytemnestra in Euripides' Iphigeneia at Aulis. (MICHAEL DANIEL)

played *Lear* and Monk played Gloucester. For that part, she won an Obie, the off-Broadway equivalent of a Tony Award.

Then Garland Wright offered her a job as part of an acting ensemble at the Guthrie Theater, where he was then artistic director. It turned out to be the perfect place for her. At the Guthrie, Monk plays roles that were written for all varieties of people, black and white, male and female. She recently played the Fool in *King Lear*. She was Linda Loman in *Death of a Salesman* and Khadjia in *The Screens*. When Wright asked her what role she had always wanted to play, she said Clytemnestra. So he put on the repertory schedule the three plays in which Clytem-

nestra appears—*Iphigeneia at Aulis*, *Agamemnon*, and *Electra*.

"I want to do anything that is possible for me to do as an artist," she told interviewer Holly Hill in *Actors' Lives*. "I will not be limited because of my race. To be limited not because of what I have in my mind, my body and my spirit to share, but because of something as simple as the darkness of my skin, is intolerable."

KATHLEEN THOMPSON

Moore, Melba (1945–)

In her eighteen months in the rock musical *Hair*, Melba Moore did more than move up from the chorus to female lead; she also grew from an ex-schoolteacher who supported herself doing background vocals and singing commercial jingles to a coming Broadway star. Since then, she has become a respected singer and actress in theater, film, and television.

Born in New York City on October 27, 1945, Moore is the daughter of singer Melba (Bonnie) Smith and jazz saxophonist Teddy Hill. She was brought up in Harlem and later in Newark, New Jersey. The pain and danger she saw around her in Harlem drove Moore into herself, making her shy, withdrawn, and able to communicate her emotions only through music. She attended the Arts High School in Newark and then Montclair State Teachers College. After graduation, she taught music at Pershing Avenue Elementary School before quitting to work in show business. She was a stand-up singer on the Catskills resort circuit for a time and was doing a background session in a recording studio when she was heard by the composers of *Hair*. They asked her to audition for a new production of the musical, and she was cast as part of the "tribe." After eighteen months, having moved to a leading role, she left to play Lutiebelle in *Purlie*, the musical version of Ossie Davis' *Purlie Victorious*. Her performance drew raves and won her a Tony Award, a New York Drama Critics Circle Award, and a Drama Desk Award.

Since then, Moore has appeared in two other Broadway musicals and five films, including *Lost in the Stars*, a musical adaptation of Alan Paton's *Cry, the Beloved Country*. She has also appeared frequently on television, including appearances on the nighttime soap *Falcon Crest*. She shared star billing in the miniseries *Ellis Island* and was the first black actress to have a situation comedy named after her. *Melba,* however, did not air for long. She also has had a successful recording career, winning two Grammy Award nominations.

More recently, Moore had a recurring role in *The Cosby Show* and starred in Duke Ellington's opera *Queenie Pie* at the Brooklyn Academy of Music. In 1993, a difficult divorce from her business partner left Moore in financial difficulties, but she is now co-writing a one-woman show called *Songs My Mother Taught Me* and is slated to appear in a revival of *Purlie*.

Melba Moore has one daughter, Charli.

KATHLEEN THOMPSON

N

Negro Ensemble Company

Some of America's finest black actors would surely have made their mark even if the *New York Times* had not asked playwright-actor-director Douglas Turner to write an article in 1966, but it helped. Turner called for the establishment of a theater company of and for black actors, playwrights, designers, and administrators. In response, the Ford Foundation supplied the funding that launched the Negro Ensemble Company in 1967.

The new group that began producing the next year in St. Mark's Playhouse was headed by Turner (who had become Douglas Turner Ward) along with producer Gerald S. Krone and actor Robert Hooks.

But **Esther Rolle**, too, was an NEC founder. So was **Frances Foster**, who with fellow black New York thespians had been conceiving such an enterprise since the 1950s. So were **Hattie Winston** and **Rosalind Cash**.

Rolle, Foster, and Winston were part of what was the nucleus of the new group. A production of two Ward one-act plays, *Happy Ending* and *Day of Absence*, was first produced at St. Mark's in 1965 and the following year went on a tour that took in Chicago (where Ward hired Mary Alice Smith, later known as **Mary Alice**, to do laundry).

The cast of NEC's first official show, Peter Weiss's *Song of the Lusitanian Bogey* in 1968, included Cash, Winston, Denise Nicholas, and Judyann Jonsson. By the time *Bogey* went on a tour to the World Theater Festival in London—NEC's first, and the first time an American troupe had been invited to the festival—Rolle and Foster had joined it.

In 1969, Nicholas would be the first to be lured away, for good, by West Coast television work. But in NEC's first, furiously prolific year of 1968, she appeared in NEC's *Kongi's Harvest* by Wole Soyinka, alongside Foster, Cash, Jonsson, Winston, Woods, and **Clarice Taylor**. Taylor, an original member of perhaps NEC's nearest historical precursor, the **American Negro Theater** of the 1940s, had also joined the company. (**Alice Childress**, an ANT actor, became an NEC playwright when her *String* was presented in *An Evening of One Acts*.) The same women—minus Foster, Rolle, and Winston—were in 1968's *Daddy Goodness*, by Richard Wright.

In the days and years ahead, these gifted women in various combinations were to be seen in *Summer of the Seventeenth Doll* and *God Is a (Guess What?)* (1968); *Ceremonies in Dark Old Men*, *An Evening of One Acts*, and *Man Better Man* (1969); *Brotherhood*, *Akokawe*, *Rosalee Pritchett*, and *The Sty of the Blind Pig* (1971); and *A Ballet Behind the Bridge* and *The River Niger* (1972).

Individually, they and several other actors, such as Barbara Montgomery and (briefly) **Phylicia Rashad**, contributed to many more shows in NEC's rich and distinguished history, which has evolved up to the present.

Mary Alice, first rejected as an NEC member, appeared in the theater's *In the Deepest Part of Sleep*, *Heaven and Hell's Agreement*, *Black Sunlight,* and *Terraces* all in 1974 (with *Terraces* directed by Foster), and then in *Zooman and the Sign* (1980).

Winston and, especially, Cash and Rolle turned to film and TV commitments during the 1970s, but Winston returned to NEC to do *The Michigan* in 1979, as did Cash the next year for *The Sixteenth Round.* Foster never strayed far from the stage or from NEC. She acted in its *Zooman and the Sign* and *Henrietta* (1985) and is still dedicated to the company's work and mission.

Between 1991 and 1993, the NEC suspended production, because of financial problems. In 1993, they produced Kenneth Hoke Witherspoon's *Last Night at Ace High.*

GARY HOUSTON

Nelson, Novella (1939–)

Novella Nelson is an actor and director with an impressive list of credits. Born in Brooklyn, New York, on December 17, 1939, she is the daughter of James Nelson and Evelyn Hines. She attended Brooklyn College and was a consultant to Joseph Papp for five years.

Nelson made her Broadway debut in *House of Flowers* and came to notice as **Pearl Bailey**'s understudy in *Hello, Dolly!,* both in 1968. She won critical acclaim for the role of Missy in Ossie Davis's *Purlie* in 1970. The next year, she directed *Nigger Nightmare* and in 1972 guided **Gloria Foster**'s performance in *Sister Son/ji,* by **Sonia Sanchez** for the **Negro Ensemble Company**

(NEC). Two years later, the Associated Press reviewer gave her credit for "animating fragments of overheard talk among beggars, hookers, schoolgirls, the lonely, lost, and frightened into an intriguing ritual of slow-motion choreographic movement and dark-lit sudden impressionistic halts" when she directed one of many shows for the Public Theater, *Les Femmes Noires.*

Over the years, she has worked as actor and director at the NEC as well as for many regional theaters, including the Alliance Theater, the Long Wharf Theater, and Seattle Repertory Theater. She has also directed at the Humana Festival.

Nelson has appeared in a number of films, including *The Cotton Club*, *The Flamingo Kid*, *The Seduction of Joe Tynan*, and *Green Card*. She has also been visible on television in, among other series, *Hawk*, *Law and Order*, and *The Equalizer* and in three soap operas—*One Life to Live*, *All My Children*, and *As the World Turns.*

A singer who has performed successfully in clubs and concerts and recorded an album entitled *Novella Nelson*, she was given the **Mary M. Bethune** lifetime award by the **National Council of Negro Women.**

KATHLEEN THOMPSON

Nicholas, Denise (1944–)

When *Room 222* went on the air in 1969, one character was a complete revelation to television audiences: Guidance counselor Liz McIntyre, as played by Denise Nicholas, was a warm, intelligent black woman with a ready wit and a sweet, independent sexiness. Those same qualities are ones this actor brings to all her roles.

Denise Nicholas was born in Detroit in 1944. In her early career, she was associated with two theaters of great significance in black theater history. One was the Free Southern Theater in Tougaloo, Mississippi, which began by bringing black versions of such classics as *Waiting for Godot* to audiences in the poor, rural South. Nicholas was one of the members who moved the theater toward producing works by and/or about black people, such as *In White America*.

The other theater was the Negro Ensemble Company (NEC) in New York, which she joined in its first year, 1968. For the NEC she acted with Moses Gunn, **Rosalind Cash**, and many others in Peter Weiss' *Song of the Lusitanian Bogey*, Wole Soyinka's *Kongi's Harvest*, and an adaptation of a Richard Wright work, *Daddy Goodness*, all in that first season.

Nicholas then turned her attention to film and television. Having appeared on television in *It Takes a Thief*, the Jack Warden–starred *NYPD*, and *The FBI*, Nicholas in 1969 captured the role of Liz McIntyre in *Room 222*. Set in Los Angeles' integrated Walt Whitman High School, this was one of the first series to deal with black characters in a nonstereotyped way. Nicholas remained with the *Room 222* until it ended in January 1974. In the meantime, she was seen in the films *Blacula* (1972) and *The Soul of Nigger Charley* (1973) and in television's *Five Desperate Women* and *Night Gallery*.

Showing versatility, she published *The Denise Nicholas Beauty Book* in 1971 and later formed her own production company, Masai Productions.

In 1978, Nicholas was back to full-time series work on CBS as Demond Wilson's wife and **Helen Martin**'s daughter in the sitcom *Baby, I'm Back*, about a man who rejoins his Washington, D.C., family after a seven-year absence. It did not last beyond a season.

Film work had resumed with *Mr. Ricco* (1975) and the second and third Sidney Poitier/Bill Cosby comedies *Let's Do It Again* (1975) and *A Piece of the Action* (1977). Television work was plentiful, including jobs on *Marcus Welby, M.D.*, *Rhoda*, *Police Story*, *Love Boat* (an episode with Robert Guillaume, Richard Roundtree, and **Pam Grier**), *Diff'rent Strokes*, *One Day at a Time*, *Magnum, P.I.*, and others.

In 1981, Nicholas married a television sportscaster and briefly used the name Nicholas-Hill. Soon thereafter, she began to move toward another, landmark wedding when she became a regular on the series *In the Heat of the Night*. As Councilwoman Harriet DeLong, she became the love interest and, ultimately, the bride of white Sheriff Gillespie, played by Carroll O'Connor. The interracial romance idea came from O'Connor, the series' executive producer, and if, in a more tolerant age, it offended few, many caught the irony of a black woman marrying the man still mainly remembered as Archie Bunker.

In 1992, Nicholas also began to write episodes for the series. Her first script involved attempts to get the city fathers of Sparta, Mississippi, to honor voter-registration activist Odessa Robbins, a black woman.

Denise Nicholas' film career has continued with *Marvin and Tige* (1983), *Supercarrier* (1988), and *Ghost Dad* (1990). In 1988, Nicholas went back to her stage roots, appearing at Crossroads Theater in *To Gleam It Around, To Show My Shine*. More recently, Nicholas has begun to appear on the series *The Fresh Prince of Bel Air* as Will

Smith's mother. She is also at work on a screenplay.

GARY HOUSTON

Nichols, Nichelle (1932?–)

"Although people know me best as Uhura, I've always considered acting the 'other' thing I do," wrote Nichelle Nichols in her 1994 autobiography *Beyond Uhura*. That may surprise casual watchers of the television series *Star Trek* and its numerous TV and film spinoffs, but to serious "Trekkers" and those who have known and worked with her, Nichelle Nichols is a singer, dancer, writer, and actor whose talents extend far beyond the image of the Starfleet communications officer who often said little more than "Hailing frequencies open, Captain."

Nichols was born in Robbins, Illinois, a small town about thirty miles southwest of Chicago. It had begun as a social experiment in 1892 and was one of the few places in America where black and racially mixed couples had any hope of ever owning land. Nichols' paternal grandfather was Samuel S. Gillespie, a white man who forsook his family fortune and changed his name to Nichols in order to marry Lydia Myers, a black woman who had been born to a family of ex-slaves. They settled down in Robbins with their three children, one of whom they named after his father. Samuel Earl Nichols grew up to become a respected figure in the community and was eventually elected mayor. His second wife was Lishia Mae Parks and their third child together was a girl they named Grace.

According to family legend, Grace could sing before she could walk, and by five she was convinced that she would someday perform on the stage. The Nicholses moved to Chicago when she was a toddler and, partly to offset the effects of childhood anemia and partly because the arts were an important part of their family life, she began to study ballet. Later, she was introduced to Afro-Cuban dancing by a woman named Carmencita Romero, whose dance troupe was hired to perform in the famous College Inn Supper Club at the Sherman House Hotel in Chicago. Grace was one of four dancers —two male and two female—who would re-create the historic appearance there by legendary black choreographer **Katherine**

While most of America may think of her only as Lieutenant Uhuru of Star Trek, *Nichelle Nichols is a gifted singer, dancer, and writer. In an encyclopedia where almost every entry has a first, hers is the first interracial kiss on network television (with William Shatner's Captain Kirk).* (PRIVATE COLLECTION)

Dunham. Grace, all of fourteen years old, had just broken into show business.

It was there that she met many of the country's greatest entertainers, including Duke Ellington, who later hired her to choreograph and perform his musical suite "Monologue Duet and Threesome." Soon she put together a solo act and, at the suggestion of her manager, briefly changed her name to Lynn Mayfair, which she hated. Because she didn't like the name Grace either, however, she asked her mother to change her first name legally. She was now Nichelle Nichols.

A short, rocky marriage to dancer Foster Johnson resulted in the birth of her only child, Kyle. After a brief hiatus, she resumed her singing and dancing career in the clubs. The grueling schedule and disturbing encounters with racism and sexism on the circuit soon convinced her to relocate to Los Angeles. She was quickly cast in a small role in the Otto Preminger–directed film *Porgy and Bess*, where she made friends with the likes of Sammy Davis, Jr., **Pearl Bailey**, **Dorothy Dandridge**, Sidney Poitier, and **Maya Angelou**.

After a number of theatrical ventures, including producing the world premiere of James Baldwin's *The Amen Corner* in Los Angeles, Nichols landed a role in an episode of the television series *The Lieutenant* in 1963. The producer—who became an intimate friend and colleague—was Gene Roddenberry. During the three years that it took Roddenberry to sell his next proposal to a network, Nichols appeared in the film *Made in Paris* with Ann-Margret and *Mister Buddwing* with James Garner. Then, while in Paris in 1966, she received an urgent telegram from her agent: "Come home immediately. . . . They're doing *Star Trek*." Thus was born Lieutenant Uhura.

While the NBC television series and subsequent *Star Trek* films made Nichelle Nichols a pop-culture icon, it did not happen without years of battles against the entrenched racist, sexist, and pedestrian attitudes of the TV honchos, not to mention the ongoing clashes of actors' egos. There are some who would argue that Uhura was little more than the "token black" on the *Starship Enterprise*. It is true that her character never developed according to Gene Roddenberry's original plan, that week after week her lines were rewritten into oblivion or simply given to the guest star. Yet, when Nichols threatened to quit after the first season, it was Dr. Martin Luther King, Jr., himself a fan of *Star Trek*, who convinced her to stay by telling her that she had "created a character of dignity and grace and beauty and intelligence" that was a role model for people of *all* colors.

Stay she did for the next 25 years. Through the first interracial kiss on network television (with William Shatner's Captain Kirk), through the years of syndication and "Trekkie" conventions, through six critically uneven but popular *Star Trek* movies, Nichols stayed. Meanwhile, she appeared in the film *Truck Turner* with Isaac Hayes, helped found the charitable Kwanza Foundation, and, through her company Women in Motion, Inc., began to write and produce educational projects for young people, incorporating music as a teaching tool.

It seems natural that "Uhura" would eventually hook up with NASA. In 1977, Nichols spearheaded a recruitment drive to encourage women and minorities to apply for the Space Shuttle Program, for which she received a Distinguished Public Service

Award. The drive resulted immediately in astronaut status for people such as Sally Ride, Guy Bluford, Fred Gregory, Judith Resnick, Ronald McNair and Ellison Onizuka, and eventually in the same for **Mae Jemison**, the first African-American woman in space.

Nichols says that while she sometimes goes for months or years without stepping in front of a camera, music fills every day of her life. She continues to produce and perform for the stage and special projects and is working on her first novel, *Saturn's Child*, to be published by Putnam's.

MICHAEL NOWAK

Norman, Maidie (1912–)

Maidie Norman was born on October 16, 1912, in Villa Rica, Georgia, to Louis and Lila Gamble. She received a B.A. from Bennett College in 1934 and a master's degree from Columbia University three years later. She also attended the Actors Lab in Hollywood from 1946 to 1949.

Norman first appeared on film in *The Burning Cross* in 1948. Throughout the fifties—not a good time for film roles for black women—she appeared in a number of films, such as *Bright Road* with **Dorothy Dandridge** and Sidney Poitier and *Torch Song*, both in 1953; *About Mrs. Leslie* and *Susan Slept Here* in 1954; and 1956's *Written on the Wind*. These were often servant roles, with a special fifties blandness. Still, Norman was skillful and professional in her execution of them. In 1962, she got a chance to chew up the scenery with Bette Davis and Joan Crawford in *What Ever Happened to Baby Jane?*

In 1968–69, Norman was an artist-in-residence at Stanford University and, throughout the seventies, she was lecturer, director, and acting teacher at UCLA. At the same time, Norman was highly visible on television, appearing in *Mannix*, *Adam 12*, *Streets of San Francisco*, *Kung Fu*, *The Jeffersons*, and others. She was also part of the cast of *Roots: The Next Generation* in 1979.

Norman was a founding member of the **American Negro Theater West**; in 1977, she was inducted into the Black Filmmakers Hall of Fame; and an award in her name is presented each year for outstanding research by an undergraduate in Black Theater at UCLA.

ANDRA MEDEA

P

Parks, Suzan-Lori (1963–)

"You should write that down, you should write that down and hide it under a rock." This line from Suzan-Lori Parks' play *The Death of the Last Black Man in the Whole Entire World* speaks of the lost history of the African American. Writing in an abstract style that uses poetry and metaphor, Suzan-Lori Parks is a unique voice in modern American theater.

Suzan-Lori Parks was educated at Mount Holyoke College, where she earned her B.A. in English and German Literature, graduating Phi Beta Kappa in 1985. While at Mount Holyoke, she participated in a master writing class with James Baldwin. In 1986, she attended The Drama Studio, London, for a year's intensive course in theater. She has been a guest lecturer at colleges all over the United States, was a writer-in-residence at The New School in New York City from 1991 to 1993, and was a playwrighting professor at the Yale school of Drama in 1995.

Her first play, *The Sinner's Place*, was produced at the New Play Festival in Amherst, Massachusetts, in 1984. Her next play, *Betting on the Dust Commander*, was first produced at The Gas Station in New York City in 1987. Both *The Death of the Last Black Man in the Whole Entire World* and *Imperceptible Mutabilities in the Third Kingdom* saw their debuts at BACA Downtown in 1990 and 1989, respectively. In 1992, the Humana Festival, Actors Theater of Louisville commissioned and produced *Devotees in the Garden of Love,* and in 1993 Theater for a New Audience commissioned *The America Play*. Most recently, Parks was commissioned by the Women's Theater Project to write *Venus*. In addition to her stage work, Parks has written screenplays and radio plays; she wrote the screenplay of *Girl 6*, produced and directed by Spike Lee.

Among many prestigious awards and grants, Parks won an Obie Award in 1990 for *Imperceptible Mutabilities in the Third Kingdom*. She is an associate artist at the Yale School of Drama and is a member playwright of New Dramatists. In 1989, the *New York Times* named her "the year's most promising playwright."

Through language and image, Suzan-Lori Parks explores the details of the African-American experience. Her characters are archetypical figures representative of a history that has often been ignored by mainstream America. Her language, often abstract and unusual, speaks in wondrous ways. "Truth rings," she told Syne Mahon in the book *Moon Marked and Touched by Sun*. "Truth as a sound and a shape that might not explain or reveal itself logically to us, but will reveal itself through our other senses."

HILARY MAC AUSTIN

Perkins, Kathy A. (1954–)

There are only two black women who belong to the United Scenic Artists Association

(USAA) as lighting designers; there is only one in set design; there are fewer than 30 African Americans out of nearly 2,200 USAA members, including set, costume, and lighting designers and hairstylists. A talented and very active lighting designer herself, Kathy A. Perkins has set out to change both that situation and our perceptions of African Americans in theater. "It's not that African Americans do not have a tradition peopled with talented, innovative designers. We do. It's just that most young people interested in theater only see 'star' roles and completely overlook the many opportunities that exist behind the scenes."

Kathy Anne Perkins was born August 27, 1954, in Mobile, Alabama, to Marion and Minerva Fletcher Perkins. One of five children, she grew up in an African-American community and participated in drama programs at church and at school. When she enrolled at **Howard University**, her ambition was to be an actor. As a theater major, however, she took courses in all aspects of the art, including technical theater. Douglas Farmun, a classmate who is now a lighting designer for NBC, noticed that she had a talent for lighting and suggested that she consider becoming a designer. She reports that her response was "Really? What's that?" but she had found her niche.

Perkins went on to the University of Michigan for a master's degree in lighting design. She told *Black Theater Network News* that, on the first day of classes, she asked another student to point her to the M.F.A. designers' classes. He directed her to the acting classes. When she pointed out his mistake, he said, "Oh, I didn't know there were any black designers." Neither, as it happened, did her teachers and textbooks.

She couldn't find any information anywhere about black designers.

In 1978, Perkins graduated as the first African American to be awarded the M.F.A. in design from the University of Michigan. She went to New York and was soon doing lighting design for the renowned Sounds in Motion Dance Company. After a year there and a number of months in Europe designing two American productions, she became a lighting instructor at Smith College in Northampton, Massachusetts. For six years, she taught all aspects of lighting and also designed or supervised the design of productions in the theater and dance department. During that time, she took a one-year leave to become a visiting scholar at Columbia University. There, she conducted research on the contributions of African Americans in the nonperforming areas of American theater.

Perkins found herself more and more interested in discovering the history of black theater artists behind the scenes. Soon her scholarly work rivaled her design work. She was designing for such major contemporary performers as Denzel Washington, **Lena Horne**, **Roberta Flack**, Helen Hunt, **Esther Rolle**, and Paul Winfield, and for theaters that included the **Negro Ensemble Company**, the New Federal Theater, and Carnegie Hall. And she was also digging into libraries and archives to find "lost" nonperforming artists of the past. Soon with the help of grants from the Ford Foundation, the National Endowment for the Humanities, and others, she had gathered a huge archive of her own.

In 1985, Perkins became resident lighting designer for the Los Angeles Theater Center, designing more than twenty productions for that theater in addition to other productions in the Los Angeles area. Then, in 1987, she became a freelance designer and worked at theaters all over the country, including Indiana Repertory, Missouri Repertory, St. Louis Black Repertory, Atlanta's Alliance Theater, and Chicago's Onyx Theater Ensemble and Victory Gardens. She also did research for PBS and for the California Afro-American Museum.

In 1989, Perkins published a landmark book, *Black Female Playwrights: An Anthology of Plays Before 1950*, which won a CHOICE Outstanding Academic Books Award. Her research also yielded dozens of articles and one more theatrical presentation of her material. In 1995, she created an exhibit of original designs, costumes, photographs, posters, and playbills that demonstrate the contributions of many talented, unrecognized black theater artists. It includes such fascinating material as set, costume, and lighting designs by sculptor **Meta Vaux Warrick Fuller.**

Perkins became an associate professor and head of the lighting-design program at the University of Illinois in 1989. Another anthology, *Contemporary Plays by Women of Color*, co-edited by Roberta Uno, was published in 1996. With Judith Stephens, Perkins is working on a third anthology, *Strange Fruit: Lynching Plays by American Women.*

"It wasn't by choice that I became a theater historian," Perkins says, "but I found something that needed to be done and nobody was doing it." Perhaps, inspired by her example, there will be others doing it in the future.

KATHLEEN THOMPSON

Perry, Shauneille (19??–)

"You must know your craft," says director and writer Shauneille Perry, "because even if no one ever finds you out, if no one else ever knows what you're doing isn't good enough, you'll know it yourself." That sort of integrity illuminates the career of this pioneer of the black theater movement.

Shauneille Perry was born in Chicago to Graham T. and Pearl Perry. Her father was Assistant Attorney General of the State of Illinois, and her mother, before marriage, was a court reporter. Her first cousin, **Lorraine Hansberry,** would also grow up to be an important figure in black theater history. Perry attended the Chicago Public Schools and then earned her B.A. in drama from **Howard University.**

While at Howard, she was a member of the Howard Players, the first group of black students to tour as part of a foreign cultural program for the U.S. State Department. She went with the group to the Scandinavian countries and Germany. During the summers, she acted in black summer stock, where she worked with such major figures as Anne Cook Reid and Owen Dodson.

Perry went from Howard to the Goodman School of Drama at the Chicago Art Institute. There, she studied directing, earning an M.F.A. She continued her training as a Fulbright scholar at the Royal Academy of Dramatic Arts and the London Academy of Music and Dramatic Art. Back in Chicago, she taught and directed at the Goodman School for two years while working as a reporter and writer for the *Chicago Daily Defender*. She taught at various colleges and universities, including A&T College of North Carolina and Dillard University in New Orleans.

At about this time, Perry had a remarkable experience when she won a trip to Paris in an essay contest. Black novelist Richard Wright had just done an adaptation of a

French play called *Papa Bonhomme* for the American Theater in Paris; Perry was cast in the play, now called *Daddy Goodness.* Years later, she would co-write the book for a musical version.

In 1960, Perry moved to New York and, for two years, concentrated on acting. She appeared in such plays as *The Goose* and *Clandestine on the Morning Line,* but ultimately the highly trained director did not find acting fulfilling enough. More and more, she moved toward directing and teaching. While she was directing plays for such groups as the **Negro Ensemble Company** (NEC) and the New Federal Theater (NFT), she was teaching at City College, Hunter College, and Queens College, and the Fieldstone School. This balancing of the professional and the academic makes Perry an unusual, almost a unique figure in black theater.

One of the first plays Shauneille Perry directed in New York was *Rosalee Pritchett* at the NEC, with a cast that included **Frances Foster**, Roxie Roker, and **Clarice Taylor**. The reviews were very positive. In the same year, 1971, she directed J. E. Franklin's *Black Girl,* a theatrical phenomenon produced by the New Federal Theater. The play's audiences quickly outgrew the space, and the show transferred to the Theater de Lys, where it ran for 247 performances. She rounded off this successful year with *The Sty of the Blind Pig,* featuring Clarice Taylor and Frances Foster, as well as Moses Gunn.

Perry has continued to work with NEC, AMAS, the New Lafayette Theater, NFT, and the Afro-American Total Theater, directing such plays as Martie Evans-Charles' *Jamimma* in 1972; *The Prodigal Sister,* by Franklin again, with music by **Micki Grant**,

in 1974; *Who Loves the Dancer* and *Keyboard* with Cleavon Little, both in 1982. Her production of *Bayou Legend* was choreographed by **Debbie Allen**, and she directed Allen's sister, **Phylicia Rashad**, as Ruth in a revival of *A Raisin in the Sun.* She remembers Rashad's being called out of rehearsal for an audition for *The Cosby Show.*

During this time, Perry was also busy as a writer. She wrote a series of short stories for a radio program entitled *Bittersweet* and also *Sounds of the City,* the first black soap opera on national radio. She has written seven plays, including *Things of the Heart: Marian Anderson's Story,* which was produced by the NFT in 1981. Her theater piece on black history and culture, called *Celebration,* tours on the National Black Touring Circuit.

These days, Perry tends to direct what she helped to create as a writer. She has published a book of short stories entitled *Pearl* after her mother, and she is working on a multicultural anthology of plays for young people.

It would be difficult to overestimate Shauneille Perry's impact on the black theater movement. Her work is marked by the professionalism she acquired by many years of training in her craft and by the passion for truth and quality that she brings to everything she does. "In the end," she says, "the things that last are the good things."

KATHLEEN THOMPSON

Preer, Evelyn (1896–1932)

"Evelyn Preer ranks first as a Movie Star," wrote Floyd J. Calvin, a reporter for the *Pittsburgh Courier,* in 1927. Preer had worked hard to earn that accolade. The daughter and the oldest of Frank and Blanch

Star of eight successful black silent films, Evelyn Preer was a leading actress with the Lafayette Players until her untimely death at the age of 36. (SISTER FRANCESCA THOMPSON)

Jarvis' three children, Evelyn Preer was born on July 26, 1896, in Vicksburg, Mississippi. While she was still quite young, Preer was taken to Chicago by her widowed mother. It was in Chicago that she received her formal education, and Chicago also was where her theatrical career had its dramatic beginnings. While street preaching for her mother, a devout member of the Apostolic Church, Preer attracted the attention of the black movie producer/director Oscar Micheaux. In 1917, she appeared in Micheaux's first black silent film, *The Homesteader*. The first of many profitable collaborations between the director and his young star, it was followed by seven other successful films: *The Brute* (1920); *Within Our Gates* (1920); *Deceit* (1921); *The Gunsaulus Mystery* (1921); *Birthright* (1924); *The Conjure Woman* (1926); and *The Spider's Web* (1926). Preer considered the latter film her best movie work.

In October 1920, Preer joined the **Lafayette Players**, who were then performing at the Lincoln Theater in Chicago. Remaining with the Players for twelve years, until her death in 1932, she became one of their most popular leading ladies and a favorite with audiences all over the country. By 1924, Preer was the star of the traveling group of Players who toured extensively through the Southern states, and she married her leading man, Edward Thompson. Their union produced one child, a daughter, Ed Eve, born shortly before Preer's death in November 1932.

Lauded by the leading black critics of the time, Preer was once referred to as "a shining jewel in Ethiope's ear." Because she was a star of the Lafayette Players, Preer performed in the leading plays of the time: *Porgy*; *Over the Hill to the Poor House*; *Salome*, in which she was advertised as "The Most Beautiful Colored Woman in the World!"; *Dr. Jekyll and Mr. Hyde*; *Madame X*; *The Chip Woman's Fortune*, written by the black dramatist Willis Richardson; *Bought and Paid For*; *Branded*; *The Warning*; *Anna Christie*; *Desire Under the Elms*; *The Hunchback of Notre Dame*; and *Rain*, to name just a few of her successes.

Evelyn Preer made several popular phonograph records and in 1924 appeared in the Broadway production of *Lulu Belle*, directed by the famous producer and playwright David Belasco. She appeared in *Shuffle Along* by Eubie Blake and Noble Sissle in 1921 and in *Rang Tang* by Miller and Lyles in 1927. Multitalented, Preer was widely acknowledged to be a pioneer for the other black actresses who were to follow her.

After her untimely death at thirty-six, Oscar Micheaux wrote of her meteoric career: "She was beautiful, intelligent . . . and a born artist . . . more versatile than any actress I have ever known . . . her early passing will leave her missed greatly by the profession." In Clarence Muse's eloquent eulogy at Preer's funeral in Los Angeles, he concluded by saying, "And so, Evelyn Preer, go on! The Lafayette Players have profited by your visit here. The world has been uplifted." It was a fitting tribute to a dedicated artist who had given her last bow and made her final exit.

SISTER FRANCESCA THOMPSON

Prendergast, Shirley (1932–)

In 1973, Shirley Prendergast became the first black woman lighting designer on Broadway with the production of *The River Niger*, as well as one of the first black women to be admitted into the lighting division of United Scenic Artists Association (USAA), the major stage-designers' union.

Born Merris Shirley Prendergast on June 15, 1932, in Boston, Massachusetts, she is the daughter of Dorita and Wilford A. Prendergast. Before working in theater, she earned a degree in microbiology at Brooklyn College. As a dancer during college, she became interested in lighting design.

During the 1960s, Prendergast attended the famous Lester Polakov's Studio and Forum of Stage Design in New York City, where she studied with some of Broadway's most prominent designers. Through the **Negro Ensemble Company** (NEC), Prendergast was provided the opportunity to design numerous productions and to develop professionally as a designer. Her first production with NEC was *Summer of the Seventeenth Doll*. In 1969, she passed the lighting examination and was admitted into USAA, Local 829.

The NEC's production of *The River Niger*, which opened at the St. Mark's Theater, moved to Broadway—allowing Prendergast to have her first Broadway show. Since the *The River Niger*, Prendergast has designed other Broadway productions, including *The Amen Corner* (1983), *Don't Get God Started* (1989), *The Waltz of the Stork* (1981), and *Robeson* (1990). She also has designed for the Alvin Ailey American Dance Theater, New York Shakespeare Festival, Crossroads Theater, the New Federal Theater, and numerous regional companies, while maintaining close ties with NEC.

KATHY A. PERKINS

R

Rahn, Muriel (1911–1961)

In theater, Muriel Rahn will always be remembered as the first Carmen Jones, a role she played in alternation with Muriel Smith on Broadway in 1943.

Muriel Rahn was born in Boston in 1911. While still a child, she moved with her family to New York. After attending the New York public schools, she went to the Tuskegee Institute in Alabama, Atlanta University in Georgia, and the Music Conservatory of the University of Nebraska at Lincoln.

Rahn's career began with **Eva Jessye**'s famous choir, which she joined in 1929. She quickly moved on to the Broadway stage, appearing in Lew Leslie's *Blackbirds of 1929* and Connie Inn's *Hot Chocolates*.

In the early 1940s, inspired by a number of successful black adaptations of classic works of theater, Billy Rose decided to produce an adaptation of Bizet's opera *Carmen*. The original setting, a Spanish cigarette factory, became a World War II parachute factory in the American South. Oscar Hammerstein wrote a new libretto and new lyrics for Bizet's music.

Hammerstein and Rose asked jazz music expert John Hammond, Jr., to help them cast the show. He assembled a remarkable group, including the two Muriels who sang the lead role at alternate performances. *Carmen Jones* opened in December of 1943 and ran for 502 performances before going on tour; the critics were enthusiastic and the show was a hit.

While she appeared on Broadway, Rahn also pursued a concert music career. She was a member of the National Orchestral Association and sang in many of its productions and performed with the Salmaggi Opera, the San Carlo Opera, and the National Negro Opera Company.

In 1950, Rahn was back on Broadway, playing the leading role of Cora in the opera version of Langston Hughes' play *Mulatto*. She also appeared in *The Ivory Branch* at the Provincetown Players Theater in 1956 and in 1959–60 was musical director for a production of *Bells Are Ringing* for the German State Theater at Frankfurt.

Muriel Rahn died on August 8, 1961, in New York at the age of fifty.

KATHLEEN THOMPSON

Randolph, Amanda (1902–1967)

Amanda Randolph was a gifted actress and singer whose talents far outweighed the opportunities she received in the course of her long stage, radio, television, and film career.

Randolph was born in 1902 in Louisville, Kentucky. Gifted with musical talent and a powerful singing voice, she began to perform at age fourteen in Cleveland's musical comedies and night clubs. She toured Europe in 1930 with the Scott and Whaley show, and in 1932, Randolph and Catherine Handy, daughter of composer W. C. Handy, sang together as the "Dixie Nightingales," appearing in several shows, including the Glenn and Jenkins Revue. During the 1930s, she performed in several hit musical revues such as *Chili Peppers*, *Dusty Lane*, and *Radiowaves*.

Randolph's film career probably began in 1936, the year she appeared in the musical short *The Black Network*. This film and others such as *Lying Lips* (1939) and *The Notorious Elinor Lee* (1940), written and produced by Oscar Micheaux and in which Randolph appeared, belonged to the genre called race movies, so-named for their focus on black American characters and plot lines designed to appeal to a black audience. Although often of poor technical quality, they offered a fairer representation of black life than did most Hollywood productions. During the 1940s, Randolph and her sister, Lillian, were featured on the long-running and extremely popular radio show *Amos 'n' Andy*. Randolph also worked on other radio productions during this time, such as *Kitty Foyle* and *Big Sister*.

During the 1950s, Randolph appeared in several Hollywood movies, including *She's Working Her Way Through College* (1952) featuring Ronald Reagan. In this film and many others, Randolph was consigned to comic roles as maids and housekeepers. Repeatedly assigned such stereotypical roles, Randolph was unable to perform to the full extent of her talent. Although many postwar films attempted to portray black American men in a more favorable light, the situation of limited roles for black women changed little during Randolph's career.

Also during the 1950s, Randolph made the transition to television. She was one of only two members of the radio cast to be accepted for the television version of *Amos 'n' Andy*, which, despite the controversy that led to its cancellation in 1955, was the first television series to feature an all-black cast. In 1953, Randolph was assigned the role of the family housekeeper, Louise, on *The Danny Thomas Show* (also known as *Make Room for Daddy*), a popular show that ran for more than a decade. She died, following a stroke, in 1967.

Despite the limited parts to which she was consigned, Amanda Randolph brought dignity to the tough-talking character she so often played. The long, cold stare directed at a foolish or pretentious character was something she had honed to perfection, as was the flagrant scorn she conveyed by a special roll of her eyes. Beyond this characterization, however, was a wealth of talent rarely drawn upon. Films such as *The Black Network* (1936), one of the few in which Randolph was given an opportunity to demonstrate her deep singing voice, suggest that, had richer roles come her way, Amanda Randolph would be much better known today.

FENELLA MACFARLANE

Randolph, Lillian (1915–1980)

Starting with the backlot movies of the 1930s contract system and continuing through to modern television, Lillian Randolph was always a trooper. Although her early acting work often had her typecast as a maid, Randolph persevered. She conducted a long and at times exhausting career that spanned film, radio, and television.

Lillian Randolph was born in 1915, thirteen years after her older sister Amanda. Her first Hollywood roles were in race movies, such as *Life Goes On* in 1938 and *Am I Guilty?* in 1940. Once established in the business, she became a regular player under the Hollywood contract system. While often a servant, Randolph maintained a level-headed comic style. She appeared in a string of light films that were cranked out of Hollywood's entertainment machine; perhaps her most memorable role in this era was that of the maid who helped pitch in to save the bank in the Christmas movie *It's a Wonderful Life* in 1946.

Randolph also did a good deal of work in radio, including playing the maid in *The Great Gildersleeves*, a popular family comedy in the 1940s. This led to a string of Gildersleeves movies in the early to middle 1940s. When the Gildersleeves series made the transition to television, Randolph went with it.

Still working at a hectic pace, Randolph found time to star in her own 1940s radio series. She replaced **Hattie McDaniel** as the star of *Beulah,* in the 1950s, played in the television version of *Amos 'n' Andy,* and in 1964, she appeared in the movie thriller *Hush, Hush Sweet Charlotte.*

By the 1970s, roles were opening up for black actresses, and Randolph began appearing in more substantial fare. She played in, among others, *The Great White Hope* (1970), *How to Seduce a Woman* (1974), *Once Is Not Enough* (1975), and *The Onion Field* (1979). Her roles also improved in television, where she was cast, in 1969, as Bill Cosby's mother in *The New Bill Cosby Show,* his earlier series. She also had parts in *The Autobiography of Miss Jane Pittman* (1974), *Sanford and Son* (1975), *The Jeffersons* (1976), and *Roots* (1977).

From the race movies of the 1930s to modern black television, Randolph was part of the evolution of Hollywood. Never one to quit, she was winning roles until the end of her life.

ANDRA MEDEA

Rashad, Phylicia (1948–)

The mother of actor Phylicia Rashad and her younger sister, **Debbie Allen**, told them always to seek "new knowledge." "There must always be some kind of program," Pulitzer Prize–nominated poet Vivian Ayers-Allen told her daughters, "some new study, some challenge to jack the mind up and make it use some of the cells it hasn't used before."

Phylicia Rashad was born in Houston, Texas, on June 19, 1948. Her mother divorced dentist Andrew A. Allen when Rashad was six. There were four siblings, including brothers Tex and Hugh. Phylicia and Debbie were high school cheerleaders, but Vivian, who developed a cultural program for Houston children, made sure hers took music, dance, and acting lessons. Influenced by a Hindu friend, she also adopted vegetarianism despite the Texan hamburger-eating culture. So did Phylicia.

At eighteen, Rashad set out for New York. A disappointing summer with the **Negro Ensemble Company** (made possible by a Howard award and $600 from Vivian) did not dishearten her, but success did have to wait.

Upon graduating magna cum laude from **Howard University** in 1970, she tried New York again, embarking on a stage career on and off Broadway that eventually would embrace *The Wiz* (as a munchkin for three and a half years), *Dreamgirls;* and *Into the Woods* (as the good witch).

Rashad married and divorced dentist William Lancelot Bowles, Jr., and had a son, William Lancelot III. She married her second husband, Victor Willis, lead singer of the rock group The Village People, in 1978 and divorced him in 1980.

Her first big career break arrived in 1983 with a recurring role in the ABC soap opera *One Life to Live.* Her second, and bigger one, came a year later, when Bill Cosby cast her to play his wife in *The Cosby Show,* in the long course of which she was hailed as America's favorite mother and won two People's Choice Awards for most popular actress on network television.

Cosby introduced her to her third and present husband, NBC sportscaster and former Minnesota Viking Ahmad Rashad. In 1985, he proposed to her on a pregame Thanksgiving broadcast, and she reached the studio to accept at halftime. They married that December, later moved to Westchester County, New York, and include in their family their daughter, Condola Phylea (named after Ahmad's mother), as well as three children from Ahmad's previous marriage.

Among her television films, all made while *The Cosby Show* was on the air, are *Uncle Tom's Cabin* (1987, which brought her a CableAce Award supporting-actress nomination), *False Witness* (1989), *Polly,* directed by her sister (1989), and *Polly Once Again* and *Jailbirds* (both 1990).

Rashad remembers other words of her mother Vivian. "The universe bears no ill to you and you bear no ill to it. And, of course, her best advice, advice to live by: Be bold, be beautiful, be free."

For Rashad, this advice would help to ensure there was life before and during—as there is after—*The Cosby Show;* for which as Claire Huxtable she was twice Emmy-nominated over an eight-season run that ended in 1992. She joined the Recruiting New Teachers board of directors in 1990 and was spokesperson both for the Cancer Information Service (1990–91), stressing

Phylicia Rashad, who was the female lead in one of the longest-running, highest-rated television series ever aired, The Cosby Show, *is also a highly talented stage actor (*Jelly's Last Jam *on Broadway) and the sister of Debbie Allen.*

early detection of breast cancer, and Save the Children (1989–91).

Leaving Claire Huxtable behind, Rashad joined the cast of *Jelly's Last Jam* on Broadway in 1993. In 1996, she again joined Bill Cosby in a new version of *The Cosby Show.*

GARY HOUSTON

Richards, Beah (1933–)

Sidney Poitier, Bill Cosby, and Robert Hooks have played her sons and grandsons; she played a grandmother in her first professional role, in 1956 off-Broadway; her career, now in its fourth decade, is still going strong. "I've been everybody's mother," says the actress, poet, and playwright with the marvelous voice.

She was born Beulah Richardson around 1933 in Vicksburg, Mississippi. Being a realist in a racist society left her no illusions, but surrounded by a close, compassionate community, Richards never entertained the idea of failure. She cites her mother, Beulah Molton Richardson, who was a seamstress and president of the Parent-Teacher Association (PTA), as her model for perseverance and community spirit; the poetry came from her father, Wesley R. Richardson. In a 1977 taped interview, Richards described him as "a minister with a gift for shaping words into images so sharp and clear that they became living and moved people to action." His daughter inherited both the gift and the will to move people.

The youngest in the family, Richards followed her sisters, Muncie and Ann, to the local school, where she remembers being inspired by a teacher named Mrs. M. A. Bell, whose great love for poetry, drama, and music gave all her students a strong sense of art. In high school, Richards shone in debating guild, drama, and Latin clubs, winning prizes and praise. There was no theater in the town, and the movie house was not open to black people, but everyone told her she was going to become a star. After high school graduation, Richards studied drama with Randolph Edmonds at Dillard University in New Orleans and centered her dreams around Paul Robeson and Marian Anderson. Although she greatly admired her English professor, Rudolf Moses, Richards left the university after one horrifying year, angered by the racism she found there.

Richards moved to San Diego, where she studied dance and apprenticed at the Globe Theater, appearing in *The Little Foxes* and *Another Part of the Forest*. She also acted and choreographed for the San Diego Community Theater, winning three Atlas Awards for her performances. After three years, Richards moved to New York, where she wrote poetry and taught at the Ophelia DeVore Charm School. In 1955, she performed at the Greenwich Mews Theater in *Trouble in Mind*; in 1956 she appeared in Brecht's *Arturo Ui*. In an off-Broadway revival of *Take a Giant Step*, Richards was cast as a cantankerous eighty-three-year-old who is not afraid to fight back; she earned her union card and the praise of the critics, only one of whom thought she looked a little young for the part. She repeated her role in the film version, which was released in 1961. Richards was the understudy for **Claudia McNeil** in *A Raisin in the Sun* in 1959 and made her Broadway debut in October of that year in *The Miracle Worker*. She subsequently toured nationally with the play and appeared in the 1962 film version. In 1961, Richards was back on Broadway as Idella Landy in Ossie Davis' *Purlie Victorious*, and she repeated her role in the 1963 film version, entitled *Gone Are the Days*.

Richards returned to California to work with the Theater of Being and Frank Silvera, who was her acting teacher, her director, and her costar in James Baldwin's *The Amen Corner*. The play opened in Los Angeles in March 1964, bringing Beah Richards more acclaim than ever. She said that prior to this time, she had merely acted at acting without really knowing what it was about—that she did not really become an actress until *The Amen Corner*. The role was Sister Margaret Alexander, who had to choose between loyalty to her storefront Harlem church and her alcoholic and wayward husband who is dying. After a successful run in Los Angeles, the play moved to Broadway, where Richards won a Theater World Award and a Tony nomination and topped *Variety*'s drama critics' poll for her performance.

In 1965, Richards began a new chapter in her career when she guest starred on the television series *The Big Valley* with Barbara Stanwyck. From appearances on *Dr. Kildare* and *I Spy* to her present recurring role on the hospital drama *E.R.*, Richards has been a familiar face on the small screen for three decades, appearing in more than 35 series and a dozen TV movies. She was a regular on *The Bill Cosby Show* in 1970–71 (as his mother, Rose Kincaid) and won an Emmy for her role on *Frank's Place*. Other appearances include *Roots II: The Next Generation*, *Ironside*, *Room 222*, *Sanford and Son*, *Murder, She Wrote*, *Benson*, *Equal Justice*, *Beauty and the Beast*, and *Designing Women*.

Richards did not give up her work on the big screen or on the stage, however, and 1967 saw the release of three feature films: *In the Heat of the Night*, *Hurry Sundown*, and *Guess Who's Coming to Dinner?* which earned her an Academy Award nomination. She enjoyed working with Spencer Tracy and Katharine Hepburn as well as with Sidney Poitier, who played her son. Other films include *The Great White Hope* (1970), *The Biscuit Eater* (1972), *Mahogany* (1975), *Big Shots* (1987), and *Drugstore Cowboy* (1989).

Onstage she performed in *The Crucible* at the Mark Taper Forum and *The Little Foxes* at Lincoln Center and on a national tour. Richards appeared in *A Raisin in the Sun* at the Inner City Repertory Company in 1968 and 1974 and in the twenty-fifth anniversary production at the Yale Repertory Theater in 1983.

She has been associated with Inner City Rep and the Inner City Cultural Center of Los Angeles since 1967. This continuing relationship has provided Richards with an oasis in which to nourish herself as an artist, as both actress and writer. Her play *One Is a Crowd* was produced by Inner City in 1971 and again in 1973, with Richards starring as Elizabeth Dundee. Much earlier, in 1957, Richards had published a poem in *Freedomways* entitled "A Black Woman Speaks"; the work is both a reproach and a plea to white women to bring an end to racism. In 1974, Inner City published *A Black Woman Speaks and Other Poems*. The following year, Richards adapted her poems to the stage in a one-woman show of the same name. She has performed this piece at theaters and colleges all over the country, including Dillard University in New Orleans and the New Federal Theater in New York. *A Black Woman Speaks*, taped by KCET-TV in Los Angeles and broadcast in 1975, won an Emmy Award. Richards's commitment to Inner City includes sharing her skills and vision as a teacher of both professionals and beginners. She teaches scene exploration and the ideal of achieving a "skinless view of life." In spite of her involvement with youth, Richards made a conscious decision not to have children of her own. (She was married in 1963 to Virginia-born artist Hugh Harrel; the couple divorced after three years.) She is committed to creating a society that welcomes all children.

The Hills/Hollywood chapter of the **National Association for the Advancement of Colored People** (NAACP) presented Richards with its Second Annual Award for

Lifetime Achievement in Theater in 1989, and her television work has earned five nominations for the NAACP Image Award. In addition to the *Theater World* Award (*The Amen Corner*, 1965), the Academy Award nomination (*Guess Who's Coming to Dinner?* 1967) and the Emmy Award listed above, Richards has received the All-American Press Association Award, 1968; the Black Filmmakers Hall of Fame Award, 1974; the NAACP Hall of Fame Image Award, 1986; and the ACE award as Best Actress on a cable TV movie or miniseries, 1986.

SHAUNA VEY

premiere of James Baldwin's *Blues for Mr. Charlie* and in the same author's *The Amen Corner* in 1965. That same year, she also acted in Douglas Turner Ward's twin bill of *Happy Ending* and *Day of Absence*, produced by Robert Hooks. That same team would, in 1968, form the **Negro Ensemble Company** (NEC), and Rolle would be a member of the original acting ensemble.

At NEC, Rolle was seen in productions of *Summer of the Seventeenth Doll* and *God Is a (Guess What?)* in 1968. She went with the latter to its London debut in 1969. In the years that followed, she appeared in many

Rolle, Esther (1922–)

Had *Good Times* not delivered Florida Evans from the identity of a maid for Beatrice Arthur's Maude, the public mind might have jelled and cast Esther Rolle in the stereotype long before memorialized by **Hattie McDaniel** and others. Not insensitive to the possibility, she has said, "It has always been a dream of mine to play a maid in a way that is dignified and strong. I'll play the maid, but I'll do it my way."

Esther Rolle was born in Pompano Beach, Florida, in 1922. She was one of eighteen children born into poverty to Jonathan Rolle and his wife. Before beginning her New York acting career, she attended **Spelman College**, Hunter College and, later, the New School for Social Research.

Her pretelevision career is distinguished. She first appeared off Broadway in 1962, replacing another actress in Jean Genet's *The Blacks*, whose producers' uncommonly generous policy let cast members come and go whenever higher-paying jobs beckoned. She appeared on Broadway in the 1964

Esther Rolle was a member of the original Negro Ensemble Company (NEC) and a Broadway veteran long before she was Beatrice Arthur's maid in the Maude *TV series. In 1991, she was inducted into the Black Filmmakers Hall of Fame.* (PRIVATE COLLECTION)

NEC productions, including *Song of the Lusitanian Bogey, Man Better Man,* and *Akokawe.* Her performance in *Don't Play Us Cheap!* which was produced, written, and directed by Melvin Van Peebles in 1972 caught the attention of Norman Lear, who cast her in the role of Florida Evans in the series *Maude,* starring Beatrice Arthur.

The role shot her into stardom. She was so popular as the straight-talking maid that she was given her own series. Because *Maude* was a spinoff of *All in the Family* —Maude Findley being Edith Bunker's cousin—the Chicago-set *Good Times,* which started in 1974, the year *Maude* ended, became television's first spinoff of a spinoff. The maid became a mother of three married to John Amos' often out-of-work James. That character was replaced by Moses Gunn as her boyfriend after Amos quit the series in 1976. Rolle herself left *Good Times* due to a contract dispute for a year (during which she played Lady Macbeth on stage while Florida's kids took care of themselves), but she returned the fall of 1978 and remained until the series ended in August 1979.

In 1979, she won an Emmy as Best Supporting Actress in a Drama Special as the housekeeper in 1978's TV feature *Summer of My German Soldier.* Back on Broadway after *Good Times* in 1980, Sam Levene and she played the title roles in *Horowitz and Mrs. Washington.* In 1989, she was Lena Younger in an American Playhouse production of *A Raisin in the Sun.* That same year, she recreated another classic role when she played the **Ethel Waters** part in *A Member of the Wedding* onstage. In 1990, Rolle was again a maid, this time in the hit movie *Driving Miss Daisy.* She has also appeared in an number of television productions, such as *The Kid Who Loved Christmas, To Dance With the White Dog,* and *Scarlett.*

Deflating the maid persona, she dons in bent and action the educator-activist hats of Mary McLeod Bethune, whom she portrayed in the 1991 one-woman play *Bethune.* (Another solo stage show was *Ain't I a Woman?*) She has campaigned for battered-women's rights, visited low-income area schools, and earned professional and public-service honors, including the NAACP's 1990 Leadership Award.

More important to her than her 1979 Emmy was her 1991 induction into the Black Filmmakers Hall of Fame, perhaps once and for all showing her peers that she had successfully played even maids with strength and dignity—"my way." The honor came, she said, "from my own . . . I believe in bonding with my own. . . . Charity begins at home, and I like what I do for my people because I love me."

GARY HOUSTON

S

Sands, Diana (1934–1973)

"Look at me. Never mind my color. Please just look at me!" Diana Sands eventually got her wish—she starred in Broadway's *The Owl and the Pussycat*, a role written specifically for a white actress. Not one line in the 1964 play was altered to accommodate or explain her race. Her sensational performance shattered the misconceptions of integration, an important subject in Sands' life. "The Negro female has been categorized as the neuter, a mammy, an exotic. Why isn't she a mother, wife . . . a woman desired . . . someone who embodies all the characteristics of American womanhood?"

Diana Sands was born on August 22, 1934, in the Bronx, New York, and was raised a Catholic. Her father, Rudolph Thomas Sands, Sr., was a carpenter; her mother, Shirley Sands, a milliner. The youngest of three, she had an older brother and a sister, Sleegie Rudolph Thomas, Jr., and Joan Crawford Sands Harris, "named for you know who." Her parents approved of her acting career and helped her during bad financial times.

Diana Sands went to elementary school in Elmsford, New York, a town with a small black minority. Racial discrimination forced the family back to Manhattan, where Sands attended the High School of the Performing Arts and made her stage debut in George Bernard Shaw's *Major Barbara*. After graduation in 1953, Sands toured as a carnival singer and then returned to New York. She there pursued her craft with devotion and persistence in $15-a-week roles at the Greenwich Mews and in show tours and lived with night jobs, daytime classes, furnished flats, and hunger.

A 1957 role in *Land Beyond the River* spared Sands from becoming a permanent key-punch operator for Con Edison. In 1958, she sang in *Egg and I* and *Another Evening with Harry Stoones*. In 1959, **Lorraine Hansberry**'s *A Raisin in the Sun* brought her a new opportunity, but "they had to come and get me. I wouldn't even audition. . . I'd given up." Her Broadway performance as Beneatha Younger led to two awards in 1959: the Outer Critics Circle Award as best supporting actress and the *Variety* Critics' Award as the most promising young actress. Sands's performance in the film version won the 1961 International Artists' Award.

In 1964, a banner year for Sands, she won an Obie for *Living Premise* and a Tony nomination for her performance in James Baldwin's *Blues for Mr. Charlie*. She also married Lucien Happersberg, a Swiss artist and Baldwin's manager (the marriage ended in divorce a few years later). Then, with controversy and opposition, Sands was cast opposite Alan Alda in *The Owl and the Pussycat*. Her performance brought her whirlwind fame and another Tony nomination. An acclaimed 1965 London production followed.

Two television Emmy nominations came for *Beyond the Blues* and for "Who Do You Kill?" an *East Side/West Side* episode. She appeared on television in *I Spy, Dr. Kildare, The Fugitive,* and *Julia;* film credits include *An Affair of the Skin, Ensign Pulver, Four Boys and a Gun, Executive Suite, Garment Jungle,* and *The Landlord.* Lead roles in *Caesar and Cleopatra, Antony and Cleopatra,* and *Phaedra* were played on tour. In 1968, she performed at the Lincoln Center Theater as Cassandra in *Tiger at the Gates,* and the title role in George Bernard Shaw's *St. Joan,* which many consider to be her finest work.

In the early 1970s, the good roles became fewer and Sands' stardom faded, though she continued to fight for effective change behind the scenes. In an interview with Maurice Peterson for *Essence* magazine (1972), Sands talked about stardom: "I did get marvelous notices and won awards, but of course, it was not possible for me to become a star." Together with Ossie Davis and others, Sands founded Third World Cinema which produced two of her last films: *Georgia, Georgia* and *Honey Baby, Honey Baby.*

In autumn of 1973, Sands was due to marry director Kurt Baker and star opposite James Earl Jones in the Third World production of *Claudine.* A sudden illness interrupted both plans. **Diahann Carroll** took the role. Sands was hospitalized at Memorial Sloan-Kettering Hospital in New York City, where she died of an inoperable tumor, the result of lung cancer, on Friday, September 21, 1973.

Diana Sands' versatile talent, persistence, courage, and vision enabled her to transcend the color barrier on stage. Her pioneering accomplishments during the tumultuous civil rights era of the 1960s are a theater legacy. She broke many barriers, but discrimination ultimately denied her the continual stardom she so richly deserved.

DELIA REYES

Sanford, Isabel (1917–)

Success did not come overnight to Isabel Sanford, but when it arrived, it arrived in style. She first acted with the **American Negro Theater** in the 1930s and held to her dream through many hard years. Finally, she became a star in the hit television series *The Jeffersons.*

Isabel Sanford was born in Harlem in 1917. Her father, a chauffeur from North Carolina, and her mother, a domestic worker, separated when she was three. She participated in class plays in grade school and later took drama classes in high school. Next, she worked with the American Negro Theater, where colleagues included Harry Belafonte and Sidney Poitier.

Theater jobs for black actresses were rare in the 1930s, so Sanford supported herself as a secretary. By night, she acted in a YMCA theater project and did stand-up comedy in Harlem nightclubs such as Cafe Society and Small's Paradise. Though she eventually appeared off-Broadway in *The Crucible,* she still made her living doing IBM key-punching. In 1959, she won a role in *Purlie Victorious* and in 1961 joined the cast of *The Blacks.*

Finally, in the early 1960s, Sanford took her three young children and moved to Los Angeles. Needing to save money, all three of them made the trip by bus. Sanford found a two-room house in an inexpensive part of town and began to hunt for acting jobs. She found a key-punching job first.

However, persistence paid off, and she began to find steady work in theater. She won a part as Tallulah Bankhead's maid in *Here Today,* not a major role but it paid the bills and enabled Sanford to tour the country. It also gave her her first real experience with Jim Crow laws. "When we were playing in St. Louis, I stopped for a sandwich in a restaurant next to the theater. The waitress leaned over and whispered, 'I'm sorry, but we don't serve coloreds here. I suggest you try the coffee shop on the other side of the theater.' What? I couldn't believe it! I could maybe understand if this was a posh place, but it was a dump!"

Returning to Los Angeles after the tour, Sanford was cast in the 1965 production of James Baldwin's play *The Amen Corner.* That show took her all the way to Broadway.

In 1967, Sanford played a small but memorable part in the film *Guess Who's Coming to Dinner* with Sidney Poitier: the maid who did not approve of him. Bit parts followed on television during the late sixties and early seventies; a semiregular role on *The Carol Burnett Show* helped pay the rent, but her career was still struggling.

Then, after more than three decades in theater and film, Sanford's big break came. In 1971, she won the role of Louise Jefferson in the hit series *All in the Family.* From 1971 to 1975, she played the mother of the family who moved next door to the all-American bigot, Archie Bunker. Her stage family proved so popular that they were given their own spin-off series, *The Jeffersons.* At times struggling in the ratings, at times riding high, *The Jeffersons* lasted for fourteen years. This series was the first long-running black series, far outstripping any black show that had gone before. Although it sometimes suffered from erratic scheduling, the show

was frequently rated among the top ten most popular shows.

In 1981 Sanford won an Emmy for her performance as Louise Jefferson. Over the years she has won several NAACP Image awards.

ANDRA MEDEA

Scott, Seret (1947–)

Seret Scott was born in Washington, D.C., on September 1, 1947. After studying at North Carolina College and at New York

Seret Scott acted in and wrote plays before she directed them in theaters around the country, including the Long Warf Theater, in New Haven, Connecticut. (CHARLES ERICKSON)

University, Scott began her career as an actor, and her performances were critically acclaimed. In 1970, she appeared in *Slave Ship* by Imamu Amiri Baraka (LeRoi Jones) and, in 1974, received a Drama Desk Award for her performance in *My Sister, My Sister*.

However, Scott became frustrated by the lack of good roles for black women. In the early 1970s, she turned to playwriting, producing *Wine and Cheese* in 1970 and *Funnytime* and *No, You Didn't* in 1972. She continued to act, appearing regularly with the **Negro Ensemble Company** in such plays as *Weep Not For Me* in 1981 and *Eyes of the American* in 1985. In reviewing the latter play, the *New Yorker* called Scott "one of the company's strongest actors."

In 1989, Scott's career changed course when she directed *Some Sweet Day* at the Long Wharf Theater in New Haven, Connecticut. Since then, she has directed in theaters around the country, including the New Mexico Repertory Theater, the Alley Theater in Houston, the Alliance Theater in Atlanta, and the Old Globe Theater in San Diego. In 1994, she was awarded a two-year residency at the Long Wharf Theater by the National Theater Artist Residency Program.

KATHLEEN THOMPSON

Shange, Ntozake (1948–)

"Somebody almost walked off wid alla my stuff" best characterizes the sentiments expressed by playwright, poet, short-story writer, novelist, and essayist Ntozake Shange (En-to-ze-ke Shong-ge). The above line from Shange's *for colored girls who have considered suicide/when the rainbow is enuf*, which appeared on Broadway in 1976, struck a chord that appealed to women of every race, class, and age.

Shange's heroines recall experiences of women who have been rejected, verbally and physically abused, and discredited. Her characters draw strong emotional responses because of their determination to survive destructive forces and to build a future that will allow women to soar. While Shange has been heralded as a leading feminist author, she is as much concerned with the plight of black men as with that of women globally. Some common themes in Shange's works include hypocrisy, racism, women's self-effacement, stereotyped roles for black people, and infidelity. Her works link race, class, and gender issues, thereby illuminating the condition of the masses of African Americans.

The oldest of four children, Ntozake Shange was born Paulette Williams on October 18, 1948, in Trenton, New Jersey. Shange's parents, surgeon Paul T. Williams and psychiatric social worker and educator Eloise Williams, provided her with intellectual stimulation and love. When Shange was eight, her parents moved to St. Louis, where they remained for five years. During her years in St. Louis, Shange was exposed to opera, music, dance, literature, and art but was also introduced to blatant racism when she was bused to a German-American school.

Shange's method of coping with the tumultuous racial tensions of the late 1950s and early 1960s was to immerse herself in the works of her favorite authors: Mark Twain, Herman Melville, Simone de Beauvoir, and Jean Genet. Shange also associated with nationally and internationally renowned musicians and singers such as Dizzy Gillespie, Charlie Parker, **Josephine Baker**, Chuck Berry, and Miles Davis, all of whom were friends of her parents and who influ-

Ntozake Shange's powerful play for colored girls who have considered suicide/when the rainbow is enuf *earned a 1977 Obie for best original play and was later nominated for Tony, Grammy, and Emmy Awards.* (LIBRARY OF CONGRESS)

enced Shange's writing; political leader W. E. B. DuBois was also a close family friend who influenced Shange. When she was thirteen, Shange's family returned to New Jersey, where she completed high school.

Always sensitive to the plight of women in a sexist society, Shange attempted suicide at age eighteen after the dissolution of an early marriage. Plagued with a deep sense of alienation and rage, Shange tried to end her life several times, including sticking her head into a gas oven, slashing her wrist, overdosing on Valium, and drinking toxic chemicals.

Though Shange's personal life was unstable, she excelled academically. She earned a bachelor's degree with honors in American studies from Barnard College in 1970 and a master's degree in 1973 from the University of Southern California, Los Angeles. After the civil rights movement of the 1960s raised her consciousness, Shange assumed an African name in 1971 that empowered her to rechannel her energies: *Ntozake* means "she who comes with her own things" and *Shange* means "who walks like a lion." It was while she was in graduate school between 1971 and 1973 that Shange discovered a black literary heritage, reading voluminously the works of Ralph Ellison, Jean Toomer, Claude McKay, Imamu Amiri Baraka, Margaret Walker, and others.

From 1972 to 1975, Shange held English teaching positions at Sonoma State College and the University of California Extension while choreographing poems with the Third World Collective, Raymond Sawyer's Afro-American Dance Company, West Coast Dance Works, and her own company, For Colored Girls Who Have Considered Suicide.

Shange's move to New York City in 1975 marked the beginning of her professional career. Her choreopoem *for colored girls* was produced professionally at Studio Rivbea in July 1975, at the New Federal Theater in 1976, at the Public Theater in June 1976, and at Broadway's Booth Theater in September 1976. Not since **Lorraine Hansberry**'s long-running *A Raisin in the Sun* in 1959 had a play by a black woman appeared on Broadway. *For colored girls* earned a host of awards—a 1977 Obie as best original play, the Outer Critics Circle Award, the AUDELCO Award, and the

Mademoiselle Award—and was nominated for Tony, Grammy, and Emmy awards.

For colored girls comprises 20 choreographed poems and vignettes that portray women in a state of pain, rage, anguish, or disillusionment. These women tell of their exploitation and resolve to stand together against pernicious men who lie, seduce, beat, and abandon them. The choreopoem ends with a laying on of hands, a self-empowering ritual that helps the women become self-confident, self-sufficient, and self-loving.

Shange's rise to fame brought with it increased speaking engagements: Between 1976 and 1981, Shange lectured and performed scenes from her Broadway hit as well as from *Sassafrass*, a 1977 novella, and *Nappy Edges*, a 1978 collection of poems, at a host of institutions, including Yale, Brown, Rice, **Howard**, Southern, and New York Universities.

Shange's writing career was secured in 1981 with the publication of *Three Pieces*, a collection of three plays: *Spell #7, A Photograph: Lovers-in-Motion*, and *Boogie Woogie Landscapes*. A prolific writer, she produced several major works in the 1980s, including the novels *Sassafrass, Cypress, and Indigo* (1982), and *Betsey Brown* (1985); two poetry collections, *A Daughter's Geography* (1983) and *From Okra to Greens* (1984); and a collection of essays, *See No Evil: Prefaces, Essays and Accounts, 1976–1983* (1984).

The major theme in Shange's works is the abuse of women and children. Her female characters survive in the face of loneliness, rejection, and rape. One scene in *for colored girls,* "Latent Rapists," focuses on women who have been raped by friends, men in prestigious positions, but who are afraid to press charges. These women fear double victimization because they live in a society that treats a woman who has been raped as the villain instead of the victim. Another scene in *for colored girls,* "Sorry," centers on the multitude of excuses that men give when they hurt women. Perhaps the most powerful scene in the choreopoem is "A Nite with Beau Willie Brown," which tells the story of an emotionally disturbed Vietnam veteran who flings his two children out of the window when his abused wife refuses to reconcile. This choreopoem had mass appeal and drew women together to discuss their abuse and be healed.

Beginning in 1981, Shange was the recipient of several honors and awards, including a Guggenheim fellowship in 1981; artist-in-residence at the Equinox Theater in Houston; a Medal of Excellence from Columbia University; an Obie Award for the Public Theater production of *Mother Courage and Her Children*, an adaptation of Bertolt Brecht's play; and an appointment to the New York State Council on the Arts Program.

While writing and performing during the 1980s, Shange also taught English at Rice University and the University of Houston before moving to Philadelphia, where she resided with her daughter Savannah. Ever undertaking new projects, Shange's *The Love Space Demands*, a collection of poems, was published in 1991; a novel, *Liliane: Resurrection of the Daughter*, was published in 1994.

Though her theater pieces are extremely experimental, Ntozake Shange carved a place for her poetry on the American stage, which has historically been dominated by males. Her most significant achievement is that she, in grand style, successfully moved her poetry from the spoken word to dramaturgy, thus popularizing the choreopoem. She blends music, dance, and poetry to characterize the black experience in America, particularly the black female experience. Her works empower women to take responsibility for their lives by learning to love themselves and to challenge their oppressors. Shange's life and works give clarification and direction to the current feminist movement.

Prior to Shange, no other playwright had drawn such an emotional response from black men and from women of every race. Her plays initiated a dialogue between men and women, a discussion that continues as sexual harassment policies are being revamped. On one level, Shange's heroines accuse men of abuse, but on another, perhaps higher, level, her characters grapple with the constraints that have been placed on black men and women in America.

"Somebody almost walked off wid alla my stuff" refers to women who have been violated by men, but the statement has also become a metaphor for the lives of poor, uneducated, dispossessed black people in America and around the world who refuse to be trampled upon and who fight mightily for a chance to seize the rainbow.

ELIZABETH BROWN-GUILLORY

Simms, Hilda (1920–1994)

As the star of *Anna Lucasta*, Hilda Simms helped break the color line on Broadway in the 1940s. This production was the first drama with a black cast on Broadway that was not a "race play," but full-bodied theater that went beyond racial lines. Hilda Simms was the star who showed the way.

Born in Minneapolis in 1920, Simms first became interested in the theater at the Uni-

versity of Minnesota; she later studied at Hampton Institute in Virginia. In 1943, she moved to New York City, which at the time was the cultural center of black America. New to the city, she still managed to win a few parts in local radio theater. What was more important, she joined the **American Negro Theater** (ANT) in Harlem.

Her first play with ANT was *Three Is a Family*. Soon she was cast as the lead in ANT's production of *Anna Lucasta*, which dealt with the daughter of a middle-class family who falls into prostitution and which was originally written for white actors. The ANT delivered a powerful production that won the attention of mainstream theaters. *Anna Lucasta* moved to Broadway in 1944, where Simms continued to star. She recreated her role in the London production in 1947. While in Europe, she sang in Paris nightclubs.

Returning to the States, she won roles in the films *The Joe Louis Story* (1953) and *The Black Widow* (1954). In New York she appeared in *The Cool World* (1960), *Tambourines in Glory* (1963), and a revival of *The Madwoman of Chaillot* (1970). Late in life, she appeared in the television series *The Nurses*.

Offstage, Simms earned a master's degree in education from the well respected City College of New York. In the 1960s she directed the creative arts program of New York State's Division of Human Rights, where she fought discrimination against black actors.

ANDRA MEDEA

Sinclair, Madge (1940–1995)

Power, presence, and virtuoso skill—those are the hallmarks of actor Madge Sinclair.

Although she sometimes has had to work with scripts that could not match her talent, she has almost always handed in a memorable performance.

Born in Kingston, Jamaica, in 1940 to Herbert Walters and Jemima Austin Walters, Sinclair was expected to live a settled life: After graduated from Shortwood Women's College with a teaching degree, she married Dean Compton, a security guard and had two sons. While teaching elementary and middle school, she performed in amateur theatrics and studied speech and drama. After six years of teaching, she decided that she could no longer wait and in 1968 left Jamaica for New York to try her luck as an actress.

Sinclair, in New York with $23 to her name, soon found a job and a place to stay and began to audition for acting jobs. Finding it difficult to get work because of her Jamaican accent, she made a deal with an American actor: If he would teach her an American black accent, she would teach him a Jamaican one. The process must have worked. By 1969 she was hired by the New York Shakespeare Festival; her acting career had begun.

Sinclair has often portrayed strong women who hold together under harsh circumstances. Her first film role was a mother whose son had been killed by a white policeman in *Cornbread, Earl and Me* in 1975. Next, she played a tough whorehouse madam in *Leadbelly* in 1976 and, later, a drug addict in *Jimmie B. and Andre* in 1980. These last two roles netted her quite a bit of criticism from the black community, not of her acting but of the roles themselves. Sinclair brushed off the criticism: Both of these characters actually existed, and it was her job, she felt, to render them as realistically as possible.

Sinclair may be best known for her role as Belle, the proud, affectionate wife of Kunta Kinte in *Roots* (1977). Her work in this landmark miniseries won her an Emmy nomination.

Although her talent often seemed better suited to film, Sinclair did most of her work on television. She appeared in minor roles in a number of shows and was a regular in the series *Grandpa Goes to Washington* in 1978. She put in an exceptional performance in the television *Guyana Tragedy: The Jim Jones Story* in 1980; while the program itself was not of the first quality, her performance in it was remarkable. By the early 1980s, Sinclair had a regular role as nurse Ernestine Shoop in the well-regarded series *Trapper John, M.D.*

Sinclair had roles in a few other feature films; perhaps the most notable of these was as the captain of U.S.S. Starship *Saratoga* in *Star Trek IV: The Voyage Home* in 1986. She also provided the voice for the Lion Queen in Disney's *The Lion King* (1994).

An actress capable of delivering finely wrought performances out of sometimes unexceptional material, Madge Sinclair was a consummate professional. She died at Good Samaritan Hospital in Los Angeles on December 20, 1995: She had battled leukemia for thirteen years.

ANDRA MEDEA

Smith, Anna Deveare (1950–)

In the 1993–94 New York theater season, one particular show boasted one of the largest and most varied casts of characters on Broadway: *Twilight: Los Angeles 1992* dealt with the violent and shocking aftermath to the trial of four Los Angeles policemen for beating apprehended motorist Rodney King. Dozens of characters, drawn from all walks of life in Los Angeles populated the stage, including police chief Daryl F. Gates, truck driver Reginald Denny, a Korean store owner, a suburban mother, and a young former gang member. Though it was remarkable enough that this cast would be found on Broadway at all, it was even more remarkable because they were all played by one performer—Anna Deveare Smith.

Born in Baltimore on September 18, 1950, the first of five children and a shy child, Anna Deveare Smith nonetheless soon manifested a keen ability to imitate other people; her siblings delighted in Anna's storytelling abilities. However, she was not to find a natural outlet for her abilities for some time. First, she needed to find a point of view to express.

After graduating from college, she says, she "left home with $80 and an overnight bag and went to California looking for a social movement." What she found was the American Conservatory Theater (ACT), the home of one of the nation's finest acting schools. There, after taking some part-time classes, she was invited to join its professional-level training program, where she earned an M.F.A. Her acting career blossomed, leading her to work in regional theaters, off Broadway, television, and film, including an appearance in the award-winning *Philadelphia*.

Acting eventually led to Smith's teaching in a number of training programs and universities, including A.C.T., Carnegie-Mellon University, Yale, New York University, and the University of Southern California and as the Ann O'Day Maples Professor of Arts at Stanford University. Among the courses she teaches is "Breaking Down Barriers: Beyond Stereotypes of Race and Gender"; as a teacher, she stresses the kind of independence that she feels as a solo performer: "I talk to them about thinking of class as a store," Smith says of her students. "You do your work in the wilderness, and you come into the store to get supplies. I believe in that type of independence, mainly because most of my career has been in independence."

Her independent spirit led Smith away from conventional theater forms and out on the road. Drawing on the oral tradition of storytellers, she began first by interviewing different people about a theme or idea; she then shaped their stories and responses into a script and edited the interview material, eventually weaving the testimony together into a dramatic tapestry. On stage, Smith, with peerless imitative skill and only a few props and costume pieces, recreates these people, shares their varying points of view, and brings them all together into a conversation that they would never imagine having with each other.

Her first performances were sponsored by educational and professional associations. In 1992 she was commissioned by George C. Wolfe, artistic director of New York's Public Theater, to create a piece about the real-life drama that took place in the interracial Crown Heights section of Brooklyn in August of 1991. Her play, *Fires in the Mirror*, gave voice onstage to the anguish, the horror, and the rage that people felt after the deaths of the young African-American Gavin Cato and the rabbinical student Yankel Rosenbaum sparked an outbreak of racial violence. The play received a special Obie Award for distinguished work off-Broadway and was nominated for a Pulitzer Prize. It was also broadcast on public television in April of 1993.

Smith staked out a unique and vital place for herself in the contemporary American theater: *Fires in the Mirror* became the first in a projected series of works she has entitled *On The Road: The Search for the American Character;* the second in the series involved the 1992 Rodney King riots in Los Angeles.

The Mark Taper Forum, Los Angeles' prestigious theater, asked Smith to create a piece examining the riots that had torn the city apart. Smith spent months researching and eventually interviewed more than 175 people. *Twilight* opened at the Taper to overwhelming acclaim in May 1993 and then moved to the Public Theater in New York and, eventually, Broadway. Since then, Smith has performed it throughout the country. Once again, she has gone on the road, sharing the experience of the people she has met. Her task, she has said, is to "perceive in the twilight" and to do whatever she can as performer, writer, and teacher "to breed people who disrupt the quiet, illuminate the twilight, build the bridges, discern pockets of justice and of peace."

RICHARD E. T. WHITE

Spence, Eulalie (1894–1981)

Unlike many early black women who wrote protest plays to promote social change during the 1920s and 1930s, Eulalie Spence wrote for entertainment and avoided racial themes. Spence was one of the most prolific and experienced black female playwrights of her time. Of her thirteen known works, at least eight have been published and seven

produced. With the exception of *Her* and *Undertow*, Spence wrote comedies about Harlem life; her themes were universal, but her characters were undeniably black.

Eulalie Spence was born June 11, 1894, on the island of Nevis, British West Indies. The daughter of a sugar planter, she was the eldest of seven girls. At the turn of the century, her father's crop was destroyed during a hurricane, and the Spence family migrated to New York City in 1902. Spence was inspired by her well-educated mother, who was a great storyteller, to become a writer.

Spence graduated from the New York Training School for Teachers and in 1937 received a B.A. from New York University and in 1939 an M.A. in speech from Columbia University. At Columbia, Spence studied playwriting and performed with the drama club.

In 1918, she joined the New York public school system and in 1927 was assigned to Eastern District High School, Brooklyn. There, until her retirement in 1958, she taught elocution, English, and dramatics, as well as heading the drama group.

Spence won numerous awards during the Harlem Renaissance for her plays: *Foreign Mail* placed second in the **National Association for the Advancement of Colored People**'s *Crisis* competition for playwriting in 1926; in 1927, Spence won the Urban League's *Opportunity* second place award for *The Hunch* and a third place award for *The Starter*. That same year, *Foreign Mail* and *Fool's Errand* were entered in the David Belasco Little Theater Tournament and won the Samuel French $200 prize. Both plays were then published by French. Spence's only full-length play, *The Whipping*, a three-act comedy, was sold to Paramount Pictures but was never produced.

Spence devoted most of her life to her students and work at Eastern District High School. Eulalie Spence died March 7, 1981, in Pennsylvania.

KATHY A. PERKINS

Stewart, Ellen (c. 1920–)

Ellen Stewart's main criterion for deciding whether to produce any given play is at once simple and mystical: "If a play is talking to me personally, if a script *beeps* to me when I'm reading it, we do it." Stewart continues to combine this straightforward enthusiasm with an uncanny ability to smooth over bureaucratic, economic, and interpersonal barriers in operating La MaMa ETC, the leading experimental theater in New York since the early 1960s.

The facts about Ellen Stewart's personal life are hazy, and she likes to keep them that way. She was born around 1920, perhaps in Illinois or Louisiana, has a son and a grandchild, and was raised in Chicago. But in 1950 she left for New York, where she felt she would have better opportunities to study fashion design. She was hired at Saks Fifth Avenue and spent her Sundays exploring New York City. On an expedition to the Lower East Side, she was befriended by a clothing merchant, Abraham Diamond, who began to promote her designs; soon she became an executive designer for Saks but had to leave her position when she became seriously ill. While recuperating in Tangiers, a friend's remark that one must "have one's own pushcart" prompted Stewart to return to New York to seek out her "pushcart": a theater of her own.

She rented a theater in the basement of 321 East Ninth Street in 1961. Cafe La MaMa began there and relocated four times over the next four years: first to 82 Second Avenue; then to 122 Second Avenue, in a loft above a laundromat; then to 9 St. Mark's Place; and then to 74 East Fourth Street, as La MaMa ETC (Experimental Theater Club), with the La MaMa Annex three doors away, at 66–68 East Fourth Street.

As a club, La MaMa originally operated on a subscription basis with Stewart constantly contributing money from her earnings as a fashion designer to keep the theater afloat. In part due to the experimental nature of La MaMa's productions and in part due to Stewart's view that long runs foster a "success-failure syndrome" harmful to developing playwrights, La MaMa's finances have often teetered on the brink of disaster. In 1966, La MaMa almost closed permanently when Actors Equity decreed that its actors could not work at La MaMa unless Stewart paid them. Equity rescinded its decree in response to her appeal.

Since then, Stewart has received several grants to support the theater and pay the actors. The move to East Fourth Street was funded by grants from the Ford and Rockefeller Foundations. She has received numerous grants from the National Endowment for the Arts over the years and, in 1985, a $300,000 MacArthur Fellowship. Her other honors include the Margo Jones Award for helping to develop new playwrights (1969, 1979), the Brandeis Award for distinguished contribution to the theater (1967), a New York State Council on the Arts Award (1973), a special Obie for achievement in off-off-Broadway theater (1980), and the Edwin Booth Award (1985), given by the

Ph.D. program in theater of the CUNY Graduate Center for a significant contribution to New York theater.

Ellen Stewart has given new playwrights the freedom to develop, and the playwrights she fostered epitomize the New York avant-garde. A brief list of her protégés includes Sam Shepard, Jean-Claude van Itallie, Rochelle Owens, Tom Eyen, Julie Bovasso, Megan Terry, Lanford Wilson, Elizabeth Swados, Israel Horovitz, and Leonard Melfi; La MaMa also fostered such important directors such as Andrei Serban and Tom O'Horgan. While rooted in the East Village theater scene, La MaMa enjoys international fame. Acting ensembles from La MaMa began touring Europe in 1965, and affiliated companies were established in London, Paris, Bogota, Tokyo, and several other cities around the world. La MaMa gave Harold Pinter his first American showing with its production of *The Room* (1962), and Stewart has brought countless other artists and companies from around the world to perform at La MaMa, the theater Elizabeth Swados has dubbed "the Marx Brothers version of the United Nations."

JOEL BERKOWITZ

Sul-Te-Wan, Madame (1873–1959)

Madame Sul-Te-Wan, born Nellie Conley on September 12, 1873, in Louisville, Kentucky, was the first African-American actress contracted to appear in one of the most pioneering and controversial films in American cinematic history: *Birth of a Nation* (1915). Her background was African-American and Hawaiian (though some thought her father was Hindu), and she was one of the "Negro Trail Blazers" of California. She did not acquiesce to false pride while experiencing seemingly insurmountable difficulties in her upward climb to be her own person. She always believed she owed it "to the future generation of Negroes to tell of this struggle that it might aid them to not lose heart."

Madame Sul-Te-Wan helped her widowed mother, a washerwoman who worked for women actors. Described as "the little lady" from childhood through adult life, she delivered laundry to women actors at the stage door and was often allowed inside to see the shows. Every time she was permitted to watch a show, she would rehearse the act at school the following day before her classmates, avowing that she too would be an actor someday.

Her mother could not afford singing or dance lessons for Madame, but actors Mary Anderson and Fanny Davenport inspired Madame. They were convinced of her talent and requested the mayor of Louisville, James Whalen, who was in charge of the Buckingham Theater, to provide the young aspirant with an audition. She was one of twenty-five "buck-and-wing dance" contestants (all African American), a special attraction at his theater. First prize was a dishpan and a spoon made of granite. Madame Sul-Te-Wan was the undisputed winner. For Madame, the prize meant confidence in her abilities and aspirations. Her mother began to allow her daughter to perform occasionally. When she was convinced of Madame's talent, she moved with her daughter to Cincinnati, Ohio, to assist the latter's career.

Madame soon became known as "the little dancing protégé of Mary Anderson and Fanny Davenport," performing on Vine Street at the Dime Museum and in a section of town called Over the Rhine in family theaters. She eventually joined the Three Black Coast company, using the stage name of Creole Nell. A major step in her career came when Fanny Davenport contacted her to help secure African-American performers for a play in which Davenport had been contracted to perform in Cincinnati. Of course, Creole Nell was a member of the cast. She eventually formed her own company, the Black Four Hundred, consisting of sixteen performers and twelve musicians. The next season she organized the Rair Back Minstrels. The company toured the East Coast with great success until "she was besieged to marry and did."

Madame Sul-Te-Wan's film debut was in the infamous Birth of Nation *(1915). Her last film was Otto Preminger's* Porgy and Bess *(1959). She was inducted into the Black Film-makers Hall of Fame in 1986.* (BEVERLY J. ROBINSON)

Madame gave birth to three sons: Otto, Onest, and James. After her marriage, she continued to work and later relocated to Arcadia, California. After two years in California and with her youngest child three weeks old, Madame's husband deserted her, and the money she had been sending home while performing on the road had not gone toward the rent, which was ten months in arrears.

An employment agent, J. W. Coleman, introduced Madame and her children before the Forum, an African-American organization devoted to cultural presentations and not-for-profit activities that assisted community members with food and shelter. When she attempted to address the men of the Forum, "she began to cry, whereupon her oldest son, who was not yet seven years, looking up into his mother's face, said: 'Mother, you are not begging. We are going to sing and earn what they give you.' He and his little brother sang and greatly impressed the Forum Club." Madame Sul-Te-Wan did not want to beg, but her situation was desperate. The local theatrical booking companies were white owned and offered excuses rather than jobs to African Americans in the early 1900s. Finally the Associated Charities of Los Angeles moved Madame and her children into town, and she was engaged at the Pier Theater in Venice, a beach area near Los Angeles. The engagement was short, which meant the money barely paid for her and her children's subsistence. Neighbors tried to assist, but Madame was not comfortable accepting charity.

Madame Sul-Te-Wan heard that a man from her hometown was directing a film that was employing African Americans. Because the booking companies claimed that they did not handle independent bookings,

Madame made a personal visit to the director-producer to plead her case for a job. His name was D. W. Griffith, and the film, *Birth of a Nation* (based on Thomas Dixon's novel *The Clansman*), was to become legendary. For Madame, it was successful employment at $3 a day in 1915, when the average American was fortunate to make that amount in a week. Her first day of work was so impressive that Griffith immediately raised her salary to $5 a day and had a separate sketch written in *Birth of a Nation*, making her the first contracted, featured African-American actor (or actress) in American film.

The new sketch "was to show the advancement of the Negro from antebellum days to this present period. . . . [Madame] appeared as a rich colored lady, finely gowned and owner of a Negro colony of educated colored citizens, who not only owned their own land, but she drove her own coach and four-in-hand." She played opposite the character actress Josephine Crowell. In her first scene as a nouveau-riche black woman immediately after the Civil War, she is finely dressed and meets Crowell on the street; Crowell shuns Madame. Insults follow, and the scene climaxes with Madame spitting in Crowell's face. "After the picture was made . . . the censor cut the part out in which she appeared as a rich colored lady, and other parts, leaving only the bitter-gall portions for the insults of the Negro race through out the nation." The film was a historical spectacle with a running time of more than three hours and broke all previous financial records. However, the censorship probably heightened the film's racial controversy; all major African-American roles (after the censoring) were played by white actors in blackface.

The African Americans who were involved were relegated to minor parts, thus encouraging the notion of racially stereotyped images.

Birth of a Nation was technically an innovative classic. While Griffith pushed the film in New York, it made its West Coast premiere in Los Angeles. Many in the African-American community objected to the racial images of Northern blacks after the Civil War moving to the South, "exploiting and corrupting the former slaves, unleashing the sadism and bestiality *innate* in the Negro, turning the once-congenial darkies into renegades, and using them to 'crush the white South under the heel of the Black South'." Portraying African Americans as eating chicken legs, drinking whiskey from bottles, and propping bare feet on their business desks as political legislators, Griffith was accused of perpetuating racial stereotypes.

Madame Sul-Te-Wan was featured in the films *The Marriage Market*, *Intolerance*, *Happy Valley's Oldest Boy*, and *Up from the Depths*. Her other films include *Narrow Street* (1925) and Josef Von Sternberg's *Thunderbolt* (1929). *Thunderbolt* was one of the earlier films to move away from the conventional images of African Americans. Madame's eccentric dress style (flowery hats, turbans, flowing beaded necklaces, and an array of cotton/silk color combinations) won her a character role as Voodoo Sue in the 1931 Will Rogers film *Heaven on Earth*, based on a novel by Ben Lucien Burman. She was also a contract cast member in the 1934 film version of *Imitation of Life* and *Black Moon* (1934). In 1938, Madame Sul-Te-Wan appeared with George Reed in Fox Pictures's major Technicolor Christmas release, *Kentucky*—one of the many racetrack films done in the 1930s. During the same era, there were attempts by filmmakers to turn the camera's eye on the social injustices of prisons. *Ladies They Talk About* (1932), for example, featured an incarcerated Barbara Stanwyck in a prison with a few blacks, who included "a darkly ominous" Sul-Te-Wan.

Madame's other films include Zanuck's *In Old Chicago* (1938), *Uncle Tom's Cabin* (1927), and, as the character Tituba, *The Maid of Salem* (1937). When she died on February 1, 1959, at the Motion Picture Country Home in Woodland Hills, Califor-

nia, several papers cited her as a pioneering actress who had performed on stage and in films for more than seventy of her eighty-five years. Sul-Te-Wan's last films included *Rhapsody in Blue* (1945), *Mighty Joe Young* (1949), *Carmen Jones* (1954), *Something of Value* (1957), *The Buccaneer* (1958), and Otto Preminger's *Porgy and Bess* (1959).

A historic painting of Madame Sul-Te-Wan is displayed at the Black Filmmakers Hall of Fame in Oakland, California, where she was posthumously inducted for her trailblazing work in theater and film.

BEVERLY J. ROBINSON

T

Taylor, Clarice (1927–)

A gifted actress of the New York black theater, Clarice Taylor has bridged eras in her life and work. Born at the end of the Harlem Renaissance, a visitor to the Apollo Theater in its heyday and an early member of the famous **Negro Ensemble Company**, she brings the richness and vitality of classic black theater to the modern audience.

Born on September 20, 1927, in Buckingham County, Virginia, Clarice Taylor was the child of Leon Taylor, a post office dispatcher, and Ophelia Taylor, a nurse. Soon after, the family moved to Harlem, where Taylor spent her childhood.

Harlem in the thirties was the black mecca of America. Still vibrating from the golden days of the Harlem Renaissance in the twenties, Harlem night life was slowed by the Depression, but it was not stopped. The Apollo Theater was the center of attraction. Jazz greats, blues greats, and comic greats such as **Moms Mabley** presented the best of black art to the best of black audiences.

When young Clarice Taylor announced to her parents that she wished to be an actress, they were frankly appalled. Respectable people might go to the theater, but they certainly did not perform in it. But the concerned parents could do nothing to dissuade their daughter.

Taylor graduated from high school and completed a year of college at Columbia University. While still a teenager, she became an early member of the **American Negro Theater**, where she first appeared onstage in *On Striver's Row* in 1942. After that, Taylor got an occasional small part in a Broadway show, such as *Rain* in 1948, but acting jobs were not enough to pay rent. She took a job at the post office when she left college, and that is how she supported herself for the next twenty years.

Meanwhile, Taylor performed in off-Broadway shows through the 1940s and 1950s. In 1955, she was highly praised by the critics for her performance in **Alice Childress'** *Trouble in Mind* at the Greenwich Mews Theater. While Broadway was the site of posh productions with huge audiences, off-Broadway was the home of smaller, more intimate theater. Much of off-Broadway consisted of progressive plays, playing to a more unconventional audience. Off-Broadway was also the home of most black theater. It was an exciting place to perform.

It also paid less; off-Broadway, sheer talent had to make up for the lack of revenue. Taylor kept her night job.

Her break came in 1967 when, at the age of forty, she was invited to become a member of the Negro Ensemble Company (NEC). At long last, she could quit the post office and become what she was meant to be—an actress. She stayed with the NEC for several years, performing in such plays as *Summer of the Seventeenth Doll, Kongi's Harvest, Daddy Goodness*, and *Akokawe*.

She was also in the premiere productions of *Five on the Black Hand Side* at American Place Theater in 1969 and of Alice Childress' *Wedding Band* at the New York Shakespeare Festival in 1972.

In 1972, Taylor moved to Los Angeles with her husband, Claude. She won minor roles in films such as *Play Misty for Me* and *Five on the Black Hand Side*. She also appeared in several television series, including *Ironsides*, *Sesame Street*, and *Sanford and Son*. She returned to Broadway in 1974, where she played Addaperle in *The Wiz* for a five-year run. When Claude died in 1977, Taylor decided to make New York home again.

In the 1980s, Taylor won the role of Grandma Huxtable in the popular series *The Cosby Show*. This role earned her an Emmy nomination in 1986 and reintroduced her to a new generation of fans.

Following up her success, Taylor decided to revive a favorite project, a re-creation of the late stand-up comic Moms Mabley. Moms Mabley was famous for playing a shabby, raffish character, always good humored and a little off color. While tame by today's standards, Moms Mabley shocked the censors in her heyday and delighted in doing so.

Taylor had watched Moms Mabley as a child in Harlem and re-created her stand-up routine in a tribute in 1981 at the Apollo Theater. Now was her chance to make the show everything it might be. Borrowing money from friends and family and with friend Alice Childress to write the script, Taylor made *Moms* an off-Broadway success. She won an Obie for her role.

Moms closed after a brief run in order to reopen a few months later. In the meanwhile, Taylor and Childress had a falling out over the script, and Taylor brought in Ben Caldwell to make changes. Childress sued for copyright infringement, and a lifelong friendship was over. The new production continued to play to rave reviews. "I feel like I've been holding on to the tail of a comet," she told *People* magazine in 1987, "while Moms is up there directing everything." That is not a bad way to feel after fifty years in the theater.

ANDRA MEDEA

Taylor, Jackie (1951–)

"I write, I direct, I produce—ain't no spare time. That's my life," says Jackie Taylor. "Leisure is half an hour before the curtain goes up, when I'm putting on my make-up."

Since 1976, Jackie Taylor and the Black Ensemble Theater have been legend in Chicago. Presenting a challenging mixture of black plays and black adaptations of classics, the theater has won a large and loyal audience. Directing and starring in many of those plays, Taylor has shown remarkable power, range, and truthfulness.

Taylor grew up in Chicago, graduating from Loyola University in the early 1970s. The city was then in the midst of a theater renaissance, and the young actor became part of the excitement at Stuart Gordon's Organic Theater, David Mamet's St. Nicholas Theater, and the Free Street Theater. It took her only a few years to realize that, exhilarating as the scene was, there was simply not enough room in it for African Americans, especially women. For a dynamic, highly motivated woman with a need to act, there was only one thing to do, and Jackie Taylor did it.

The Black Ensemble Theater has not been Taylor's only venue. She has continued to perform at the Goodman, Victory Gardens, and the other important Chicago theaters. She has also appeared in such Chicago-made films as *Cooley High* and *Losing Isaiah*, as well as the television movie *The Father Clements Story*. But she has spurned Hollywood—where her brother, Meschach Taylor, has costarred in two major comedy series—and anything else that would take her away from the theater she created.

In that theater, she has directed more than fifty plays in the last twenty years. She has acted the roles of Medea, Anna Lucasta, Blanche Dubois in *A Streetcar Named Desire*, and Amanda in *The Glass Menagerie*. She has written or co-written such plays as *The Other Cinderella*, *Great African Queens*, *Only the Strong Survive*, *Precious Lord Take My Hand* (the life of gospel great Thomas Dorsey), and *Muddy Waters (The Hoochie Coochie Man)*.

At the same time, Taylor has worked with young people in Urban Gateways, Centers for New Horizons, and other artist residency programs. She created a theater program in 1993 for the Little City Foundation, a group that works with mentally challenged students.

The Black Ensemble Theater has made its home for many years on Beacon Street in Chicago's uptown area. Recently, its address changed; it is now officially, by order of mayor of the city of Chicago, on Jackie Taylor Street.

Jackie Taylor is the mother of one daughter, Tynea Wright, who is a prelaw student at Fisk University.

KATHLEEN THOMPSON

Taylor, Regina (1960–)

Onto the television screen in 1992 came a luminous presence, a character of reserve and intelligence who clearly viewed life as a search and a treasure. She was a maid. In playing Lilly, of *I'll Fly Away*, Regina Taylor reached through the stereotype to the reality of the thousands of black women who have filled that role in life.

Regina Taylor was born in Dallas, Texas, to Nell Taylor, a social worker in the Social Security Administration. When Regina was in the second grade, Nell Taylor was transferred to Muskogee, Oklahoma. At that time, schools were still segregated in Oklahoma; then, in 1972, Alice Robertson Junior High School was integrated, and Taylor, a seventh-grader, was one of the first group of black students to enter the school. "I was feeling like this idealistic child of Martin Luther King," she told *People* magazine in 1992, but the experience was far from an ideal. The first day contained a rejection by a white classmate that was so emotionally brutal that Taylor ended feeling, "How can she hate me when she doesn't know me?"

In spite of this atmosphere, Taylor's talent and imagination emerged early in her life. She began to write plays and musicals; in fact, when she entered Southern Methodist University, she planned to be a writer. After an acting class, she changed her mind and began to study theater.

Though Taylor did one television program—*Crisis at Central High*—while she was still in college, she started at the bottom when she moved to New York after graduation. She auditioned, did some stage work, and in 1989 finally won a role in the film *Lean on Me*. She played a recovering crack addict. In the television movie *Howard*

Beach: Making the Case for Murder, she played a district attorney. In 1991, she won the role of Lilly.

The critical reaction to *I'll Fly Away*, in which Taylor costarred with Sam Waterston, verged on the ecstatic, but NBC did not feel they were getting high enough ratings. The series was dropped. However, in a remarkable tribute to the quality of the show, PBS picked it up. Taylor and Waterston were reunited in 1994 on an episode of *Law and Order*.

Taylor did not abandon her early aspirations to be a writer when she turned to acting. She wrote and starred in a one-woman show, *Escape From Paradise*, that opened on Broadway in 1994.

KATHLEEN THOMPSON

Teer, Barbara Ann (1937–)

Barbara Ann Teer, award-winning actor and director, producer, writer, educator, cultural leader, businesswoman, real estate developer, and founder/executive director of the National Black Theater Company, was born June 18, 1937, in East St. Louis, Illinois, to Fred L. and Lila (Benjamin) Teer. She received her B.S. in dance education in 1957 from the University of Illinois with honors; did further study in dance in Germany, Switzerland, and Paris; and studied acting with Sanford Meisner, Paul Mann, Phillip Burton, and Lloyd Richards. Additionally, she studied at the University of Wisconsin, University of Connecticut, Bennett College, Sarah Lawrence College, Mary Wigman Studios, and for four years at the Musical Academy of Dramatic Art.

Her Broadway credits include the controversial African musical *Kwamina*, for which she worked as the dance captain for Agnes De Mille (who won a Tony Award for choreography), and *Where's Daddy* by William Inge at the Billy Rose Theater. She was the winner of the Drama Desk Vernon Rice Award in 1964–65 for outstanding achievement off-Broadway in *Home Movies* and later appeared in twelve off-Broadway productions: *The Experiment, Who's Got His Own, Day of Absence* and *Experimental Death Unit I, The Living Premise, Does a Tiger Wear a Necktie?, Young Lady of Property, Missing Rattlesnakes, Funnyhouse of a Negro, The Owl and the Pussycat,* and *The Prodigal Son*. Her television credits list three appearances on *Camera Three, Kaleidoscope,* the soap opera *As the World Turns, The Ed Sullivan Show, The David Susskind Show,* and Joseph Mankiewicz's *A Carol for Another Christmas*. Her movie credits have among them Sidney Lumet's *The Group* and *The Pawnbroker* and Ossie Davis's *Gone Are the Days*. Her dance tours traveled to Brazil with the Alvin Ailey American Dance Theater, Chicago with the Duke Ellington show, Las Vegas with the **Pearl Bailey** show, Canada with Get Aboard the Jazz Train, and New York City with the Louis Johnson Dance Company and the Henry Street Playhouse Dance Company.

Prior to taking the boldest step in her theater career, founding the National Black Theater Company (NBT) in Harlem in 1968, Teer had grown dissatisfied with the lack of respect for black culture in American professional theater. In 1967, she and Robert Hooks founded the Group Theater Workshop in Harlem to refocus their talents toward the black community. When this endeavor evolved into the founding of the **Negro Ensemble Company** (NEC), she was inclined to establish her own company, which (with NEC) became one of the most prominent theater companies in the country during the black revolutionary-theater movement of the late 1960s and early 1970s. In the NBT, Teer saw the opportunity to develop an art form that would address the immediate concerns of African-American people. Her endeavor to reflect the collective personality (ethos-soul) of African Americans through theater was enhanced in 1972 by a Ford Foundation Fellowship to sponsor her visit to Africa to further her research. She spent four months in western Nigeria acquainting herself with the Yoruba culture and extended her study to South America, the Caribbean islands, and Harlem.

Out of this quest evolved Teer's ritualistic theater, developed and taught through the "Black Art Standard"—sometimes known as "Teer Technology of Soul"—as a technique for teaching "God Conscious Art" at the National Black Theater. Teer has written, directed, and produced several productions reflecting her "Black Art Standard," including *The Ritual* on the television show *Soul* in 1970, *Change/Love Together/Organize: A Revival* (1972), *We Sing a New Song* (1972), *Sojourn into Truth* (1976), and *Softly Comes the Whirlwind, Whispering in Your Ear* (1978). She toured in Haiti, Bermuda, Trinidad, Guyana, and Nigeria. More recently, she produced the ritualistic drama *The Legacy* by Gordon Nelson at the 1989 National Black Theater Festival. Additionally, she directed *Me and My Song* for the Black Heritage series on NBC television and wrote, directed, and coproduced the award-winning film *Rise: A Love Song for a Love People* (1975), based on the life of Malcolm X. Her off-Broadway directing credits include Joseph Walker and Jo Jackson's *The Believers*, Douglas Turner Ward's award-winning *Day of Absence*, and Charles Russell's *Five on the Black Hand Side*.

Teer's boldest accomplishment, developing real estate for the arts, promises to be the most ambitious building project of any traditionally black arts organization in history. After the NBT's 137th Street home was destroyed by fire in 1983, Teer purchased property on 125th Street and Fifth Avenue for NBT to develop a new theater in the Harlem community: the National Black Institute of Communication through Theater Arts (NBICTA). This $10-million theater is the first revenue-generating black arts theater complex in the country according to Teer and combines commercial, retail, and office space with theater-arts activities.

Teer's talent, vision, and commitment to her community and to uplifting African-American theater arts have been recognized extensively. She is the recipient of more than thirty awards, citations, and memberships including *Who's Who in America* (1991); distinguished membership in **Delta Sigma Theta Sorority**'s National Commission on the Arts (1991); Legends in Our Time, *Essence* magazine (1991); Citation, the J. Raymond Jones Democratic Club, Barbara Ann Teer Day, East St. Louis, Illinois (1991); AUDELCO (Audience Development Committee) Special Achievement Award (1989); Kwanza Expo Award (1989); Acknowledgment Award, Breakthrough Foundation New York Youth at Risk; Sojourner Truth Award, Harlem Women's Committee/New Future Foundation, Inc. (1987); and the Monarch Merit Award, National Council for Culture and Art (1984).

LINDA NORFLETT

Thomas, Edna Lewis (1886–1974)

Born in 1886 in Lawrenceville, Virginia, Thomas first came to acting prominence with the Lafayette Players, a group that existed from 1917 to 1932. Sister M. Francesca Thompson says that "this was the first major professional black dramatic company in America." Thomas made her debut on November 8, 1920, at the Putnam Theater, Brooklyn, in F. H. Wilson's *Confidence*, a vehicle of the Quality Amusement Corporation, the contractual name for the Lafayette Players.

Seven months later, on June 11, 1921, the *New York Age* recorded her being cast in the principal female role of Elsie Tillinger in *Turn to the Right* with the Lafayette Players in New York City.

It was during the 1920s, however, and the fervent Harlem Renaissance that Thomas received considerable recognition. A part of the wealthy A'Lelia Walker's social circle, Thomas mingled with artists, musicians, writers, actors, underworld characters, and leading citizens at one of Walker's three splendid residences. Carl Van Vechten, *bon vivant*, writer, photographer, and Negrophile, supported Thomas and served other artists of color through his wealth, media contacts, and vast photographic collection.

A "handsome" woman, according to actor-director-promoter Carlton Moss, this performer of color, fair-skinned enough to be mistaken for white, "rubbed shoulders with the dominant group." Eventually, she came to the attention of young filmmaker Orson Welles and actor-director John Houseman and finally, after a half-century, went on to Hollywood and Broadway to be cast in minor roles.

Her first exposure outside the Lafayette Players came on May 15, 1923, when the Ethiopian Art Theater cast Thomas as Adrianna's sister in a jazz version of Shakespeare's *The Comedy of Errors*, staged in a circus tent at the Frazee Theater, New York City. Percy Hammond, critic of the *New York Herald Tribune*, referred to the then thirty-seven-year-old actor as an "ingenue," giving her "a magnificent review," according to an interview Thomas gave scholar Richard France in 1972. Alexander Woollcott, also a major critic, called the troupe "an industrious darky" one.

Expansive and unflinching in a daring career against all odds for a woman of color, Thomas saw the footlights again in 1926 when producer David Belasco cast her in a small role in his production of the realistic drama *Lulu Belle* by Charles G. MacArthur and Edward S. Sheldon. Lenore Ulrich and Henry Hull, both white, played the courtesan and the male lead, respectively. Larry Barretto, in *Bookman*, observed that "an enormous cast [mainly African American] . . . must have depopulated several cotton-growing states, not to speak of emptying Harlem's black belt nightly." In a letter to Van Vechten, Thomas wrote from Chicago on October 21, 1927:

> Carlo darling . . . *Lulu Belle* went over big—every critic (except one) praising the work of Miss U. in the most extravagant fashion. The odd man (*Tribune*) laid off until yesterday, when he used much space warning the natives against so filthy a play. The result of which will be, I hope, a forced extension of our ten weeks here. . . . Affectionately, Edna

The actor also crossed the boards in vaudeville and, according to *Variety*, was in

Edna Thomas came to prominence with the Lafayette Players and went on to perform on Broadway and in films. Among her roles was that of the Mexican woman in Tennessee Williams' A Streetcar Named Desire, *which she played in the original Broadway production, several subsequent revivals, and in the film version. She is seen here in her dressing room during the 1951 revival of the Williams play.* (GRIFFITH J. DAVIS)

the Theater Guild's production of Dorothy and DuBose Heyward's *Porgy*, the 1927 play on which the 1935 Gershwin opera *Porgy and Bess* was based. However, her name does not appear in cast listings.

With the waning of the Harlem Renaissance and the onset of the Great Depression, Thomas and her husband, Lloyd Thomas, met with hard times. Finally Thomas worked again, playing Maggie in Donald Heywood's *Ol' Man Satan*, which opened at the Forest Theater on October 3, 1932, after a year's rehearsal; this was the longest rehearsal period on record, excluding *Sing for Your Supper*, produced by the Federal Theatre. Such abuse of actors made Thomas an activist; she gave her copy of *The Revolt of the Actors* to unionizer Frederick O'Neal.

In 1933, Thomas played the forgiving wife of the preacher's son at Hope Baptist

Church in Hall Johnson's *Run, Little Chillun:* Sis Ella's marriage is threatened by the temptress Sulamai from a pagan cult across the river. The volatile and controversial *Stevedore*, a play by Paul Peters and George Sklar about the unionizing of Louisiana dock workers, followed; Thomas played Ruby Oxley, the romantic interest. Congress labeled the play "a Communistic lynch drama."

With such stellar performances and recognition by critics and audiences, Thomas became a leading figure in the Federal Theatre's $46 million effort under the aegis of Franklin Delano Roosevelt's Works Progress Administration (WPA) project. In 1936, Orson Welles chose Thomas to play Lady Macbeth in his voodoo adaptation of Shakespeare's tragedy; she was fifty years old. The work opened to mixed reviews, intensely hot controversy, and standing-room-only crowds that had to be quelled by riot police squads. This was her first major classical role. Roi Ottley of the *New York Amsterdam News* wrote, "In Edna Thomas's last scene as Lady Macbeth, she literally tore the heart of the audience with her sensitive and magnificent portrayal of the crazed Lady Macbeth." *Newsweek* also was favorable, but arch-conservative Percy Hammond declared, "Miss Thomas impersonated Lady Macbeth with a dainty elegance that defied all traditions except those of the WPA."

Other Federal Theatre vehicles for Thomas included the part of the slave girl, Lavinia, in a 1938 black version of George Bernard Shaw's *Androcles and the Lion* opposite P. Jay Sidney as the romantic interest, the captain. Six months after this play opened, Congress closed the Federal Theatre, urged on by threatened Broadway producers who feared "welfare" theater and communist infiltration.

The government theater led to roles on Broadway—Sukey, a mulatto slave girl, in *Harriett*, with Helen Hayes, in 1943–44; Mamie McIntosh in Lillian Smith's novel-turned-play, *Strange Fruit*, produced by José Ferrer in 1945; and the Mexican woman in Tennessee Williams' *A Streetcar Named Desire*, both on stage in 1947, 1950, and 1951 and on the screen in 1956.

Her opportunities were few, although she was well known in limited circles of Boston and New York. She spent her retirement years in New York City, where she died of a heart condition on July 22, 1974.

GLENDA E. GILL

Tyson, Cicely (1939–)

The achievements and contributions of Cicely Tyson are a testament to the substantial gains made by African-American women in film and theater. Her parents, William and Theodosia Tyson, immigrated to the United States from Nevis, the smallest of the Leeward Islands in the West Indies. Her father was a painter and in between jobs sold fruit and vegetables from a pushcart. The family settled in East Harlem, New York, where Cicely, one of three children, was born on December 19, 1939. Her parents divorced when she was eleven and Cicely grew up with her mother, who was devoutly religious. It was at church that her talents began to develop. She sang, played the organ, and taught Sunday school in the Episcopalian and Baptist Churches. Theatrical entertainment, such as movies, was strictly forbidden by her mother as sinful; the ability of the actor to capture and potentially sway an audience in an other than ordinary space could be mistaken for godliness.

After graduating from Charles Evans Hughes High School, she took a job as a secretary before she was asked by Walter Johnson, her hairdresser, to model hairstyles. He encouraged Cicely to pursue modeling, and she eventually enrolled in the Barbara Walters Modeling School, earning $65 an hour as a model. When the *Ebony* fashion editor Freda DeKnight discovered Cicely Tyson through an interview, she developed Tyson to become one of the top models in the United States.

Her first starring role on stage was in *Dark of the Moon*. This 1957 production was directed by Vinnette Carroll at the Harlem Young Men's Christian Association (YMCA). It was written by Howard Richardson and William Berney and was produced by the YMCA Drama Guild in association with the Little Theater players and the Harlem Showcase. In 1959, *Dark of the Moon* was presented at the Equity Library Theater with Cicely Tyson, James Earl Jones, **Isabel Sanford**, and choreography by Alvin Ailey. Her next performance was in *Moon on a Rainbow Shawl* (1962), written by Errol John and directed by George Roy Hill. This time, she shared the stage with Vinnette Carroll, whom she respected as an important teacher of theater. The New York production was the winner of an Obie Award, and Tyson received the prestigious Vernon Rice Award for her role as Mavis.

When Jean Genet's *The Blacks* appeared off-Broadway (1961–62), directed by Gene Frankel, Cicely Tyson was again honored with the Vernon Rice Award, this time for her portrayal of Virtue. Frankel's epochal directing established an innovative standard for off-Broadway theater. The play had a

stellar cast that included Tyson, James Earl Jones, **Helen Martin**, **Maya Angelou**, Roscoe Lee Browne, Godfrey Cambridge, and Louis Gossett, Jr. An ensemble of many of these African-American actors was later formed to develop one of the oldest continuous black theater companies today, the **Negro Ensemble Company**. Though she had begun a film and television career, Tyson never forgot the stage. Films broadened her acting experience and further tested the

Magnificently exemplifying a new awareness of black beauty and dignity, after The Heart Is a Lonely Hunter *(1968) Cicely Tyson refused film roles rather than appear in parts that were not positive in their image, attitude, and expression. She broke that hiatus with a stunning performance in* Sounder *(1972) as Rebecca Morgan (pictured).* (DONALD BOGLE)

training that she began with Lloyd Richards in 1959, the same year she filmed *Odds Against Tomorrow* and *The Last Angry Man*.

She made her major television debut in Paule Marshall's *Brown Girl, Brownstones* (1960) and then did a series of Sunday morning dramas. She also was cast for a *Camera Three* television production, *Between Yesterday and Today*. When the prominent actor George C. Scott saw her performance in *The Blacks*, he recruited her for the 1963–64 season television show *East Side/West Side*, establishing Cicely Tyson as the first black regular on a television series. Unfortunately, the television series did not utilize her talents as an actor; fortunately, the stage did allow her to explore and display her artistry. In 1962, she appeared in the stage production *Tiger, Tiger, Burning Bright* and in 1963 in the off-Broadway production of *The Blue Boy in Black*, directed and produced by Ashley Feinstein.

In 1963, Tyson performed in *Trumpets of the Lord* (directed by Donald McKayle). This off-Broadway production was adapted by Vinnette Carroll from folk sermons and a prayer from James Weldon Johnson's *God's Trombones* and was revived in 1968. (Tyson performed in both productions.) Other theater credits include *A Hand Is on the Gate* (1966); *Carry Me Back to Morningside Heights* (1968); the off-Broadway production of *To Be Young, Gifted, and Black* (1969); and *Desire under the Elms*, performed in Lake Forest, Illinois (1974). Between her stage, film, and television performances, she honed her craft by taking courses at New York University, Lee Strasberg's Actors' Studio, and the Paul Mann workshop.

Cicely Tyson's television appearances on *Slattery's People* (1965); *I Spy* (1965, 1966); *The Guiding Light* series (1967); and *Cowboy in Africa* (1966, 1967) were mere preludes to her stunning performances in the 1968 film *The Heart Is a Lonely Hunter* and as Rebecca Morgan in *Sounder* (1972). The several-year gap between films resulted from Tyson's refusal to accept parts that were not positive in their image, attitude, and expression of black people. In *The Heart Is a Lonely Hunter*, based on the novel by Carson McCullers, the role of the doctor's daughter had been especially tailored for her by the screenwriter. *Sounder* was Tyson's first film after her decision not to participate in films exploiting stereotypes. As Rebecca Morgan, she played a faithful, dignified, strong, loving wife of a sharecropper. While some African Americans were critical of the 1940s setting of *Sounder* and its Southern historical base, Tyson was adamant in her belief that the characters were drawn from lives of people "who have been through those kinds of years, [and] are the foundation upon which we are standing today."

The 1970s saw Cicely Tyson emerge as one of America's leading dramatic performers. She brought a refreshing image of black women to the screen by portraying perseverance, pride, and strength in a variety of settings. For her critically acclaimed performance in *Sounder*, she was named Best Actress by the National Society of Film Critics and was nominated for an Academy Award. Her ability to absorb a role as part of an organic process in the art of acting is (as she has often learned and stated) "getting into the cells, and fibre, and being of the character." Her absorption process was truly put to the test when she was cast in the television drama *The Autobiography of Miss Jane Pittman* (1974), in which she portrayed 110-year-old Jane Pittman. Born into slavery and subjected to discrimination in a racist and hostile society, Jane Pittman finds in old age the courage at last to strike out at injustice. For her performance, Cicely Tyson received excellent reviews and numerous awards, including Emmy Awards as Best Lead Actress and as Actress of the Year. Her agent, Bill Haber, lauded her performance but questioned what she could possibly do after *Sounder* and *Miss Jane Pittman;* he believed that she had "acted herself clean out of the business."

Cicely Tyson returned to the stage in 1976 for the Broadway production of *The River Niger*, and that same year she received her fourth **National Association for the Advancement of Colored People** Woman of the Year Award. The following year, she returned to television in *Wilma* (the story of **Wilma Rudolph**, played by Shirley Jo Finney). Subsequent television roles include the mother of Kunta Kinte in *Roots* (Emmy nomination as Best Actress); **Coretta Scott King** in the miniseries *King*; **Harriet Tubman** in *A Woman Called Moses*; and Chicago schoolteacher **Marva Collins** in a television movie. Most recently she appeared in a television miniseries produced by and starring **Oprah Winfrey**, *The Women of Brewster Place* (1989) and in the film *Fried Green Tomatoes* (1991).

Other awards and honors include an Honorary Doctor of Humane Letters from Lincoln University, an honorary Doctor of Fine Arts from Loyola-Marymount College, and honorary doctorates from Atlanta and Pepperdine Universities. She has been honored by the Congress of Racial Equality (CORE), the NAACP, and the **National**

Cicely Tyson poses here with the two Emmy Awards she won for her performance in the title role of the 1974 drama The Autobiography of Miss Jane Pittman, *an account of a black woman's life from slavery to defiance at the age of 110.* (PRIVATE COLLECTION)

Council of Negro Women. In 1974, she received the Best Actress award at Jamaica's First Black Film Festival (for *The Autobiography of Miss Jane Pittman*). She was inducted into the Black Filmmakers Hall of Fame (1977), and in Chicago, Operation PUSH declared a Cicely Tyson Day. In 1974 Cicely Tyson was the first actor of any race or sex to be honored with a day by the Harvard University Faculty Club.

She was the first vice president of the board of directors of the Dance Theater of

Harlem, a trustee of the American Film Institute, and a Board of Governors member of Urban Gateways (an organization that exposes children to the arts). Tyson is also the former wife of the late jazz trumpeter Miles Davis.

BEVERLY J. ROBINSON

U

Uggams, Leslie (1943–)

In the early 1960s, the only black regular on a network television show was Leslie Uggams. This teenager with a beautiful smile was already a seasoned performer when she began to appear on *Sing Along With Mitch*, a weekly musical revue hosted by Mitch Miller on NBC.

Uggams was born in the Washington Heights neighborhood of New York City on May 25, 1943, to parents familiar with show business. Her father, Harold, an elevator operator and floor waxer, had sung with the Hall Johnson Choir, and her mother, Juanita, had been a chorus girl at the famous Cotton Club. Little Leslie first sang in public when she was six, and her mother insisted that she take dancing lessons to develop poise. She went to a public school and then transferred to the Professional Children's School in the fourth grade. As a child, she appeared on several TV variety shows and played **Ethel Waters'** niece in the series *Beulah*. When she was nine, she sang at the Apollo Theater in Harlem, and the *Variety* critic praised her "stage savvy."

In 1958, on the TV quiz show *Name That Tune*, Uggams won $25,000 and the attention of Mitch Miller, who was then an executive with Columbia Records. He signed her to a recording contract, and her first album was released in October 1959. In January 1961, they began to work together on *Sing Along With Mitch*. At the time,

many whites felt threatened by the idea of integration, and Miller emphasized Uggams's wholesome sweetness in order to avoid alienating viewers of his family-oriented program. Her father recalled that Miller "sold her into the American home. He fixed it so no one resented her." His

In the early 1960s, Leslie Uggams was the only black regular on a network television show— Sing Along With Mitch. *She has been seen in starring roles ever since.* (PRIVATE COLLECTION)

marketing tactics paid off: before the show ended in 1964, several polls rated her the best female singer on television, and she won the *Radio and TV Daily* award in that category twice. Between 1961 and 1963, she also studied at the Juilliard School of Music, and in 1962 she appeared in her first film, *Two Weeks in Another Town.*

Uggams returned to the weekly television spotlight in 1969, hosting her own variety show, but the series was canceled after only ten weeks. She felt this was because the people who had watched her on the Miller show "didn't want to see me grow up."

But, of course, grow up she did, and her achievements make the failure of that series look insignificant. As a guest star, she appeared on TV variety shows and in dramas including *I Spy* (costarring Bill Cosby), *The Girl from U.N.C.L.E.*, and *Marcus Welby, M.D.* She also continued to make records and to sing in clubs, where she had been very

successful since her debut in late 1963. In 1967, she starred on Broadway as Georgina in *Hallelujah, Baby!*, a musical about the history of the civil rights movement. (**Lena Horne** had originally been cast in the role but had quit during rehearsals.) Although the show's reviews were not good, Uggams' were terrific; one critic thought she might be "the greatest thing to happen to musical comedy since the invention of the orchestra pit." She played major roles both in Ossie Davis' film *Black Girl* (1972) and in two TV miniseries, *Roots* (1977) and *Backstairs at the White House* (1979). In 1983, she won an Emmy as Best Hostess of a Daytime Variety Series for *Fantasy.*

Uggams, whom Rex Reed once called "a kind of sepiatone Shirley Temple," may have known her greatest fame as a child, but as a woman she built a career that testifies to her talent and perseverance.

INDIA COOPER

W

Walker, Aida Overton (1880–1914)

Variety called Aida Overton Walker "easily the foremost Afro-American stage artist" of her day. The leading black female cakewalk dancer and ragtime singer at the turn of the century, she electrified audiences with her talent, brought more authentic black songs and dances to Broadway musical theater, and became one of the first black international superstars.

She was born Aida Overton on February 14, 1880, in New York City, the second child of Moses and Pauline Whitfield Overton. In her teens, she joined the traveling chorus of the Black Patti Troubadours. She met and married George W. Walker at the beginning of his successful stage career with Bert Williams; Aida Walker choreographed the Williams and Walker shows, played female leads, and emerged as a sensational attraction in her own right.

Williams and Walker's ragtime musicals with all-black casts superseded minstrelsy and so helped change the nature of American vernacular entertainment. Aida Walker took major roles, beginning with *The Policy Players* in 1899 and continuing in *Sons of Ham, In Dahomey, Abyssinia,* and *Bandanna Land.* In 1903, *In Dahomey* went to London for a command performance at Buckingham Palace; Aida Walker sang and danced for the royal family.

When George Walker's illness forced him to retire from the stage, Aida Walker con-

Aida Overton Walker was a pioneer actress, singer, and dancer who was one of the most popular entertainers of the late 1880s and early 1890s. She brought dignity to the cakewalk and other dances originating in black culture. (DONALD BOGLE)

tinued in *Bandanna Land,* wearing his flashy clothes and singing his numbers. She went on to appear in various productions, including, in 1912, a spectacular vaudeville

215

The leading black woman ragtime singer at the turn of the century, Aida Overton Walker electrified audiences with her talent, brought more authentic black songs and dances to Broadway musical theater, and became one of the first black international superstars. (RICHARD NEWMAN)

performance of *Salome* at Oscar Hammerstein's Victoria Theater.

Aida Walker died in New York City as a result of a kidney infection on October 11, 1914.

RICHARD NEWMAN

Ward, Valerie Grey (19??–)

Perhaps the town where she was born inspired Val Ward to "start things." Mound Bayou, Mississippi, was founded by former slaves in 1887; located 100 miles southwest of Memphis, Tennessee, it is the second oldest all-black town in the United States. This is where Valerie Ward was born and where she grew up.

She moved to Chicago in 1951 and attended Wilson Junior College. From 1966 through 1967, she was the director of theater for the Chicago Committee on Urban Opportunity and in 1969 became the first director of the African-American Cultural Center at the University of Illinois Champaign/Urbana. At the same time, she was pursuing a career as a performer. During the mid- to late 1960s, she appeared in the films *The Monitors* and *Medium Cool* and wrote her own one-woman show *I Am a Black Woman*, which she has been touring since 1966.

In 1968, Ward founded the groundbreaking and influential organization, the Kuumba Theater. A word found in several African languages, *kuumba* here bears the Kiswahili definition of "creativity"; Kuumba was one of the first black theaters in Chicago and became Ward's life and creative outlet for the next twenty years.

Kuumba began as a collective of artists on the south side of Chicago, dedicated to developing plays with African-American themes, perspectives, and voices. This workshop organization soon became an official theater company and began its long history of producing original plays and musicals. Ward was involved in either directing or producing pieces such as *Sister Son/ji*, by **Sonia Sanchez**; *Ricky*, by Eugenia Collier; *Five on the Black Hand Side*, by Charles Russell; *The Little Dreamer: A Nite in the Life of Bessie Smith*, by Ed Shockley; and *Brownsville Raid*, by Charles Fuller. The Kuumba Theater production of *The Image Makers* by Eugene Perkins was performed at the World Festival of Black and African Artists (FESTAC) in Lagos, Nigeria, in 1978. In 1979, its production of *The Amen Corner* by James Baldwin, which Ward produced, directed, and performed in, toured to the National Black Theater Festival at Lincoln Center in New York City.

In addition to her directing, acting, and producing, Ward wrote many Kuumba Theater productions, including *The Heart of the Blues*, which toured to the Montreal International Jazz Festival in 1985. Collaborating with her husband Francis Ward, she adapted her play *Precious Memories: Strolling 47th Street* for television; produced by Chicago public television, it was shown nationally on PBS in 1988, and the next year Ward and all twenty-one actors in the production won Chicago Emmys for their work. In 1990, she narrated the film *The Onliest One Alive* (an account by the lone survivor of the 1979 Jim Jones massacre in Guyana) for national public television.

A mother of five and grandmother of six, Valerie Ward has influenced and provided opportunities for an entire generation of Chicago artists. She has enabled the black community in Chicago to see images of themselves, their history, and their art. She is the mother of a great deal more than her children.

HILARY MAC AUSTIN

Warfield, Marsha (1955–)

As a comedienne, she is tough, foul-mouthed, and lewd—and she *likes* it that way. Unlike so many black women who were reshaped and repackaged to make it in show business, Marsha Warfield has told the jokes that she wanted in the way she wanted to tell them and has changed her

style for no one. Still she has became a success.

Marsha Warfield was born in 1955 and grew up on the South Side of Chicago in a comfortable, middle-class family. Her father left the family while she was still a little girl, but her mother, Josephine, remarried to James Gordon. Josephine had a steady job with the telephone company, and James was a computer programmer with the city library system. Together, they hoped to raise their daughter for a conventional, middle-class life.

Marsha Warfield didn't turn out that way. A lackluster student in high school who felt like she never fit in, she sat in the back of the class and cracked jokes. "Humor was my shield and my weapon," she said. She graduated from Calumet High School at the age of seventeen and joined her mother working at the telephone company; she married at eighteen. Neither job nor marriage lasted very long.

By the age of twenty, Warfield was divorced and unemployed and had no idea what to do with herself. She decided to try her luck as a stand-up comic. After her first night on stage, she knew what she wanted to do with her life.

Making a living at stand-up comedy was another matter. Although performing regularly around Chicago, she was still barely making ends meet. Her act was brash and bawdy, and she refused to clean it up even to get paying jobs. She had the kind of humor that made women howl, while offending a good number of men in the audience—not that she was afraid of offending women, too. Her scathing comments on the war between the sexes were simply too much for many Chicago crowds.

In 1976, Warfield moved to Los Angeles, where audiences knew how to appreciate her. She was still broke, but at least her reception was better. A fellow comic landed her a role with *The Richard Pryor Show*, but that show closed after a short run. Then came her big break: In 1979, she won the famed San Francisco National Stand-Up Comedy Competition. There still was no money, but at least she had a reputation.

The victory at the comedy competition helped Warfield gain a few small parts. She acted with Cicley Tyson in *The Marva Collins Story* and had a bit part in *Mask*. Because she still refused to tame her act, most of her comedy work was on the cable channels. She appeared in *Teddy Pendergrass in Concert* and *Comic Relief*. Finally, she caught the attention of the creator of the popular television series *Night Court*. At first, she was booked to share a rotating role, but soon she was asked to join the regular cast.

As the bailiff, Roz Russell, Marsha Warfield could finally win mainstream acclaim. The character was tough and scathing without blue lines to make the critics gasp. As an *Ebony* writer put it, "She has elevated the cynical look to an art form. Hers is an expression that could make killer sharks flee to safer waters."

When *Night Court* went off the air, Warfield had a brief stint as the host of her own talk show, where she showed her own likable personality without losing her edge. She then went on to play a doctor in the television series *Empty Nest*.

Success agrees with Marsha Warfield: She now leads a comfortable life in West Hollywood, and she still refuses to clean up her act. She donates scholarship money to high school students from the South Side of Chicago and does occasional guest spots on prime-time television.

Friends and family report a softer side to the comic, an underside to the tough exterior. Even Warfield remarks on it: She tells the story of a time when she was trying to survive as a starving comic and came off stage, thoroughly discouraged. ". . . I was standing by the bar and this guy came up to me and said, 'I know you don't know me and I don't know you, but I've been watching comedians for a long time and I'm so proud of you.' I burst into tears. It was such a nice thing for somebody to say."

Marsha Warfield is tough, vulnerable, and complex—her own woman through and through—and a remarkable success story.

ANDRA MEDEA

Washington, Fredi (1903–1994)

An actress, writer, dancer, and singer, Fredi Washington (Fredericka Carolyn Washington) was born in Savannah, Georgia, on December 23, 1903. Her education began in Cornwells Heights, Pennsylvania, at St. Elizabeth Convent. She then attended the Egri School of Dramatic Writing and the Christopher School of Languages, where she pursued her early interests in civil rights, casting, writing, dancing, and singing.

Her career began as a dancer in nightclub engagements: She made her first cabaret appearance in New York at the age of sixteen as a member of the Happy Honeysuckles. From 1922 to 1926, she toured with one of America's first musicals, *Shuffle Along*, written by Flournoy E. Miller and Aubrey Lyles with music by Noble Sissle and Eubie Blake. Following this production, she adopted the stage name Edith Warren and was cast as the lead in *Black Boy* (1926) with Paul Robeson. It was difficult to find work in New York, so she toured Europe as a dancer. **Florence Mills** and **Josephine Baker** had already begun to pave the way for other African Americans in Europe. Some of her European engagements included the Gaumont Palace and Chateau Madrid (Paris); Casino (Nice); Green Park Hotel (London); Casino (Ostend), Trocadero, and Floria Palast (Berlin); Barberina Cafe (Dresden); and Alkazar (Hamburg). She was cast in *Sweet Chariot* (1930) in New York, followed by *Singin' the Blues* (1931) and *Run, Little Chillun* (1933).

Washington also started a film career between stage performances and appeared in *Black and Tan Fantasy* (1929), an all-black musical short with Duke Ellington, *The Old Man and the Mountain*, and *The Emperor Jones* (1933). Yet, the stage was her first love. When she appeared in *Mamba's Daughters*, the *New York Times* critic Brooks Atkinson wrote that Fredi Washington "beautifully plays the part of Hagar's talented granddaughter . . . with intelligence as well as charm."

One of Washington's primary concerns was the relationships that existed between black and white women. She brought to the screen a new conception of African-American women in general that was best exemplified in her role as the mulatto daughter who passed for white in the movie *Imitation of Life* (1934). Thematically, the film was probably the first Hollywood attempt to portray the struggles of racially different women with similar financial woes. Claudette Colbert and **Louise Beavers** are both single heads of households; both have daughters; both are determined to keep a roof over their heads. The association of

The citation for Fredi Washington's 1975 induction into the Black Filmmakers Hall of Fame reads, in part: ". . . a black girl in search of a black role. The parts she wanted were rarely given to her because of her green eyes, long silky hair and fair complexion." (SCURLOCK STUDIO)

these two women during America's Depression occurs through domestic employment: the mistress (Miss Bea, played by Colbert) and the maid (Delilah, played by Beavers). Washington's performance as the daughter (Peola) and that of Beavers as the mother who helps a white employer become rich by teaching her how to fry griddle cakes were two of the finest of the time. The story was wrought with melodrama, but when Washington and Beavers were paired in their one-on-one scenes, the film's power was said to "transform Hollywood trash into something unique and often powerful." So convincing was Washington's portrayal of the tragic mulatto that many African Americans believed Fredi Washington in real life must have been antiblack. Friends like Bobby Short and her sister's husband, Congressman Adam Clayton Powell, Jr., said Washington never hid behind the lightness of her complexion; the only times she passed for white was when she was traveling in the South with Duke Ellington and his band. None of them were allowed to go into ice-cream parlors; according to her friend Jean-Claude Baker, she would go into the parlors,

Fredi Washington's performance in Imitation of Life, *as a young black woman who passes for white, was so powerful that it caused her problems in real life. In spite of her strong commitment to the black movement for equality, she was often thought of as a woman who denied her heritage.* [DONALD BOGLE]

buy ice cream, and take it outside to the band. "Whites screamed at her, 'Nigger lover!'" She always maintained a very strong sense of racial pride. Parvenu Otto Kahn offered to sponsor her dramatic education if she would change her name to a French one because he believed that this would free her of the burden of race to become a star. She declined, stating "I want to be what I am . . . nothing else."

Washington's commitment to equal rights was as strong as her commitment to her craft as a performer. She was one of the founders of the Negro Actors Guild and was the guild's first executive secretary in 1937–38; she was theater editor and columnist for the *People's Voice* (a New York weekly published by Adam Clayton Powell, Jr.), administrative secretary for the Joint Actors Equity-Theater League Committee on Hotel Accommodations for Negro Actors throughout the United States, and the registrar for the Howard da Silva School of Acting.

Washington also performed on the radio and television program *The Goldbergs*, a comedy series about a Jewish immigrant family, in addition to specials for National Urban League on CBS. After her major film performance in *Imitation of Life*, she appeared in *Drums of the Jungle* (1935) and *One Mile From Heaven* (1937), and was casting consultant for the screen version of *Cry, the Beloved Country* (1952) and for the stage productions of *Carmen Jones* and *Porgy and Bess* (1943). Washington appeared on stage in *Lysistrata* (1946), *A Long Way From Home* (1948), and *How Long till Summer?* (1949).

Fredi Washington believed in performance excellence and human rights and in herself and her heritage as an African American; she never denied who or what she was. She gave her best unselfishly to make room for others.

She was inducted into the Black Filmmakers Hall of Fame in Oakland, California, in 1975, which described her as "a black girl in search of a black role. The parts she wanted were rarely given to her because of her green eyes, long silky hair and fair complexion. She didn't look black enough to play the kind of roles Hollywood wanted, and Hollywood wasn't prepared to put this sophisticated, well-schooled black woman into a part which would do much more than mirror the conflicts of the Depression-era mulatto."

Her marriage to Lawrence Brown, a trombonist with the Duke Ellington Orchestra, ended in divorce; her second husband, Dr. Anthony Bell, died in the early 1980s. She is the sister of **Isabel Washington**—the actress, singer, and first wife of Congressman Adam Clayton Powell, Jr. Fredi Washington died on Tuesday, June 29, 1994, in Stamford, Connecticut, of pneumonia, which developed after a stroke. She was buried in Stamford beside her second husband.

BEVERLY J. ROBINSON

Waters, Ethel (1896–1977)

In her autobiography, actress and blues singer Ethel Waters wrote, "'Stormy Weather' was the perfect expression of my mood, and I found release in singing it each evening. When I got out there in the middle of the Cotton Club floor, I was telling things I couldn't frame in words. I was singing the story of my misery and confusion, of the misunderstanding in my life I couldn't straighten out, the story of the wrongs and outrages done to me by people I had loved and trusted."

Although the song "His Eye Is on the Sparrow" gave Ethel Waters visibility when she toured with evangelist Billy Graham after she retired from a thirty-year career in clubs, theater, and films in the late 1950s, Waters was best known for launching the Harold Arlen song "Stormy Weather" in a Cotton Club extravaganza in 1933.

Waters indeed had a hard life. Born on October 31, 1896, as a result of the rape of twelve-year-old Louise Anderson, Waters (who took her father's surname) lived in the slums of Philadelphia and Chester, Pennsylvania, raised by her grandmother, a live-in housekeeper. She would not gain the affection and admiration of her mother until much later in her life.

Her professional debut as the five-year-old baby star in a church production inspired her and led to performances throughout her youth. At age thirteen Waters was urged by her mother into a short-lived marriage to twenty-three-year-old Buddy Purnsley, after which she supported herself doing domestic work in hotels, singing before mirrors to an imaginary audience.

At a local Halloween party in 1917, Waters caught the attention of Braxton and Nugent, producers for a small vaudeville troupe, who offered her a job. Billed as Sweet Mama Stringbean in appearances in Philadelphia and Baltimore, she became the first woman to perform W. C. Handy's "St. Louis Blues."

Following her success as Sweet Mama Stringbean, Waters went on to perform with the Hills Sisters, touring and singing blues standards of the day. She continued to work as a blues singer on the Southern vaudeville circuit, often for the TOBA (Theater Own-

Ethel Waters became the first black woman to star in a Broadway drama in Mamba's Daughters *(1939), then stunned the theatrical community with her powerful performance in* The Member of the Wedding *(1950). Both she and Julie Harris repeated their Broadway roles in the 1952 film version.* (DONALD BOGLE)

ers Booking Association or, as it became known in the trade, Tough on Black Asses). She also performed during this time at Chicago's old Monogram Theater and in tent shows.

In 1919, when Harlem was the center of a national black renaissance, Waters arrived in New York, where she became one of the leading entertainers in the clubs and on stage. Her initial New York club appearances were at the small Edmund's Cellar, a basement dive patronized by shady characters (Waters later described it as "the last step on the way down"). Her stint there,

however, resulted in her first recordings for Black Swan Records in 1921. For that label owned by Harry Pace (which produced "race" recordings), Waters recorded many songs; her major hits were "Down Home Blues" and "Oh Daddy."

Waters continued to record throughout the 1920s, performing blues and fast-tempo jazz songs as well as sweet, beautiful ballads, bringing refinement and elegance to her blues style both on record and in live performance. Also during this period, Pace sent Waters on tour with the Black Swan Troubadours, a band directed by Fletcher Henderson, one of the most sought-after band leaders at the time; this was certainly a career move that benefited Waters. The singer signed a ten-year recording contract with Columbia Records.

Waters declined an invitation to tour Paris, and in 1925 **Josephine Baker** replaced her while Waters established her career by touring all over the United States and recording hit after hit.

Her second career, as an actress, began in 1927 in Broadway musicals: *Africana* (1927), *Blackbirds* (1930), and *Rhapsody in Black* (1931). *On With the Show* in 1929 was Waters' first film, followed in 1930 by *Check and Double Check*, a film featuring the characters of Amos and Andy.

Waters was thirty-four in 1930 when she went to Europe for a rest. By the time she returned, the Depression was at its peak, and the golden era of the theater was about to begin. During this time her second marriage, to Eddie Matthews, ended.

In 1933, among other entertainment luminaries, Irving Berlin came to see the Stormy Weather Show at the Cotton Club. When he heard Waters, backed by the Duke Ellington Orchestra, sing the title song, he signed her for the musical *As Thousands Cheer*, a new revue produced by Sam H. Harris for which Berlin was writing the music. Waters became the first black to perform in the all-white Broadway hit, singing Berlin originals that included "Heat Wave" and "Harlem on My Mind." Her career took off. A Radio City Music Hall version of the Stormy Weather act was staged. Waters subsequently appeared in the revue *At Home Abroad* (1935). She established herself with new power on the stage in 1939 as the first black woman to star in a Broadway drama with the lead role of Hagar in *Mamba's Daughters*, receiving seventeen curtain calls on opening night.

The 1940 role of Petunia in the all-black stage musical *Cabin in the Sky* featured Waters performing at her best, singing Vernon Blake's "Taking a Chance on Love"; she excelled again in the 1943 film version with **Lena Horne**. Other films Waters is known for were *Tales of Manhattan* (1949), *Pinky* (1949), and *The Sound and the Fury* (1959). For her performance in *Pinky*, she was nominated for an Academy Award as Best Supporting Actress. In 1950, she appeared on Broadway in Carson McCullers' *The Member of the Wedding*, and she repeated her performance in the 1952 film version.

Tall and big-boned, yet slender and attractive, Waters developed a tough assertiveness as a child that continued throughout her career, allowing her eventually to negotiate top salaries and to withstand the injustices and harshness of being a black entertainer. She was always a conflicting mixture of bawdiness and piety, rawness and sweetness. Her life was a mixture of success and sadness; it was mainly through song that Waters found solace. Waters's

grandmother, who had raised her, died before seeing her accomplishments on stage and screen, but Waters did win the love she sought from her mother before she died. Ridden by debt and plagued by problems with the IRS whenever she hit a career slump, Waters sang and made club appearances. She died in 1977 following a long bout with cancer.

EVAN MORSE

West, Cheryl (1957–)

Good playwrights do not always live in New York, and they are not always nonconformist. Cheryl West is a critically acclaimed playwright from Champaign, Illinois, who believes in hard work and the American Dream.

Born in Chicago and raised in the nearby suburbs, she came from a family that believed in education and hard work. Brought up by a single mother with solid blue-collar values—playwriting was considered a "luxury occupation"—West earned degrees that could help her get a job: First, a B.A. in criminal justice and then master's degrees in rehabilitative administration and journalism. Only after she had established herself as a social worker did she turn her attention to plays.

Her first play, *Before It Hits Home*, was a powerful drama about AIDS in a black family. The play debuted in Seattle in 1989 and toured the country. A critical success, it often met with controversy in the black community. The actors who portrayed gay males were even booed by audiences in Washington, D.C.; however, it was dynamic theater. Director Spike Lee bought the film rights.

Her next play, *Holiday Heart*, was another success. This was a drama about a young girl who was abandoned by her mother and taken in by a kind stranger. The show deftly handles vast social issues in a deep, funny, and oddly nonpolitical fashion. With productions in Cleveland, Seattle, and Syracuse, the play finally opened off-Broadway at the Manhattan Theater Club. In addition to her movie option with Spike Lee, West also has been commissioned to do a screenplay for **Oprah Winfrey**'s Harpo Productions.

She has remained refreshingly unaffected by her success. "You can't rely on other people to tell you who you are [as an artist]," she told *Essence* in 1994. "If you listen to them, you'll have to believe the good *and* the bad. The only thing you can really rely on is what I call the midnight owl, that voice you hear when you're just alone, working. That's what will tell you when you've done good work."

ANDRA MEDEA

White, Jane (1920?–)

"There was a sense" Jane White says of Harlem before and just after World War II, "that *if* you kept your nose clean, and if you *went* to school, and you *held* a good job, and you *made* a little money, and you washed and ironed your clothes—that it was all going to turn out all right. . . . It came as a shock to me that there were barriers against my becoming one of the great stars of all time."

Jane White was born into a prominent family: Her father was Walter White, National Secretary of the NAACP for nearly twenty-five years and was as famous a leader as Martin Luther King, Jr., would be

several decades later; her mother, the beautiful Leah Gladys Powell White, gracefully and graciously managed their spacious apartment in one of the most expensive buildings on Sugar Hill in Harlem. For some time, their home was called "the White House of Black America."

As a child, Jane White showed James Weldon Johnson her paper dolls and listened to George Gershwin play *Rhapsody in Blue* on the piano in their living room. Her parents entertained Langston Hughes, Countee Cullen, Claude McKay, and Thurgood Marshall, as well as presidential candidate Wendell Wilkie and great Russian director Sergei Eisenstein. She graduated from Smith College and then moved back into her parents home.

In 1945, José Ferrer directed a stage adaptation of Lillian Smith's novel *Strange Fruit*, the story of an interracial love that ends in tragedy in the South. Ferrer's friend Paul Robeson suggested White for the role of Nonnie Anderson, the young black woman who loves and is loved by a white man. The Broadway production was the beginning of White's stage career.

Her career, however, was not what she had dreamed of. In the late forties, the Theater Guild rejected her as Joan of Arc because "St. Joan was a blonde Frenchwoman, and we just can't buy a Negro girl in that role." There were few available substantial roles specifically for black women, and Jane White, in spite of her talent, beauty, fame, and aristocratic background, was not considered for the others.

Still, in the 1950s, White would appear on Broadway in *Take a Giant Step* with Louis Gossett and **Helen Martin**; *Once Upon a Mattress* with Carol Burnett; and *Shadows Move Among Them* with Earle

Hyman. In the 1960s, she acted with the New York Shakespeare Festival in *Coriolanus*, *Troilus and Cressida*, and *The Trojan Women*. White appeared in the film *Klute* in 1971.

In the late 1960s, she married Alfredo Viazzi and lived for a few years in Rome. Upon their return to New York, White and Viazzi opened three Italian restaurants, which he ran. For about a year, she played the role of Nurse Holliday in the television soap opera *Edge of Night*. In the late 1970s, Bobby Short worked with White to put together an act of songs, cabaret tunes, and monologues from her stage roles, which had an enthusiastic reception at Town Hall before White took it on tour.

More important to White, she finally came to terms with her feelings about herself and her heritage. For a long time, she told *Ebony* in 1978, "I was in a sort of racial limbo. I was seeking identity. But thank God I've broken out and now I'm *here*. I *am* a black woman, and my recognition of that has a lot to do, I think, with a kind of 'essential iron' that I inherited from my father."

KATHLEEN THOMPSON

Winfrey, Oprah   (1954–)

Oprah Winfrey is a talk-show host, actress, and cultural phenomenon. Her success could almost certainly never have happened at any time in the past; that it has happened at all must be attributed to a combination of history and her own unique talents.

Winfrey was born on January 29, 1954, to Vernita Lee and Vernon Winfrey. When her parents, who were not married, separated, she went to live with her maternal grandmother on a farm. Although life was austere, the young girl thrived. She learned

to read before she was three and was in the third grade by the age of six. At that point, she went to live with her mother in Milwaukee. Vernita Lee managed a subsistence-level existence with income from welfare and domestic work, and she had little time to supervise her daughter. Between the ages of nine and twelve, Winfrey was repeatedly subjected to sexual abuse by a cousin and then by other men close to her family. She began to have such serious behavioral problems that Lee gave up and sent the girl to her father in Nashville.

Life changed dramatically. Vernon Winfrey was a respected member of his commu-

Oprah Winfrey is a phenomenon: both an Academy Award–nominated actress and an Emmy-winning talk-show host and producer, she is one of the most successful women in the history of entertainment. (PRIVATE COLLECTION)

nity, and he put his daughter under the strictest guidance. Soon, she was excelling in school again and in extracurricular activities such as speech and drama and the student council. While she was still in high school, a local radio station, WVOL, hired her to broadcast the news. She attended Tennessee State University on a scholarship she had won in an Elks Club oratorical contest.

While in her freshman year, Winfrey won the titles of Miss Black Nashville and Miss Black Tennessee and was a contestant in the Miss Black America pageant. This led to a job offer from the local CBS television affiliate, WTVF. In 1971, she became Nashville's first woman coanchor. She was still in the job when she graduated from college. Shortly thereafter, in 1976, she was offered a job at WJZ-TV, the ABC affiliate in Baltimore, Maryland.

The management at WTVF in Nashville had enjoyed great success with Winfrey by allowing her to be herself. The management at WJZ tried to remake the young broadcaster into a more acceptable mold, and her first year at the station was rocky as a result. The situation improved greatly when she was switched to cohosting the morning talk show, *Baltimore Is Talking*, with Richard Sher. Winfrey did the show for seven years, with ever-increasing popularity. Then, in 1984, she moved to Chicago to take over *A.M. Chicago*, a talk show that was in serious trouble in the ratings. It aired opposite Phil Donahue, a Chicago favorite, and none of its many hosts had been able to make a dent in his audience.

It took a month for Winfrey to equal Donahue's ratings. This was in a city notorious for its racial problems—not the ideal milieu for a black woman. It took three months for Winfrey to surpass Donahue in the ratings. A year and a half after Winfrey's arrival in the windy city, *A.M. Chicago* expanded to an hour and became *The Oprah Winfrey Show*. Winfrey is smart, thinks fast on her feet, and reveals her own life and personality in a way that makes people identify with her.

In 1985, Winfrey was cast in the film version of **Alice Walker**'s *The Color Purple*, directed by Steven Spielberg. Her performance earned her an Academy Award nomination. She has since continued her acting career in film and on television, forming a production company, Harpo Productions, to develop her own projects. In 1989, she bought her own television and movie production studio. That same year, she donated $1 million to Morehouse College in Atlanta, Georgia, one of many contributions to the community.

In 1989, Winfrey produced a miniseries based on **Gloria Naylor**'s novel *The Women of Brewster Place*; its success led to the creation of a short-lived network dramatic series, *Brewster Place* (1990). Winfrey herself appeared in both the miniseries and the drama as the long-suffering Mattie Michael. Meanwhile, for her work on *The Oprah Winfrey Show*, Winfrey received three Emmy Awards, two (in 1987 and 1991) as outstanding host of a talk/service show and one (in 1991) as supervising producer of the outstanding talk/service show. (The show itself also received Emmys in 1987 and 1988.) She was awarded the NAACP's Spingarn Medal in 1994.

In the 1990s, Winfrey emerged as one of the most powerful people in show business. She is also one of the richest women in America, earning $40 million every year from her talk show alone. A *Redbook* article in 1993 pointed out that "Her personal worth exceeds the gross national product of some countries."

All of this has as its base Oprah's show, her ability to empathize with her audience and her willingness to talk about her problems and her past as openly as she asks her guests to do. However, as Winfrey approached her fortieth birthday, there seemed to be a change in her perspective. Perhaps the first sign of this came when she stopped talking about a lifetime weight problem and then conquered it by replacing a negative and potentially self-destructive dieting regime with a positive style of exercise and healthful eating. Then in June 1993, she announced that she would not be publishing her much-anticipated life story. She explained that, though it had been good for her to work on the book, it would not be good for her to publish it. Finally, she announced that her talk show would have a new slant.

"The time has come for this genre of talk shows to move on," she said, "from dysfunctional whining and complaining and blaming. . . . We're all aware that we do have some problems and we need to work on them. What are you willing to *do* about it? And that's what our shows are going to be about."

It is interesting to see the audience that loved to moan with Winfrey build and grow with her. It is quite certain that she will find ways of working and creating in the future.

KATHLEEN THOMPSON

Winston, Hattie (1945–)

From abandonment as a child in Mississippi to a luxurious home in New York's Upper East Side, Hattie Winston has been the mas-

ter of her fate. An award-winning actress in New York theater and Hollywood, she has always been the form and figure of a class act.

Born in Greenville, Mississippi, in 1945, Hattie Winston grew up believing that the aunt who raised her was truly her mother. In fact, her mother left by the time she was two, and her father left soon after. At the age of fourteen, Winston left Mississippi to live with relatives in New York. Her New York relations did not know what to do with her, and she was soon taken in by the parents of her best friend.

Flourishing in her new-found family, Winston won a fine arts scholarship to **Howard University**, after which, she returned to New York to make her way as an actor. It was not easy finding work as a black actor in the early 1960s, but she was cast in *The Prodigal Son* in 1965.

At that time, Winston and others were studying acting under Robert Hooks, and together they formed the famous **Negro Ensemble Company** (NEC). With NEC, she got the exposure she deserved in plays such as *Song of the Lusitanian Bogey*, *Summer of the Seventeenth Doll*, *Kongi's Harvest*, and *God Is a (Guess What?)*, all in 1968. This season was followed by *Man Better Man* and *Sambo* in 1969, and *The Me Nobody Knows* and *Billy NoName* in 1970.

Later stage appearances included both NEC productions and others, including *The Great MacDaddy* in 1974 and *A Photograph* in 1977. One busy season, she played in *The Michigan* late in 1979, followed in 1980 by a role in **Ntozake Shange**'s adaptation of *Mother Courage and Her Children*, produced by the New York Shakespeare Festival. For her work in *The Michigan* and *Mother Courage and Her Children*, Winston won two Obie awards in one year, a rare feat.

Winston has also appeared in several Hollywood productions, including the film, *Sweet Love, Bitter*, in 1968. She later co-starred in the television series *Nurse*. To young viewers, she is perhaps best known as Valerie the librarian in PBS's *The Electric Company*. During the 1980s, Winston also became one of the leading voice-over actors in commercials.

In 1984, Winston appeared on Broadway in *The Tap Dance Kid;* three years later, she appeared with **Vinie Burrows** in the latter's *Her Talking Drum* at American Place Theater. A review of that show in the *New Yorker* said, "Hattie Winston . . . no matter how serious or even lamentable the occasion, cannot help being humorous, seductive, and charming."

When she joined Actor's Equity, several of Winston's friends urged her to change her name. She refused. She later explained, saying "One day I'll be starring on Broadway and the marquee outside the theater will read Hattie Winston starring in . . . whatever. At the end of the performance, a very tall and distinguished woman is going to come backstage. She's going to say, 'I'm your mother.'" Success may bring happiness, but it does not erase the memory of sorrow.

ANDRA MEDEA

Woodard, Alfre (1953–)

Until the late 1980s "my agent used to tell me, 'Alfre, this part isn't for you—it's for a cute black girl,'" actress Alfre Woodard recalls. Since then, she thinks, black actors with African features "like myself have altered Hollywood's narrow standards of beauty by not going away or even getting angry about it. We just had to be hired." And hired and hired and hired. Today, Woodard is one of the most respected and most frequently employed black women in her profession.

Woodard was born in Tulsa, Oklahoma, on November 8, 1953. She has a brother and a sister, both older. Her father, Marion H. Woodard, was an interior decorator and an oil driller before retiring; her mother, Constance, a homemaker, died in 1993. Woodard was fifteen when she appeared in her first play, at Bishop Kelly High School. "It was as if I had been doing the breaststroke all my life and then somebody put me in the water and I went, 'Ahhh! This is it!'" She graduated cum laude with a B.F.A. in drama from Boston University in 1974 and then worked on Broadway as an understudy and in productions at the Public Theater in New York and the Arena Stage in Washington, D.C. After appearing in *for colored girls who have considered suicide/when the rainbow is enuf* at the Mark Taper Forum in Los Angeles in 1977, she worked in television and movies. Soon, she was well known and highly regarded in the entertainment industry, not only for the quality of her performances but for her professionalism and hard-working, thorough approach to her craft. However, she was far from famous. When the Academy Award nominees were announced in 1984, many moviegoers probably asked themselves, "Who's Alfre Woodard?" Playing a rural Southern servant named Geechee in *Cross Creek*, a 1983 movie that drew very small crowds at the box office, she had earned a Best Supporting Actress nomination. The *Los Angeles Times* called it "the biggest surprise" on the list. It was also the first time since 1967 that a black woman had been nominated in that category.

Woodard believes "everyone must earn her right to be on earth. What I hope to do with my work is to give people a sense of being nurtured, even if it's just a laugh. That's my service." Maybe it's coincidence, but she has portrayed many nurturing, caring women. Her performance in *Hill Street Blues* as the mother of a child killed by a police officer won her a 1984 Emmy as Best Supporting Actress in a Dramatic Series. In *Unnatural Causes*, a 1986 TV movie, she had the role of a Veterans Administration counselor investigating the effects of Agent Orange on soldiers who served in Vietnam. As Dr. Roxanne Turner on *St. Elsewhere* in 1985–87, she earned two Emmy nominations. One of her finest performances is in the excellent 1992 film *Passion Fish*, as the caregiver for a young woman confined to a wheelchair.

In Spike Lee's 1994 film *Crooklyn*, she plays a character based on Lee's own mother; Carolyn Carmichael is a schoolteacher in the Bedford-Stuyvesant neighborhood of Brooklyn, married to an unemployed jazz musician, and has five lively children to raise. She won an ACE Award for her portrayal of Winnie Mandela on HBO, a role for which her careful research included listening to tapes of Mandela's voice so that she could reproduce her accent; she even traveled to Zimbabwe to meet with South African women. Woodard herself is interested in politics and cofounded the antiapartheid group Artists for South Africa. She has won NAACP Image Awards for *Mandela* in 1988 and for *A Mother's Courage* in 1990.

But Woodard does not limit herself to playing empowered or maternal black women. For instance, in the pilot for the hugely successful TV series *L.A. Law*, for which she won another Emmy, her character was a rape victim dying of leukemia, and in 1989 she returned to the Public Theater to play Paulina in Shakespeare's *The Winter's Tale*. The most important question she asks herself when deciding whether or not to accept a role is, "Is this something that my mother and father wouldn't be ashamed to watch?" She looks for scripts "that will make me run, fly, leap and jump all in the same character."

Like all fine actors, Woodard isn't afraid to share important parts of her emotional and mental life with her characters, and through them with her audience. In real life, though, she is a notoriously private person who gives few interviews. Family life is extremely important to her. She is married to Roderick Spencer, an actor, writer, and producer, and the couple has a daughter, Mavis.

INDIA COOPER

Chronology

1619

Twenty Africans, three of them women, are put ashore off a Dutch frigate at Jamestown, Virginia.

1600s

There is little theater in the colonies. Where it exists, it is performed almost entirely by white men.

1776

First black gospel singing by an organized choral group is heard at a black Baptist church in Petersburg, Virginia.

1778

A federal law outlaws theater of any kind.

1781

Los Angeles, future home of the motion picture industry, is founded by forty-four settlers, at least twenty-six of whom are black women, men, and children.

1820

The African Grove Theater is founded to present productions of Shakespeare and other classics. Black men and women perform together in the company.

1823

Failing to find a white woman who will play in blackface, Edwin Forrest casts a black washerwoman to play in *The Tailor in Distress*.

1830s

The minstrel show, based on African American music and dance, becomes popular. The performers are all white men.

1835

Actor **Adah Isaacs Menken** is born in Chartrain, Louisiana, to Auguste Theodore, a "free man of color."

1851

Elizabeth Taylor Greenfield, "the Black Swan," makes her singing debut in Buffalo, New York. She is the first black woman concert singer and the first to have a career of any kind on the stage.

1854

Elizabeth Taylor Greenfield gives a command performance at Buckingham Palace for Queen Victoria.

1857

Adah Isaacs Menken, as a white woman, makes her theater debut as Pauline in *The Lady of Lyons*.

1860–1865
The Civil War.

1861
Adah Isaacs Menken opens in *Mazeppa*, in which she rides onstage wearing a body stocking and strapped to the back of a horse. The role makes her the highest-paid female actor on record at the time.

1865
After the Civil War, black male entertainers begin to form minstrel troupes, including Lew Johnson's Plantation Minstrel Company and the Georgia Minstrels.

1875
Anna and Emma Hyers found the Coloured Operatic and Dramatic Company to present musical plays about the black experience.

1884
Actor **Rose McClendon** is born in Greenville, South Carolina. She will be called the "Negro first lady of the dramatic stage."

1885
Flora Batson becomes star singer with Bergen Star Company.

1890
The Creole Show begins the transition from minstrel show to musical comedy when it incorporates a chorus line.

1896
Sissieretta Jones' Black Patti Troubadours opens its first season. The troupe will eventually perform musical comedies such as *A Trip to Africa*, in 1909.

1898
Bob Cole produces *A Trip to Coontown*, the first full-length musical comedy written, directed, performed, and produced by African Americans. The presence of women in the cast helps to distinguish the musical from a minstrel show.

1899
New York has more legitimate theaters than any other city in the world. It has forty-one, while London has thirty-nine, and Paris a mere twenty-four.

1903
Aida Overton Walker, one of the first black women to star in musical comedy, has one of her biggest successes in *In Dahomey*. The Broadway cast also includes **Abbie Mitchell**, **Anita Bush**, and **Hattie McIntosh**.

1904
Abbie Mitchell's acting career takes off with a song when her performance of "Mandy Lou" in *The Southerners* stops the show night after night.

1906
Walker and Williams' *Abyssinia* opens on Broadway with Hattie McIntosh and Aida Overton Walker in principal roles.

1909
The Theater Owners Booking Association (TOBA) is organized to present black vaudeville. It will be responsible for sparking the careers of many black women, including **Ma Rainey**, Susie Edwards, and **Ethel Waters**.

1910
Jackie "Moms" Mabley begins her performing career in a minstrel show on the Theater Owners Booking Association Circuit.

1915
Anita Bush founds the Anita Bush Players, opening *The Girl at the Fort* at the Lincoln Theater in Harlem.

1916
The Anita Bush Players move to the Lafayette Theater and become the **Lafayette Players**. They will continue to produce, in various venues, until 1932.

The NAACP produces **Angelina Weld Grimké**'s play *Rachel*. It is the first successful, fully staged, professional production of a play by a black playwright.

1917
Inez Clough and Opal Cooper score personal triumphs in Ridgely Torrence's *Three Plays for a Negro Theater*. Both women are on George Jean Nathan's list of best performances of the year.

Evelyn Preer makes her film debut in *The Homesteader*, the first film by Oscar Micheaux.

1919
They That Sit in Darkness, a play by **Mary Burrill**, is published in the *Birth Control Review*. It is the first known play by a black woman to deal with a feminist issue.

1921
Shuffle Along heads **Florence Mills** (a lead) and **Josephine Baker** and **Adelaide Hall** (chorus girls) toward stardom.

Howard University establishes a Department of Dramatic Art.

Anita Bush stars in *The Crimson Skull*, the first black western film.

1922
Florence Mills opens in *The Plantation Revue* in Harlem before moving to Broadway.

1922
Louise Evans is the first black woman admitted to the United Scenic Artists Association.

1923
Laura Bowman and Evelyn Preer star in Willis Richardson's one-act play *The Chip Woman's Fortune*, the first nonmusical play by a black playwright on Broadway.

1924
Florence Mills wows them in *Dixie to Broadway*, which is based on her London hit *Dover Street to Dixie*.

1925
Josephine Baker is a sensation in *La Revue Nègre* in Paris, launching a legendary European career.

1926
The Krigwa Players are founded in New York to present black plays to black audiences. In the next few years, the group and its affiliates in other cities will produce the plays of many black women playwrights.

Rose McClendon and Abbie Mitchell star in *In Abraham's Bosom*. Its white playwright, Paul Green, will win a Pulitzer Prize for the script.

Florence Mills captivates London in *Blackbirds of 1926.*

1927

Ethel Waters, billed as "the world's greatest colored comedienne," opens in *Africana. Time* magazine says, "In Harlem, she is queen. In Manhattan, she stops the show."

Evelyn Ellis plays Bess in the play *Porgy,* upon which Gershwin's opera *Porgy and Bess* was based. Other important black women in the remarkable cast include Rose McClendon and **Georgette Harvey.**

Florence Mills dies. More than 150,000 people crowd the streets to make her funeral the largest in Harlem history.

1928

The first of the *Blackbirds* revues opens in New York. It will showcase a number of black performers, including Adelaide Hall and Aida Ward.

1929

Regina Andrews and **Jessie Fauset** are among the group who form the Negro Experimental Theater in the basement of the New York Public Library.

1930

The Green Pastures opens on Broadway.

1931

The play *Fast and Furious: A Colored Revue in 37 Scenes* opens on Broadway. **Zora Neale Hurston** and Jackie "Moms" Mabley collaborate to write and perform scenes.

Ethel Waters and **Valaida Snow** star in *Rhapsody in Black,* a show that significantly broke away from minstrel stereotypes and blew away its audiences.

1933

Ethel Waters is the only black cast member in Irving Berlin's *As Thousands Cheer.* She stops the show with "Heat Wave" and sings "Supper Time," about an African-American woman whose husband has been lynched. She is now the highest paid woman on Broadway.

1934

Osceola Archer makes her Broadway debut in Elmer Rice's *Between Two Worlds.*

Louise Beavers and **Fredi Washington** set a standard for screen realism in their scenes in *Imitation of Life.*

The Gertrude Stein–Virgil Thomson opera *Four Saints in Three Acts* opens with a black cast. The members of the cast are gathered from New York's black churches.

1935

Rose McClendon and Dick Campbell found the Negro People's Theater.

Rose McClendon stars as Cora in Langston Hughes' *Mulatto,* which has a record run for a nonmusical play by a black author. It is her last role.

Lillian Hellman's *The Little Foxes* is a triumph on Broadway with Abbie Mitchell in the role of Addie.

Gershwin's *Porgy and Bess,* with libretto by Dorothy and DuBose Heyward, opens at the Alvin Theater. **Eva Jessye** is choral director, and **Anne Wiggins Brown** creates the role of Bess. The cast also includes Georgette Harvey and Abbie Mitchell.

The landmark *Negro History in Thirteen Plays* is published. It is a collaboration between **May Miller** and Willis Richardson

Rose McClendon, with John Houseman, heads the Negro Unit of the Federal Theatre

Project for the Works Progress Administration.

1936

Rose McClendon dies. **Mercedes Gilbert** takes over for her in *Mulatto*. Muriel Rahn and Dick Campbell found the Rose McClendon Players.

Edna Thomas plays Lady Macbeth in Orson Welles' production of *Macbeth* set in Haiti.

1939

Hattie McDaniel wins the Academy Award as Best Performance by a Supporting Actress for *Gone With the Wind*. She is the first black actor to win an Oscar.

Ethel Waters makes her dramatic debut in *Mamba's Daughters* to almost universal critical acclaim. The one critical holdout, Brooks Atkinson, recants after an ad in the *New York Times*, signed by Judith Anderson, Tallulah Bankhead, et al., asks him to reconsider.

1940

The **American Negro Theater** is founded by Abram Hill and Fred O'Neal. Among its members are **Helen Martin**, **Ruby Dee**, and **Hilda Simms**, who stars in its biggest hit, *Anna Lucasta*, in 1944.

Ethel Waters and **Katherine Dunham** star in the all-black musical *Cabin in the Sky* on Broadway.

1941

Helen Martin and Evelyn Ellis play principal roles in the black classic *Native Son* on Broadway.

1942

Anne Wiggins Brown returns to Broadway with a new production of *Porgy and Bess*.

1942

Lena Horne makes her film debut in *Panama Hattie*.

1943

Ethel Waters and Lena Horne star in the film version of *Cabin in the Sky*. It is one of Horne's few speaking roles.

Carmen Jones opens on Broadway with Muriel Smith and Muriel Rahn alternating in the title role. The black adaptation of Bizet's opera *Carmen* is a triumph.

1944

Hilda Simms scores a triumph in the title role in *Anna Lucasta*, the American Negro Theater's Broadway hit.

1945

Strange Fruit, adapted from the novel by white author Lillian Smith, introduces **Jane White** in a story of interracial love and violence.

1946

The Rose McClendon Memorial Collection of Photographs of Distinguished Negroes is established at Yale and Harvard universities.

Pearl Bailey makes her Broadway debut in *St. Louis Woman* and steals the show from the leads.

1950

Ethel Waters pulls off another dramatic tour de force in Carson McCullers' *The Member of the Wedding*.

Evelyn Ellis directs and stars in an all-black *Tobacco Road* presented at the Apollo Theater.

Alice Childress adapts Langston Hughes' *Simple* stories in *Just a Little Simple*, the first play by a black woman to appear off-Broadway.

Juanita Hall is the first African American to win a Tony award. She wins for her portrayal of Bloody Mary in *South Pacific*.

1952

With *Gold in the Trees*, Alice Childress becomes the first black woman playwright to have an off-Broadway production of an original script.

1953

The film *Bright Road* is released, starring **Dorothy Dandridge** in her first movie role. Mary Elizabeth Vroman wrote the screenplay, basing it on her own short story. She thus becomes the first black woman in the Screen Writers Guild.

1954

House of Flowers showcases Pearl Bailey, Juanita Hall, Josephine Premice, and **Diahann Carroll**.

Eartha Kitt receives raves for her first real dramatic performance on Broadway in *Mrs. Patterson*.

Dorothy Dandridge appears in film version of *Carmen Jones*. She is the first black woman to be nominated for an Oscar in the Best Actress category.

1955

Alice Childress' *Trouble in Mind*, starring **Clarice Taylor**, is produced at the Greenwich Mews Theater. Playwright and actor both receive raves, and Childress becomes first black woman to receive an Obie.

1957

Lena Horne has a huge personal success in a weak musical called *Jamaica*.

1959

Lorraine Hansberry's *A Raisin in the Sun* makes theater history as the first play by a black woman on Broadway. The stellar cast includes Ruby Dee, **Diana Sands**, and **Claudia McNeil**.

Dorothy Dandridge plays Bess in the film version of *Porgy and Bess*.

1961

Jean Genet's *The Blacks* provides a jumping-off place for an entire generation of black actors, including **Cicely Tyson, Cynthia Belgrave**, and Helen Martin.

Ellen Stewart founds the La MaMa Experimental Theater Club, an off-off-Broadway theater that will make theater history.

1962

The lovely *Moon on a Rainbow Shawl* features **Vinette Carroll** and Cicely Tyson. In the 1970 revival, Carroll will direct.

Singer/actor Diahann Carroll stars in a racially mixed cast in the musical *No Strings*.

1963

Gloria Foster makes her mark in *In White America*.

Cicely Tyson appears regularly in the dramatic series *East Side/West Side*.

1964

Diana Sands wows Broadway in *The Owl and the Pussycat*, scoring a hit in a role that was not written for a black actor.

The critically praised cast of James Baldwin's *Blues for Mr. Charlie* includes Diana Sands and **Rosetta LeNoire**.

1964

Billie Allen is powerful in the lead role of Adrienne Kennedy's *Funnyhouse of a Negro*, the first play by a black woman other than Alice Childress to appear off-Broadway.

Lorraine Hansberry's *The Sign in Sidney Brustein's Window* opens shortly before the playwright dies.

1965

Beah Richards plays her most important stage role in James Baldwin's *The Amen Corner*.

The first production of the **Negro Ensemble Company** is a pair of one-acts —"Happy Ending" and "Day of Absence" —and include in their casts **Barbara Ann Teer, Hattie Winston, Esther Rolle,** and **Frances Foster.**

1966

Nichelle Nichols is Lieutenant Uhura in the cult classic television series *Star Trek*.

1967

Pearl Bailey heads the all-black cast of *Hello, Dolly* on Broadway, for which she receives a special Tony.

Leslie Uggams dazzles critics and audience alike in *Hallelujah, Baby*, a survey of black history with a racially mixed cast.

Vinette Carroll forms the Urban Art Corps to train minority theater artists.

1968

Diahann Carroll, in *Julia*, becomes the first black star of a television situation comedy since the days of *Beulah* and *Amos 'n' Andy*.

Vinie Burrows' one-woman show *Walk Together Children* opens at the Greenwich Mews Theater to great acclaim. It becomes a black theater classic in touring and revival productions.

The longest-running drama of the season off-Broadway is *To Be Young, Gifted, and Black*, adapted from the writings of Lorraine Hansberry.

The Negro Ensemble Company (NEC) is founded. Women who are original members include Esther Rolle, Frances Foster, Hattie Winston, and **Rosalind Cash**.

Barbara Ann Teer founds the National Black Theater Company (NBT).

Ellen Holly is the first black woman in a principal acting role on daytime television as Carla on *One Life to Live*.

1970

Lorraine Hansberry's *Les Blancs*, her final work, opens after her death.

Melba Moore breaks into the big time as Lutiebelle in *Purlie*, the musical version of Ossie Davis's *Purlie Victorious*. She won Tony, Drama Desk, and Theater World awards and topped *Variety's* Drama Critics Poll.

In *Boesman and Lena*, Ruby Dee gives what Clives Barnes considered one of the finest performances he has ever seen. She won both the Obie and the Drama Desk Awards.

1971

Georgia, Georgia is released, making **Maya Angelou** the first black woman to have an original screenplay produced.

J. E. Franklin's landmark play *Black Girl* premieres at the New Federal Theater and then moves to Broadway, where it runs for 234 performances. Later, it is made into a film.

Mary Alice makes her Broadway debut in *No Place to Be Somebody*.

1972

Micki Grant's *Don't Bother Me, I Can't Cope* opens off-Broadway, directed by Vinette Carroll. Grant wins Obie and Drama Desk awards. The show moves to Broadway, making Carroll one of the first black women to direct on the Great White Way.

Alice Childress codirects her own script, *Wedding Band*, at the Public Theater. Ruby Dee, **Hilda Haynes**, and Clarice Taylor contribute to the positive reviews.

The first black woman to join the Directors Guild of America, Sue Booker wins an Emmy Award for producing *As Adam Early in the Morning*.

Diana Ross makes her film debut in *Lady Sings the Blues*. For the same film, Elizabeth Courtney is the first black woman nominated for an Academy Award for Costume Design.

1973

Valerie Capers wins a Tony for her role as Lena Younger in *Raisin*, the musical version of *A Raisin in the Sun*.

Shirley Prendergast designs lights for the NEC's *The River Niger*, becoming the first black woman lighting designer on Broadway.

Ten films with largely black casts, including *Sounder* with Cicely Tyson, are nominated for Academy Awards.

Cicely Tyson wins two Emmy awards for her performance in *The Autobiography of Miss Jane Pittman*.

1974

Diahann Carroll receives an Academy Award nomination as Best Actress for *Claudine*.

Critically acclaimed *My Sister, My Sister* wins **Seret Scott** a Drama Desk Award and Barbara Montgomery an Obie.

Esther Rolle begins five-year run as Florida Evans in *Good Times*.

1975

The Jeffersons begins its fourteen-year run with **Isabel Sanford** and **Marla Gibbs**.

Beah Richard's one-woman show, "A Black Woman Speaks," appears on television and later wins an Emmy.

1976

for colored girls who have considered suicide/when the rainbow is enuf by **Ntozake Shange** opens at the New Federal Theater, quickly moves to the Public, and ends up on Broadway for a total run of 867 performances.

Vinette Carroll and Micki Grant collaborate again, with Alex Bradford, on *Your Arms Too Short to Box With God*, dazzling Broadway and sixty-six tour cities.

Marsha Warfield makes her film debut in *Car Wash*.

1977

The miniseries *Roots* draws huge audiences and highlights such actors as **Madge Sinclair**, Cicely Tyson, Leslie Uggams, and **Olivia Cole**.

1978

Nell Carter is a smash hit in *Ain't Misbehavin'*.

1979

Roots: The Next Generation features more fine actors, including Ruby Dee, Diahann Carroll, **Carmen McRae**, Beah Richards, **Irene Cara**, and **Pam Grier** in one of her early serious roles.

Esther Rolle wins an Emmy as Best Supporting Actress in a Drama Special as the housekeeper in *Summer of My German Soldier*.

1981

In *Dreamgirls*, **Jennifer Holiday** stops the show every night with "And I Am Telling You I'm Not Going" and, according to *The New York Times*, makes "Broadway history."

Judith Jameson leads a smashing cast in *Sophisticated Ladies*, the first hit musical with Duke Ellington music.

Lena Horne: The Lady and Her Music opens on Broadway. It will be the longest-running one-woman show on Broadway to date and win Tony, Drama Desk, and Drama Critics Circle Awards.

Isabel Sanford wins an Emmy for her performance in *The Jeffersons*.

1982

Kathleen Collins is the first African American woman to direct a feature-length film, *Losing Ground*, which she also wrote.

1983

Julie Dash directs the award-winning film *Illusions*.

1984

The Cosby Show premieres with **Phylicia Rashad** as the independent, unflappable lawyer-mother.

1985

The film of **Alice Walker**'s *The Color Purple* garners Oscar nominations for **Whoopi Goldberg**, **Oprah Winfrey**, and **Margaret Avery**.

Marla Gibbs takes *227*, a play by Chicago playwright Christine Houston, to television as a series.

Frances Foster receives a special Obie Award for Sustained Excellence of Performance.

1986

Toni Morrison's *Dreaming Emmett* is presented at the Capital Repertory Theater.

Madge Sinclair plays a starship captain in the film *Star Trek IV: The Voyage Home*.

1987

Mary Alice wins a Tony for her performance in August Wilson's *Fences*.

1988

From the Mississippi Delta by **Endeesha Ida Mae Holland** is nominate for a Pulitzer Prize.

1989

Oprah Winfrey acquires her own television and movie production studio, Harpo, becoming the first black woman and only the third woman in U.S. history to own her own production company.

Illusions, a short film by filmmaker Julie Dash in 1983, is named Best Film of the Decade by the Black Filmmakers Foundation.

Gloria Naylor's novel *The Women of Brewster Place* is produced as a television movie by Oprah Winfrey, who also appears in it with such actors as Olivia Cole and Mary Alice.

Ruth Brown wins a Tony for her performance in *Black and Blue*.

1990

Whoopi Goldberg wins an Academy Award in the Best Supporting Actress category for her role in *Ghost*. She is the first black woman to win an Oscar since Hattie McDaniel.

In Living Color premieres, giving black women—Kim Coles, T'Keyah "Crystal" Keymah, and Kim Wayans—a chance to do satiric sketch comedy on television.

1991

Daughters of the Dust, written, produced, and directed by Julie Dash, is the first feature film by an African-American woman to have a national release.

Esther Rolle is inducted into Black Filmmakers Hall of Fame.

Regina Taylor costars in the very fine dramatic series *I'll Fly Away*.

1992

Anna Deavere Smith's one-woman show *Fires in the Mirror* ignites off-Broadway and earns a Pulitzer nomination.

Helen Martin is inducted into the Black Filmmakers Hall of Fame.

1993

Angela Bassett stars in *What's Love Got to Do With It*, the film based on the life of **Tina Turner**.

Leslie Harris is the first African-American woman director to have a major commercial film release, *Just Another Girl on the IRT*.

Anna Deavere Smith's *Twilight*, a play about the Los Angeles riots following the Rodney King verdict, opens at the Mark Taper Forum in that city to overwhelmingly positive reviews.

1994

Halle Berry integrates Bedrock in the comedy film *The Flintstones*.

1995

Mary Alice and Gloria Foster star as the **Delaney sisters** in *Having Our Say* on Broadway.

1995

Whitney Houston and Angela Bassett are the first two black women actors to receive "above the title" billing for their roles in the movie version of **Terry McMillan**'s novel *Waiting to Exhale*.

Bibliography

General Books Useful to the Study of Black Women in America

Reference Books

African-Americans: Voices of Triumph. Three volume set: *Perseverance, Leadership,* and *Creative Fire.* By the editors of Time-Life Books. Alexandria, Virginia, 1993.

Estell, Kenneth, ed., *The African-American Almanac.* Detroit, Michigan, 1994.

Harley, Sharon. *The Timetables of African-American History: A Chronology of the Most Important People and Events in African-American History.* New York, 1995.

Hine, Darlene Clark. *Hine Sight: Black Women and The Re-construction of American History.* Brooklyn, New York, 1994.

Hine, Darlene Clark, ed., Elsa Barkley Brown and Rosalyn Terborg-Penn, associate ed. *Black Women in America: An Historical Encyclopedia.* Brooklyn, New York, 1993.

Hornsby, Alton, Jr. *Chronology of African-American History: Significant Events and People from 1619 to the Present.* Detroit, Michigan, 1991.

Kranz, Rachel. *Biographical Dictionary of Black Americans.* New York, 1992.

Lanker, Brian. *I Dream a World: Portraits of Black Women Who Changed America.* New York, 1989.

Logan, Rayford W., and Michael R. Winston, eds. *Dictionary of American Negro Biography.* New York, 1982.

Low, W. Augustus, and Virgil A. Clift, eds. *Encyclopedia of Black America.* New York, 1981.

Salem, Dorothy C., ed. *African American Women: A Biographical Dictionary.* New York, 1993.

Salzman, Jack, David Lionel Smith, and Cornel West. *Encyclopedia of African-American Culture and History.* Five Volumes. New York, 1996.

Smith, Jessie Carney, ed., *Notable Black American Women.* Two Volumes. Detroit, Michigan. Book I, 1993; Book II, 1996.

General Books about Black Women

Giddings, Paula. *When and Where I Enter: The Impact of Black Women on Race and Sex in America.* New York, 1984.

Guy-Sheftall, Beverly. *Words of Fire: An Anthology of African-American Feminist Thought.* New York, 1995.

Hine, Darlene Clark, Wilma King, and Linda Reed, eds. *"We Specialize in the Wholly Impossible": A Reader in Black Women's History.* Brooklyn, New York, 1995.

Jones, Jacqueline. *Labor of Love, Labor of Sorrow: Black Women, Work, and the Family from Slavery to the Present.* New York, 1985.

Lerner, Gerda, ed. *Black Women in White America: A Documentary History.* New York, 1972.

Books about Black Women in Theater Arts and Entertainment

Bogle, Donald. *Brown Sugar: Eighty Years of America's Black Female Superstars.* New York, 1980.

Brown-Guillory, Elizabeth, ed. *Their Place on the Stage: Black Women Playwrights in America.* Westport, Connecticut, 1988.

————. *Wines in the Wilderness: Plays by African American Women from the Harlem Renaissance to the Present*. New York, 1990.

Gray, John. *Blacks in Film and Television: A Pan-African Bibliography of Films, Filmmakers, and Performers*. Westport, Connecticut, 1990.

Haskins, James. *Black Theater in America*. New York, 1982.

Hatch, James V. *The Roots of African American Drama*. Detroit, Michigan, 1991.

Hill, Errol, ed. *The Theater of Black Americans*. New York, 1990.

Hill, George, Lorraine Raglin, and Chas Floyd Johnson. *Black Women in Television. An Illustrated History and Bibliography*. New York, 1990.

Hughes, Langston, and Milton Meltzer. *Black Magic: A Pictorial History of the Negro in American Theater*. Englewood Cliffs, New Jersey, 1967.

Kellner, Bruce, ed. *The Harlem Renaissance: A Historical Dictionary for the Era*. New York, 1984.

Notable Women in the American Theater: A Biographical Dictionary. Robinson, Alice M., Vera Mowry Roberts, and Milly S. Barranger, editors. New York, 1989.

Null, Gary. *Black Hollywood*. Secaucus, New Jersey, 1975.

Perkins, Kathy A. *Black Female Playwrights: An Anthology of Plays Before 1950*. Bloomington, Indiana, 1989.

Sampson, Henry T. *Blacks in Blackface: A Source Book on Early Black Musical Shows*. Metuchen, New Jersey, 1980.

Sampson Henry T. *The Ghost Walks: A Chronological History of Blacks in Show Business, 1865–1910*. Metuchen, New Jersey, 1988.

Smith, Sharon. *Women Who Make Movies*. New York, 1975.

Toll, Robert C. *Blacking Up: The Minstrel Show in Nineteenth-Century America*. New York, 1974.

Toll, Robert C. *On With the Show*. New York, 1976.

Woll, Allen. *Dictionary of the Black Theater*. Westport, Connecticut, 1983.

Contents of the Set

(ORGANIZED BY VOLUME)

Dance, Sports, and Visual Arts

Dance

Sports

Visual Arts

Education

Religion and Community

Social Activism

Science, Health, and Medicine

Contents of the Set

(LISTED ALPHABETICALLY BY ENTRY)

Index

Page numbers in **boldface** indicate main entries. *Italic* page numbers indicate illustrations.